M]

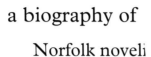

a biography of

Norfolk noveli

C000225928

✦❖❖❖✦

Marion Aldis and Pamela Inder

Larks Press

Published by the Larks Press,
Ordnance Farmhouse,
Guist Bottom, Dereham NR20 5PF
01328 829207

larks.press@xlnmail.com

www.booksatlarkspress.co.uk

British Library Cataloguing-in-Publication Data
A catalogue record for this book is available
from the British Library

ISBN 978 1 904006 69 5

Acknowledgements

We have done our best to read all Mary E. Mann's novels and short stories, published and unpublished, typed and hand-written, even those she labelled 'not for publication'. Our grateful thanks go to the staff in the **Norfolk Record Office** for getting out the as yet uncatalogued boxes of her papers – all thirty-two of them – time and time again as we worked our way through them.

But it is to **Mary Fortune**, who spent such a great deal of time researching Mary E. Mann for a book of her own, that we give greatest thanks. She has been enormously generous in sharing her research with us. Without her help a great deal of this biography could not have been written. We are also grateful to **Adrian Money**, Mary E. Mann's great-great-grandson, who has shared family memories and stories with us, and to Patience Tomlinson who shared her knowledge of Mary Mann with us.

We should also like to thank the staff of the **British Library**, **the Reverend Michael Langan**, the archivist at **Marlborough College**, **David Napier** and **Richard Wilson** for their help and support.

Sources

Most of the information in this biography comes from the collection of Mary E. Mann's papers and mss in the Norfolk County Record Office, MC2716 or ACC20.2002 boxes 1-32. We have also consulted the trade directories published by Kelly, Piggott and White. Other information comes from Mary E. Mann's published novels and short stories and from Mary Fortune's unpublished interview with the late Diana Hyde.

Autobiography of Sir Albert Munnings , NCRO.

Strand Magazine – 1891-1893. In authors' personal collection.

The Assassin's Cloak, an anthology of the world's greatest diarists. Edited by Irene and Alan Taylor. Canongate Books 2001. In authors' personal collection.

History of Norwich by Frank Meeres, - Phillimore 1998

Illustrations

Pictures on p.22 and p.100 are printed by courtesy of Picture Norfolk, Norfolk Millennium Library. The picture on p.102 is printed by courtesy of Marlborough College, and on p.208 by courtesy of Wilsford Church.

Pictures on pages 9, 16, 38, 96, 118, 190, 223 are photos by the authors.

The remainder are published by kind permission of the Norfolk Record Office.

CONTENTS

Errata

Illustrations

The illustration on p. 22 is Shropham Vicarage, not Town Close House

The illustration on p.38 is Town Close House not Church Farm

The captions on p.118 should be reversed – the top illustration is Ivy Cottage, the lower, Mill Farm

Only the illustration on p.38 is printed by courtesy of Picture Norfolk; that on p.22 is the authors' own.

Text

p. 41 'George Budd' should be 'Thomas William Budd'

p. 161 'there was a general election' should read 'there was a change of government'

p.166 'Clara Fisher' should be 'Ursula Fisher'

Notes on money

It is never possible to be entirely accurate when converting historical prices to their modern equivalents. The figures below are based on the conversion tables provided by the National Archives and give some idea of the changing value of £10 worth of modern (2005) money at various points in Mary E. Mann's lifetime.

1850 £585–30p 1900 £570–60p
1860 £431–60p 1910 £570–60p
1870 £457–00p 1915 £430–60p
1880 £483–10p 1920 £212–10p
1890 £598–90p 1930 £234–20p

Chapter 1. Setting the scene.

'They were striving to draw over the rigid legs of the doll the grey calico nightgown of which they were stripping it when I saw them last. Their fat, dirty little hands trembled with their eagerness ...' Only the 'doll' with which little Evangeline and Randolph Hodd were playing was actually the corpse of their still-born baby brother. Worse still, their mother was unrepentant when the visitor from the Vicarage remonstrated with her. 'Other folkes' child'en have a toy, now and then, to kape 'em out o' mischief,' she protested. 'My little 'uns ha'nt. He've kep em quite for hours, the po'r baby have; and I'll lay a crown they han't done no harm to their little brother.'

The shocking revelation comes in the last few lines of a story called *Little Brother,* and it is the more powerful because the author does not judge Mrs Hodd. The woman was a neglectful mother with a dirty home, an uncaring husband and twelve children: she was uneducated, malnourished, exhausted and had just given birth – we are left to decide for ourselves why we are so horrified and whether we should really blame her for taking the opportunity to have a bit of peace and quiet.

The tale is beautifully crafted, spare, macabre and thought-provoking. It is even more chilling because we know that the author, Mary Elizabeth Mann, based most of her writing on real-life events – so almost certainly, somewhere in Norfolk, sometime in the late 19th century, a labourer's child – or children – were found playing with a dead baby.

Mary E. Mann, (or 'MEM' as she signed herself and as we shall call her throughout this book) was a celebrated novelist in the 1890s and early 1900s. A few of her novels have recently been republished but she is now largely unknown – though not entirely so. She has a following in her home county of Norfolk, and in the 2009 edition of *The Oxford Book of English Short Stories*, edited by A.S. Byatt, *Little Brother* is included alongside tales by H.G. Wells and Rudyard Kipling, Charles Dickens and Thomas Hardy.

In a career that spanned more than thirty years, Mary E. Mann wrote thirty-three novels, hundreds of short stories, some of which she collected and published in book form, and fourteen plays, at least two of which made it to the London stage. By no means everything she wrote was as memorable as *Little Brother*, but she had an original mind and a considerable talent and she deserves to be much, much better known.

✦❖❖❖✦

She was born Mary Elizabeth Rackham in Norwich in 1848, but she was known to her family and friends as 'Polly'. Eighteen forty-eight was a seminal year in European history. Across the continent there were a series of republican uprisings. Even in Britain some relatively minor skirmishes took place in London, Manchester and Bingley as the Chartists revived their attempts to get the government to accept the six-point 'charter' they had drawn up a decade before. Britain already had a rudimentary parliamentary democracy but the Chartists wanted to extend the franchise to all adult men, to introduce a secret ballot and other measures to enable men of all social classes to stand for parliament. They were unsuccessful, but the fact that these uprisings happened at all heralded the idea that a change to the old order was desirable, and might one day come about. Not that the adult Mary Elizabeth would have sympathised with the revolutionaries: she believed people should know their place and be content with their lot. She claimed she was not interested in politics, and she would be an old woman before she was able to vote, but her sympathies were Conservative

Nonetheless, the world would change dramatically in her lifetime: old certainties and ways of life that had held sway for generations would be swept aside, the class system would begin to crumble and women's role in British society would change out of all recognition. She would live to see the coming of the first cars, the first aeroplanes, the telegraph, the telephone, typewriters, electricity, cinemas and wireless sets. Women would learn to ride bicycles and drive cars; they would wear skirts that showed their legs and go out without wearing a hat and gloves. Respectable young girls would earn their own livings, live apart from their families and travel round the country unchaperoned. They could become doctors and politicians, smoke cigarettes, eat in cafés, divorce their husbands and control their own fertility. It was a lot to get used to.

When Polly Rackham was born, Britain was the most powerful nation on earth. The idea of this as a godly land of 'Christian soldiers' fighting righteous wars had become embedded in the British way of thinking and the myth was embodied in the cult of 'muscular Christianity' – a concept first expressed in *Tom's Brown's Schooldays*, written in 1857 in the wake of the Crimean War, and in its sequel, *Tom Brown at Oxford*, where sport is extolled as a builder of manly character, teamwork, chivalry and moral fortitude – qualities that were believed to make Britons great. The men who administered the largest empire the world has ever seen had, supposedly, learnt these values on 'the playing fields of Eton,' and the schools Polly's brothers attended would do their best to inculcate those same values in the sons of the middle class.

Britain was also well-established as the world's first industrial nation. Raw materials from the colonies were shipped home to be transformed into cotton cloth and cane furniture, medicines and mackintoshes, bicycle tyres and brass candlesticks, silk handkerchiefs and cigarettes, chocolate and cheap jewellery - and a host of other products that Victorian consumers had learnt to want. Norwich, the Rackham's home town, was a vibrant industrial city, second only to Manchester in the number of its mills weaving silk, wool, linen and cotton. But there was a cost to be paid for that sort of prosperity and a government report published in 1848 recorded that a fifth of the entire population of Norwich were listed as paupers. Wages in the twelve main factories, which between them employed almost 4,000 people, were very low: an adult man could earn up to fourteen shillings a week, a woman earned just eight shillings for the same hours of work, a youth only two. Cloth was exported and the river through Norwich was constantly clogged with traffic. There were also iron works, dye works, tanneries, big shoe-making factories, coach-making works, tin-plating works, breweries, soap and chemical works, brick and tile-makers with huge kilns and, of course, the celebrated Colman's mustard factory. The entire city was engulfed in suffocating noxious fumes and smoke which permeated everything, and on damp and foggy winter days a choking blanket of cloud settled over the city. Industrialisation led to miserable conditions for the working class – but to prosperity for the country as a whole.

Little Polly Rackham was born into a country unique in Europe in that it already had a thriving middle class of manufacturers and merchants. It was not the aristocracy who created the Industrial Revolution, but intelligent, often self-educated, men from the middle and lower classes – men like Stephenson and Watt, Arkwright and Brunel, Boulton and Wedgwood. But it was the Crimean War – which started when Polly was five years old – that did more than any other single event in the mid-nineteenth century to advance the middle-class ideal of meritocracy and cause people to question the unassailable right of the aristocracy to lead. It was not just the military blunders made by the army's aristocratic leadership – most famously the disastrous Charge of the Light Brigade – but their almost criminal negligence in failing to provide for the troops. Without sufficient food, warm clothes or shelter to survive the freezing winter, thousands perished from cold, exhaustion and disease. Florence Nightingale volunteered her services and was eventually given permission to take a group of thirty-eight nurses to Turkey. She found the conditions in the army hospital in Scutari appalling. The men were kept in rooms without blankets or decent food. War wounds accounted for just one death in six; diseases such as typhus, cholera and dysentery were the main reasons why the death-rate was so high.

Florence Nightingale's contribution has been grossly exaggerated, but she became an important symbol. The legend of the 'Lady with the Lamp' was retold in schoolbooks, histories and biographies. It contained the basic elements of the middle-class Victorian ideal: a Christian narrative about maternal care, good works and self-sacrifice; a moral one of self-improvement and the salvation of the deserving poor; a domestic tale of cleanliness and good housekeeping; a story about individual determination.

Polly Rackham's family was solidly middle class and these were their values. Her father, William Simon Rackham, was a draper and cloth merchant in Norwich, like his father before him. He had married Mary Ann Elizabeth Smith, his partner's sister and another cloth merchant's daughter, and they had seven children. Polly was the second child and the only girl.

William Rackham was a cultured man and understood the value of learning – his sons were sent away to school, and his daughter was given the best education Norwich could provide. Not that she was ever expected to need to earn her own living. Norwich was full of working women – women servants, women working in factories, washerwomen, shop assistants, seamstresses, women working with their husbands in a huge variety of trades and some even running their own small businesses. But as a girl from a respectable middle class family, Polly's role in life was to find herself a husband and have his babies; spinsterhood was not a fate to be contemplated and there were few careers open to girls like her. Polly's education was intended to develop her interests and to turn her into a suitable companion for her husband, preferably one who would keep her in comfort and not expect her to work alongside him. Her grandmother might have helped her husband in his business, but her mother stayed at home and ran her household, as Polly herself expected to do.

In her early years the family lived on Pottergate Street in Heigham, in a comfortable three-storey Georgian house which opened straight on to the street, as did all the other houses in the road. It was just round the corner from St Swithin's Church in St Benedict Street where the family worshipped. In the 1851 census, taken when little Polly Rackham was a toddler, the family had two live-in servants. Their nearest neighbours were two unmarried ladies of independent means who also had a servant, and Edward Nicholls, a brazier (brass maker), whose wife, Rebecca, worked as a cap-maker. The Nicholls also took in lodgers. There were houses of different sizes along Pottergate Street, and though a respectable area, it was somewhat mixed. It was certainly not as sought after a place to live as the outer suburbs or the pretty riverside village of Thorpe St Andrew.

The Rackhams' house in Pottergate
We cannot be certain which was their
house but, working from the census,
this seems the most likely

Norwich was the county town, a cathedral city, and, in the 1850s, a city with a lively cultural and religious life. There were two public libraries as well as many smaller subscription libraries, a museum with 'an extensive and interesting collection of antiquities and curiosities' and the East of England Art Union for the 'encouragement and promotion of the fine arts.' There was a large theatre, an Assembly Hall and a Choral Society, a Harmonic Meeting and a Glee Club, all of which gave recitals. On Dereham Road there was the West End Retreat with acres of gardens and a hall and galleries designed by Paxton, where exhibitions and concerts were held. The Horticultural Society held annual exhibitions in the Corn Exchange and there were various parks and gardens around the city, including a small menagerie in Kensington Gardens at Old Lakenham. Regattas and 'water frolics' were held on the river each summer. There were newsrooms – though these would only have been frequented by men – and three local newspapers representing the views of the main political parties – Whig, Tory and Radical. William Rackham probably subscribed to the Tory *Norfolk Chronicle and Norwich Gazette*. There were lecture series, and sermons to listen to in the various churches. Norwich was well supplied with shops of all kinds, there were regular markets and an annual fair with side-shows and roundabouts.

These were the aspects of Norwich that Polly Rackham would have known. But there were parts of her city with which she would have been much less familiar. Down the narrow mediaeval back streets, which today's tourists find so attractive, lay stinking, insanitary courts and alleys inhabited by the city's poor. A report on the state of sewage in parts of Norwich, made in 1840 for a parliamentary commission into sanitation in major cities, makes grim reading. The commissioner describes visits he made to several families in the weaving districts of Norwich. The following account is typical.

'There were twelve houses in [the court] *of two rooms each. There were no back premises to any of them. A row of eight houses occupied one side of the court; the other was occupied by a stable and slaughter-house. At the bottom, or lower end of the court, were four houses... Immediately facing the entrance to the house* [of the weaver he was visiting] *was the privy, used by the whole of the inhabitants of the court; by the side of it was an open bin, into which all the refuse matter was thrown, and into the bottom of which the soil from the adjoining privy drained. Some rain had fallen on the night previous to my visit, and the contents of this open cesspool, oozing through the walls, were streaming sluggishly down the path to the house. A part of this filthy fluid was absorbed by the ground, but some parts of it not infrequently found their way into the house, the floor of which, as if to invite its entrance, was nearly a foot lower than the ground outside...'*

As early as the 18th century there was a piped water supply in Norwich – for those who could afford it – but the water was not pure, and contaminated water caused and spread disease. The first half of the nineteenth century saw cholera epidemics which brought about scenes of horror in towns around the country. In many graveyards, heaps of bones and partially rotted bodies would be dug up to make way for even more burials, causing an additional health hazard. Cholera first struck England in 1831, killing some 30,000 people in an outbreak lasting the best part of a year, and thereafter there were frequent epidemics. In 1850, when Polly was two years old, there was a move to supply clean water to many parts of the city, but the city councillors turned down its full implementation on the grounds of expense. The situation got worse as factories continued to expand, but it wasn't until 1867, when she was nineteen, that the councillors succeeded in bringing clean water to most of the city. In 1870 they also built a network of much-needed sewers to dispose safely of the gallons of 'night soil' produced by a population of over 80,000 people, which until then had been fouling the river and running in gutters the streets.

And dirty drinking water and lack of sanitation were not the only problems faced by the city's poor. Mothers had to contribute to the family income, so many, many children, too young to work in the mills and factories, were left alone during the day to fend for themselves at home or out on the streets. Schooling was not compulsory – nor was it free. The risks were obvious. In 1873 children under five accounted for 25% of all deaths – the causes given by the coroners were: insufficient or unsuitable food, burns and scalds, indifference to cleanliness, scanty or insufficient clothing, polluted water – and drugs. Opium was an over-the-counter remedy and 'Godfrey's Cordial' was a cheap and sure way to quiet the incessant crying of starving babies and children, while 'gin 'n' laudanum' was a way of alleviating the dire misery that was daily life for their parents.

Little Polly Rackham's family were relatively prosperous, but diseases emanating from the poorer parts of town were an ever-present risk. In a world without antibiotics where doctors had only a rudimentary understanding of disease and how to treat it, childhood was a gamble, even for the well-to-do. However, Polly and her brothers were lucky: all seven of them survived into adulthood.

Willy and Polly Rackham c.1851-2

Chapter 2. Pretty Polly Rackham

Sheringham, 1928. In a large, draughty house on a cliff top an old lady sits at her writing desk. The town below her was originally a picturesque and flourishing fishing village, and the coastline, unusually rugged for Norfolk, is often swept by high seas and gales. There is a fine sandy beach, the town has an exceptional record for sunshine and in recent times has developed into a thriving holiday resort. MEM has lived there for the past twelve years and is now eighty. She is still very much mistress of her own domain, though the day-to-day running of the household is now in the hands of her younger daughter, Margery, a quiet, self-effacing spinster of fifty-two. Her eldest daughter, Bertie, is fifty-four and also living at home. Bertie was once a beautiful, vivacious girl, her mother's favourite, but she is now a restless, unfulfilled artist, eking out a precarious living as an illustrator. She and Margery are now merely the ageing spinster daughters of their more famous mother - and Bertie finds it galling.

MEM is still upright, with white hair in a high bun bound with a velvet ribbon. She wears a thick patterned cardigan, and her dark skirt is short enough to show her ankles – a concession to the fashion of the times - but her demeanour is that of a Victorian lady. She is still active, out and about most days accompanied by one of her girls, but her horizons have narrowed. Someone has persuaded the former authoress to record her earliest memory and she is thinking back to when she was three years old … At last she picks up her pen. She still writes fluently and with obvious enjoyment, an accomplished writer using careful literary language.

'Things I Can Remember

I can remember the first time I went to church. Seventy-seven years ago. Is that a record I wonder? Truly my appearance there was brief and inglorious. I ended up being carried out, yelling in my father's arms to the vestry, where from a window looking into the dismal city churchyard a pussy cat engaged my attention and my tears were stayed. It was the mournful peal of the organ or the sudden appearance of my former friend the parson in a white nightshirt in the box across the way that had upset my infant susceptibilities. After that came years of standing up on the cushioned seat of the square room that was our pew, my father's arm round me, while I pretended to follow with his pointing finger the words of the psalms. And well do I recall that finger pausing upon the verse, *"The valleys shall also stand so thick with corn that they shall laugh and sing"* and his whisper, *"beautiful, beautiful"* in my ear. My poor father, city bred, whose heart was ever in the country.

When my mother, and her half dozen little ones knelt in prayer I thought it a matter of pride that my father did not need to do so but stood up in the corner of the pew just hiding his face for a few minutes in the tall hat that he held. Speaking of that same hat, by the way, I remember an awful occasion when bouncing down from my perch on the seat beside him, I sat into it with disastrous results.

The church was heated by a stove which stood in the aisle by our pew door, and round it, until the service began, all the old women from the free seats used to cluster. Their fires at home, I fear, were not generous ones, for they were all 'on the parish'. None could have looked on the prospect of an old age pension as a foretaste of the heaven about which they had come to hear. At the first notes of the organ they scuttled reluctantly off to the cold quarter at the bottom of the church; to gather round the stove again at the conclusion of the sermon for a last warming of cold hands, and a greeting from the gentry in the pews.

We always began the service by the chanting by a half dozen girls who, seated in the organ loft, formed our choir, with 'I will arise and go to my Father' and I, who so loved my own father, thought it most beautifully appropriate. The pulpit was a three-decker, and I was always glad when my friend the parson, having put off his nightshirt and arrayed himself becomingly again in a black frock, would appear in the highest tier. For at that juncture my mother would produce from her pocket refreshment for encouragement to her little ones to keep quiet and hold on to the end. I suppose there are biscuits called *Ratafias* still? A *Ratafia* used to be dealt out to each of us from that kind hand. Our friend up aloft had us directly under his eye, and his eye winked at the *Ratafias*, though naturally he did not approve. I remember a summers day when, a sudden storm coming, how long and wearisome we thought his sermon; I learnt afterwards that he had prolonged it hoping that the showers would pass and we children should not get wet going home.

The service of the Holy Sacrament was held once a month only. An occasion much appreciated by us as there was no sermon. But even without a sermon how long and tedious seemed the morning prayers. Nothing was spared us in those days – the Litany, all the psalms for the day, the Communion Service. How little we understood of it all. But I for my part was busy with many interests of my own. On the Great East window behind the altar were two small rounds of painted glass; those had an extraordinary

13

fascination for me, and I was satisfied in my own mind that one day my dear friend the parson would take them down and give them to me. Why I so loved them, why I so ardently desired them who shall say! But how brilliant was their blue and crimson and gold when the sun shone through them into my covetous upturned eyes.'

MEM never forgot those windows. She described a similar one of 'crimson and amethyst and gold' in *Mrs Carabey's Curious Dream,* a short story she published in 1913.

'I told no one that my heart was set upon the possession of those bits of coloured glass; nor did I ever, until this day, when I write it down, reveal to mortal ear the fact that a certain old man in the free seats at the west end of the church meant to murder me. He was a very ugly old man, and I now believe that to have been his only crime; that and the fact that instead of attending to the prayers his eyes were fixed on his little victim, gazing fearfully at him over the top of the big pew. Why were they so fixed I wonder; did I only imagine it, or did the sight of a little girl so tenderly encircled by her father's arm really hold a fascination for him. Memories of something he had lost perhaps or more possibly of something he had never had.

Is the old church there still I wonder? I believe I heard years ago that services are no long held there. Strange to think of it silent and deserted, squalid looking amid its squalid streets. It was only as a child that I knew it. I would like just once to see it again. Yet could I more plainly than I see it now: the group of old women clustered round the stove, the dear forms of mother and children in the great square pew, the little girl mounted on the padded seat the protecting arms around her, how the sun shines through the painted panes of the great window. Now sound the first wheezing notes of the organ, here comes, duly apparelled in his nightshirt, our friend the parson; he mounts the reading desk across the aisle and hark, hark, the sweet singing voices, " I shall arise and go to my Father."'

✦✛✙✦✙✛✦

The first service she describes may have been memorable because they were new to that church – St Swithin's in St Benedict Street. Willie, Polly, Harry and George were all baptised there *together* on October 3rd, 1852. Perhaps the family were new to the area, perhaps they were recent converts from non-conformity – we have no way of knowing.

The younger children in the family – the twins and Eddie – were baptised there as babies in 1855 and 1863 respectively.

Things I Can Remember shows that even as a child little Polly Rackham noticed, or was perhaps encouraged to notice, the layers of society and what it was like to be in a lower one than her own. It indicates that she was part of a loving family; her mother took biscuits to church to bribe her small children to sit quietly through the lengthy services rather than simply telling them to keep quiet. It also suggests that even as young as three, little Polly was imaginative and easily frightened. The parson's robes become an 'almost ghostly nightshirt' and the pulpit a 'closed box,' an ugly old man becomes a possible murderer. She remembers that her father sat with his arm round her - William Rackham was a gentle man and had a close relationship with his only daughter.

The Rackham household, like a great many Victorian households, was a large one, with parents, children, relatives, visitors and servants. In the Rackham's strata of society a husband was expected to provide for his wife and family; only poor women went out to work. Not that women like Mrs Rackham lived idle lives – they had plenty to do supervising the servants, helping the cook, entertaining their husbands' business contacts and teaching their children the ways of polite society. Polly eventually had six brothers, but William, just two years older than her, was her constant companion and friend when they were young. They played together and, until she was six, they attended the same school.

A story called *Willy and I* that she wrote in the early 1900s is autobiographical in many respects, showing her close relationship with her slightly older brother, and is another window into her early life – MEM doesn't even bother to change their names. Willy is her eldest brother, William Simon Rackham, named after their father, and always called Willie (usually spelt with an 'ie' not a 'y') in the family. The little girl in the story is called Polly, the name by which MEM was known to all her family and friends.

This story is probably set in or near their house in Unthank Road, as sometime in the early 1850s the Rackham family left the house in Pottergate Street where MEM was born and moved there to a big detached house of yellow brick with two-storeyed bay windows on either side of the front door with its stylised portico. Unthank Road was away from the town centre, cleaner and more prestigious than Pottergate Street and the houses were large. In the 1861 census the

15

Rackham family of five boys and Polly, was living there with three servants. Today the front has been tarmacadamed and is used as a car park, but originally it would have been a small front garden, as described in the story. Their neighbours included a Baptist minister,

The Rackhams' house on Unthank Road to which they moved c.1854 and where *Willy and I* may have been set

school teachers, a boys' school, a clerk and an oil and coke merchant. The house in *Willy and I* is probably an amalgam of this house and the taller, more densely built houses in the neighbouring streets.

'When we were little – Willy and I, oh such weary long years ago, we lived in a big house, in a long quiet street in the old town of Norwich. Now although the house was so big there was allotted to it only a small square of garden; a garden exquisitely kept and fostered, a garden to smell the roses in …holding father's or mother's hand, even, wondrous treat, to take our tea in, sometimes sitting demurely, we two, with a couple of dolls and a few lead soldiers from Willie's last box for company, at the little round table … beneath the red may-tree. A garden that was the delight of our city bred father, who protected the sprouting mignonette seeds from depredation of snail and slug, who trained with tenderest care the slender shoots of sweet pea and canariense, who tied and pruned and watered with his own hands when office hours were over. A broken toy would have been as great an offence as a stray cat in the treasured spot …a footmark on the verbena bed, a kicked stone on the gravel walk were punishable offences. No room for us two children there. And so, beside the nursery where our toys and books were kept and where our soberer hours were passed, there was given up to our use at the top of the house a large attic, which we called our play room.

It is quite desirable for children to run wild at times, to shout, to scream, to jump... for girls as well as boys ... I don't for a minute advise you to copy Willy and me in aught – for we were often a naughty pair...

We had not many toys there. Looking back I think we spent our time mostly in struggles on the floor, rolling over and over each other with screams and shouts and roarings as of wild animals emphasising that we were not Willy and his little sister Polly, but a great large lion and a huge black bear in mortal combat. We played at French and English too. It takes a lot of yelling from lusty lungs, a lot of stamping and jumping on hollow boards for one little girl to represent at all adequately a mighty and victorious army .... [Willy was Napoleon in this game]... *as we always grew tired at last we sat down quietly upon the floor and looked through our closed window at the window opposite.'*

One day when they are sitting at the window a man chats to them from the house opposite - he is a lodger in the house next door and his window is directly opposite their playroom window. He seems interested in them and sympathetic. They tell him they would like to have a kitten – but they are not allowed a dog or a cat because animals might spoil Papa's garden. The man pretends to think about this and then suggests that they could have a little cat and keep it in their play room. He could get them one and bring it to them when their parents are out and he suggests that he get a plank to bridge the gap between his room and theirs so he can get the cat to them without having to knock on the door and anyone knowing. That night their parents are away, and the outcome, of course, is obvious. The next day it is discovered that overnight the house has been broken into and jewellery, silver plate and other valuable items stolen – and the children find a dead kitten in their playroom.

'We had a policeman in the house all morning... Willy free from nursery rule, trotted about proud of his courage and daring, and coming upstairs to report 'progress' to me, who would not leave the playroom.

"All the bars of the doors and shutters were untouched, the thief must have been let into the house," the policeman said, and our father, who trusted all his servants, was furious with the policeman.'

Eventually it dawns on the parents that Polly is nowhere to be seen and they ask Willy where she is. He has to tell them and Polly's mother walks steadily up to the attic and enters the room.

' *"Where is my little girl, and what is she hiding away for? And what have you got in your lap, and why are you crying Polly"*, she asked. *Then she turned back my little skirt which hid it, and there was the kitten. Sobbing wildly, I flew up and pushed it into her arms.*

"The man...the man at the window promised it," I cried incoherently... *"And I wanted it because it was so unhappy....and we left the window open – and I loved it so. And it had to walk the plank....and Willy and me thought it was asleep, and I picked it up ...and it was dead."'*

The mystery of how the burglar got in is solved but the stolen goods are not recovered. The children are not punished – except by themselves – for their foolishness, their sadness for their lost kitten, and the dire distress they have caused their parents.

In the last paragraph of the story MEM describes going to her old home again as an adult and writes about her sadness that the indomitable brother, who wanted so much from life, is no longer with her. *'I made a pilgrimage to that wide street the other day, and stopped before that big old house where we two had lived as children, where I had played so contentedly second fiddle to Willy who was so eager to act the leading part, so determined to enjoy, to do, to conquer; Willy –*

> *Whose part in all the pomp that fills*
> *The circuit of the summer hills*
> *Is that his grave is green!*

I stepped into the narrow passage between the houses, and looking up saw that the present neighbours ... had slung a rope across from window to window, upon which towels hung to dry. I could see the projecting ledge of the window through which our little faces used to peep and the projecting ledge upon which the kitten had shivered and mewed ... and then came home and wrote this story.'

But before the family moved to Unthank Road, Willie and Polly Rackham went to a school in Pottergate Street as 'day boarders'.

Schooling in England was not compulsory until 1870 when a law was passed setting up a framework of education for all children between the ages of six and twelve. But the Act was not taken up in all areas, and would not be fully enforced for several years. There were also objections to the whole concept of 'universal education' on the grounds that teaching the working poor to think might make them dissatisfied and rebellious. In *Astray in Arcady*, published in 1910, MEM has Mrs Chisholm articulate this idea – and what is more, she herself appeared to agree with it. Others thought it undermined the authority of the Church of England which, in 1811, had established the National Society for Promoting the Education of the Poor in the Principles of the Established Church in England and Wales, with the aim of providing a church school in every parish. Education in these 'National' schools was not free and many parents could not afford even the one penny a week for their children's' education that the schools demanded, and which went to augment the teachers' salaries. Teachers in the National schools did at least have some training and textbooks were published specifically for their use. There were also regular inspections. But every parish did not have a National school and the type and quality of educational provision throughout the country was very variable. Many small schools were run by vicars in their own homes – to support their miserable stipends rather than to teach the word of God. Boys from respectable families whose parents considered them too delicate or sensitive for the rough and tumble of boarding school tended to be educated in this way. There were also Sunday Schools, run by volunteers, which taught basic reading, writing and arithmetic to working children who otherwise had no access to education. Then there were dame schools run by women who were not themselves highly educated. Some taught children a local trade – lace making or straw plaiting for example – and little else; some taught the three 'R's; others did not provide much more than a baby-sitting service. It was not until the Education Act of 1880 that education in England became genuinely compulsory – and free.

William Rackham's children were privileged; their parents could afford to pay for their education, even if the first establishment they chose was a pretty dreadful place. It was a dame school, owned by Mrs Henry Priest, wife of Henry Raven Priest, the wine merchant, and was listed as a 'Preparatory Establishment for Young Gentlemen'. The advertisements that appeared regularly in the Norwich papers made it sound quite attractive:

The unremitting *Personal* attention the *Pupils* receive from *Mrs Priest* both in the *School* and in the Domestic arrangements of her

Establishment, where they are entirely treated as *Parlour Boarders,* gives it completely the character of a well-organized *Private Family. Latin etc taught by competent Master*

It was only a few doors away from the Rackhams' house in Pottergate Street and Polly's parents seem to have persuaded Mrs Priest to take her, along with Willie – 'a miserable, frightened little girl, sitting on a tiny, green-painted form pushed against the wall – the one little desponding female (taken to oblige an old friend of Mrs Priestley's) in that desponding society of little males' as MEM described herself in a short story, *The Coming of King Ackerman.* In it Mrs Priest is thinly disguised as 'Mrs Priestly'. Like a great many Victorian schools Mrs Priest's was not a happy place, and the assistant mistress, Miss Paraman, then a young woman in her mid-twenties, seems to have been thoroughly sadistic. Her father had been the City Gaoler and her mother had been matron at the gaol – perhaps she had inherited her lack of compassion from them, or perhaps it was something she had had to acquire because of the awful things she had seen at the prison as a child. Inspection of private schools was not mandatory and what went on in many of them makes grim reading. Ghastly as it was, Mrs Priest's school was not exceptional in its cruelty.

We know about her school because in or around 1903 a Mr Hibgame wrote to MEM congratulating her on her book *Gran'ma's Jane* (published in 1903) which he had just read, saying that it brought back vividly to him his early life in Norwich, fifty years previously. He had attended Mrs Priest's school for five desperately miserable years, and the memory haunted him. He was regularly beaten, made to stand on his book box wearing a dunce's cap, or in the stocks, a contraption of pieces of wood that held the victim's feet in the uncomfortable 'first position' of dancers. He was locked in cupboards for hours on end, and was always hungry; the boys' meals consisted mainly of boiled mutton, bread and rice pudding, though they ate in the same room as Mr and Mrs Priest and Miss Paraman who were served much more interesting dishes. Being sent to bed with only bread and water was a frequent punishment. 'Now I come to think of it I feel sure that for some time I was the only boarder Miss Paraman had, for I can remember all the day boys going home in the afternoon and leaving me alone. I had to sit in the school room window and look at the country in the distance over the house tops and count the windmills ...' he wrote. Later in the letter he describes some of the things that happened in the school and assures MEM that he 'has not over drawn them...I have purposefully omitted many of the things concerning the whippings and beatings etc ...'

This letter prompted MEM to write *Memories of Ronald Love* which will be discussed in more detail in Chapter Six. In a letter written to her nephew, Tom Ordish, in 1904 MEM says ironically, 'I too had the privilege of tuition under the "tender" rule of Paraman and Priestly.' and she tells him she remembers the place well – 'the boxes, the stocks, the boy lying under Paraman's chair. I had an abject terror of the women though they were both kind to me.' She described them both in the novel. Miss Paraman was large, pale and sandy haired and, in a letter to her nephew, MEM said how unpleasant it was to hold her 'bony hand encased in its silk glove' when the class was taken out for a walk, as she always had to do because she was the only girl in the school.

Mrs Priest, who was in her mid-50s when Polly attended her school, is depicted as an old lady, fat, pale and intimidating. She extended 'her large white hand encased in a white mitten; her large face was white also; the hair arranged in flat curls upon her temples, was white, she wore a cap of much quilled net tied beneath her chin with broad white ribbons, over her ample bust, white muslin was crossed.' MEM also wrote of her with her 'white lashed lids and snappy voice' taking a spelling lesson and 'encouraging' the boy nearest her with smacks about the head from the lesson book in her hand. Miss Paraman was much more vicious and MEM describes one boy 'being whacked on head and trembling hands by the gigantic paper knife Miss Paraman carried for the purpose' for failing to write the letter 'x' properly.

When they were old enough, Willie and most of his brothers were sent, as boarders, to the Grammar School in Wymondham. A few of the letters that Willie sent to Polly from there still survive. Many of them describe long walks that he has taken, and not very much else. In one letter he talks of playing football in the snow and accidentally hitting an old lady on the head with the ball, *'which she kept!'* He also mentions that his younger brothers have been in trouble but he does not elaborate on what they have done.

On February 26th 1861 Willie wrote to Polly in French (he was about fifteen then, she thirteen) – and asked her to reply in French, which she did. He was impressed – and wrote back, 'I almost showed it to Monsieur Emerique, but I did not. Never say I don't consider your feelings.' The letter that he wrote shows a very good knowledge of French – and so did Polly's so she must have been well taught – perhaps she had a governess for a while after she left Mrs Priest's. We know that she went on to attend Mrs Dunnett's school in Surrey Street which opened in 1858. Polly was a bookish child who remembered that she drove her mother to distraction by sitting *inside* the fender to read by the light of the fire, and who was totally disinterested in needlework and crochet and the sort of pastimes Mrs Rackham thought suitable for a young girl.

A letter from her brother John from Wymondham in May 1870 suggests that the Rackhams may have been growing short of money, because he says he thinks he and his brother will be able to make their winter coats last until next year 'as it is almost summer'. In another letter in April 1871 he requests 'Dear Polly' to ask their mother to send shirts immediately as they have none to wear. Either Mrs Rackham was neglecting her growing sons' needs or the family had financial problems.

Town Close House where the Rackhams lived from 1865-1881

In 1865 the Rackham family moved again, this time to Town Close House. William Rackham took a thirty year repairing lease on the property at £75 a year, which was something of a bargain, though the

22

house itself does not seem to have been in very good condition. It was a huge rambling property, set in eight acres of land, with stables, yards, outbuildings, huge gardens and some pasture land; Polly's father was beginning to realise his dream of being a country gentleman and he acquired dogs and horses to live up to the image. The house had been built as a farmhouse in the mid-18th century, but in the 1820s the then owner, Jeremiah Ives, had extended and modernised it. Within a few years Town Close and Ipswich Road were being developed with high quality housing and by the 1840s it had become a fashionable area in which to live.

A year after they moved to Town Close House, William Rackham pulled out of his partnership with Chamberlins, the big drapers in the Market Place. He had only been a junior partner with a very small share of the business, but nonetheless Chamberlins were a successful firm and deciding to go it alone with his own warehouse as his only source of income was probably not his best business decision. The family may have been hard-up because his business was not doing as well as he had hoped and, at the same time, he had over-reached himself by taking on a mansion and a small estate.

They were a close-knit family in those early years. A letter to Polly from her brother William in 1868, when he was no longer living at home and was working as a solicitor in an office on Banks Plain, reinforces this. He congratulates her on the lodgings she has found in Great Yarmouth for their annual family holiday and asks her to get him accommodation nearby. He was twenty-two, living independently, but he still wanted to share his family's summer holiday. One letter that Polly wrote on an earlier holiday survives. She was about ten and writing to her father at her mother's behest. The letter is very, very neatly written – nothing slapdash for her father. The family had already arrived in Great Yarmouth for the annual holiday and he is to join them shortly with their maid, Martha. Polly wrote, 'Mother has told me to say that we brought the beef with us as she thought you would not want the trouble of bringing it.' It would seem that they were providing their own food. She also tells him about the walk they had been on and how her little brother John, then aged about three, had cried because he didn't like walking up hills.

Such snapshots of MEM's childhood are few and far between, but there are descriptions of 1860s Norwich in *Gran'ma's Jane* that tell us about the city she knew as a little girl. Jane's grandparents and their house were based on Polly's own. The 'tea-room at Orford Hill is a living memory with me and my poor Gran'ma, with the milk-blue eyes, and poor, bullying tender hearted Gran'pa … until I was about six years old I was escorted, a small snivelling visitor, to spend every Saturday… the gloom of the place used to lie like a shade about my small feet as I walked there, and the sadness of them all sank into my very bones … [W]hile I wrote it I thought a good bit of Willie … and I put a good many phrases to Gran'ma's mouth I knew he would recall.' We don't know whether Willie ever read *Gran'ma's Jane*; he died the year it was published. The grandparents must have been her father's mother, Maria, née Ling, and her second husband, Robert Sheppard.

On St George's Day in Jane's – and MEM's – childhoods, men dressed up as 'Snap the Dragon' and attempted to bite the hats off children's heads. If 'Snap' got your hat you had to pay him to get it back. Norwich Fair was another exciting annual event with sideshows, stalls selling toys and sweets and 'Norfolk fair buttons', a type of sweet biscuit. When she was a very old lady MEM's cousin sent her some as a treat. Like Jane, Polly Rackham probably had dancing lessons and attended the annual Children's Ball in St Andrew's Hall. Before she set out for this event 'Jane was made by her elders to place her silk-shod feet in first, second and third positions before she left, she went through the polka, the waltz, the varsovienne steps, she held out her tarletan skirts and courtesied [sic] to the floor.' The children's ball was evidently quite a formal affair.

It is from the letters from Polly's friends, both male and female, that we get our only other insight into her life before she married, and begin to hear for the first time the cadence of their speech and see the relationship she had with people other than her immediate family. These are not literary documents. They are full of the enthusiasms of youth – and its swings of emotion from the heights to the depths. Many of the letters are undated but we do get some idea of the friendship between the young people and, in particular, how they were all in awe of MEM and her talent. To all of them she was 'Polly', but to her closest friends, both male and female, she was 'Poppie' or 'Pops'.

Polly's girl friends all seem to have attended Mrs Dunnett's school. Mrs Dunnett was the wife of James Dunnett, an accountant, and the couple had three sons and a daughter. At census time in 1861 they had three little girls aged between nine and thirteen as live-in pupils, but Polly and her friends seem to have been day girls and there were probably many more of them.

24

In *Gran'ma's Jane*, little Jane is sent to 'Mrs Bennett's Establishment for Young Ladies' which is based on Mrs Dunnett's school – even the owners' names are similar. MEM describes the white scrubbed floorboards in the schoolroom, the narrow benches and tables where the girls sat to work. They each had a bookshelf and their books were 'veiled in the green jaconet lining [a cheap fabric] with which all the school books were clothed.' She mentions in particular *Brewer's Guide to English History, Delille's French Grammar* and Tasso's *Gerusalemme Liberata* – which is interesting in view of Rachel's letter below. There were no organised games, 'No tennis in those days, or hockey, or cricket for schoolgirls. A game of Les Graces, perhaps, of battledore and shuttlecock for the more actively inclined.' 'Les Graces' involved whirling a beribboned hoop round in a circle towards your opponent who tried to catch it on a wand. The action was a bit like throwing a frisbee. It was pretty and graceful to watch and was thought especially suitable for young girls. In their breaks the girls 'sauntered about with their arms around each other's waists or sat reading under the trained branches of the willow tree.' MEM describes how Jane was dressed for school. 'The curls were tucked away into a net now, and were surmounted by a queer little brown mushroom shaped hat, tied with brown ribbons beneath her chin. She wore a tiny crinoline and side-laced boots, and a pearl grey jacket with wide sleeves.' This is probably how young Polly Rackham and her friends dressed for school.

The female friends with whom she kept in touch were Annie Rising, Nellie Edgar, Julie Woolbright, Isabel Mear, Rachel Taylor, Mary Lee and Kate Nichols and they were all from very respectable families: Nellie's and Kate's fathers were surgeons, Rachel's and Julie's were attorneys, Isabel's was a master builder, Mary's was a painter, though Nellie's and Julie's fathers had both died when the girls were little.

It is from her friend Rachel's letters that we gain the clearest impression of MEM's personality as a schoolgirl and young woman. They were both highly intelligent and Mrs Dunnett worked them hard: they were studying Italian. In one letter Rachel asks Polly how she is getting on with the work Mrs Dunnett has asked them to prepare saying that she has 'prepared 40 stanzas of Tasso's cantos for next Monday' adding that she is going to be at Mrs Dunnetts at 10.30 and is looking forward to seeing Polly there and chattering about, 'friends, bonnets, and young men'. This makes it sound very much as if the older pupils only came in for certain lessons and were not there the whole time.

In another letter Rachel is arranging a walk with Polly saying that she is so looking forward to it but is concerned 'lest we should laugh when we are together if we meet anyone we know and when there is an elevation of a chimney pot...' This sounds like some sort of in-joke but it does suggest Polly Rackham was fun to be with. Rachel's language was never commonplace and her letter ended with an irreverent nod to their Italian lessons, 'Addie a rivederce la nostra fidele amica.' She seems to have been the most lively and enthusiastic of the group. In a letter from Cromer one holiday she writes 'I have bathed three times. Oh splendid! Beautiful! Glorious!' She also often uses what was then modern slang; 'My dear little Pops, you are an absolute brick to give me such a splendid present' runs one letter, and she saw no need to be polite. When their friend, Julie Woolbright, got engaged, she was incredulous. 'I cannot understand people falling in love with people they have known for so long'. Rachel herself never married but stayed at home with her mother and siblings until she was in her forties. It is also interesting to catch a glimpse of the different lives the girls lived. Rachel's family appear to have been very strict: in one letter she describes how they have ruled that she can only write to her friends on Saturdays, for example, and in another she breaks off an arrangement to meet because she is 'not allowed out.'

Nellie Edgar also seems to have been quite lively and her family obviously encouraged her to be adventurous. There is a letter from her when she is obviously at some sort of avant garde girls' camp near Canterbury; she talks about picnics in the woods, getting wet and muddy, going nutting and blackberrying and, most daring of all, not wearing their crinolines.

MEM stayed in touch with Kate Nichols for most of her life, but as a girl Kate seems to have been somewhat in awe of Polly Rackham. In one letter she replies to an accusation that she has not returned a book she had been lent: 'You know Polly,' she wrote, 'I am so afraid of you that I can't write naturally.' Kate was a strong-minded and talented young woman and it is hard to imagine that she was really so nervous of her friend. Though she longed to be a painter her real skill lay in etching and she became one of the first women members of the Royal Society of Etchers. Kate's father ran his own lunatic asylum – there was some conflict with the Rackhams when he wanted to open it opposite their house in Town Close – and after his death Kate had a comfortable private income. She was a flamboyant character with dramatic looks, who went on sketching tours all over the country and abroad and could afford to send her work to exhibitions in Europe and America. She founded the Woodpecker Art Club in 1887 to which both MEM and her artist daughter later belonged. Kate Nichols was also the first president of the Norwich branch of the RSPCA and kept an extraordinary collection of pets in her studio; her particular favourite was a pet rat who used to accompany her to church in her handbag! MEM wrote a short story, *The Eerie*, based on Kate's eccentricities. It was published in 1912.

Mrs Dunnett was obviously very fond of her girls and Rachel, Kate and Polly were her particular favourites. One letter shows that after they had left school she tried to arrange a meeting of the three them with her at her house, 'I should so like to have with me at the same time three of the "olden time." ' Sadly for her it doesn't seem as if they found a date when they were all in Norwich and free. Polly kept in touch with her for some years after she left school and Mrs Dunnett was on visiting terms with Mrs Rackham.

Isabel Mear wrote regularly to Polly and her letters often make dismal reading. Much to Isabel's distress, she and her sister, Emily, were transferred from Mrs Dunnett's to a school run by the Reverend Thomas Sutton and his third wife, Caroline, at Marton Vicarage, near Gainsborough, in Lincolnshire. There were four Sutton daughters still living at home and Isabel had to share a bed with one of them. There were seven other boarders and she 'didn't care much' for any of them. The Suttons seem to have spent a lot of time on Bible study – Isabel describes the regime in some detail – and church music. Presumably the Mears were keen for their girls to have a strong religious education. The Suttons also seem to have taken young women with problems: in one letter Isabel describes how one girl was taken for a walk and had some sort of a breakdown – she thought it was something to do with a failed love affair. Isabel's letters are written in a rather overblown style that she perhaps felt would impress the already literary and erudite Polly.

After leaving school Isabel became a governess, first to the Freeman family in Hingham and then to the Reverend Dashwood's two children, thirteen year old Anna, who she described as 'clever', and seven year old Edmund, at Billingford, a tiny village near East Dereham. While she was there her mother became very ill, and though the Dashwoods were kind, Isabel was miserable and wrote to MEM. 'I felt so horrid, more like hearing the doorbell at school than anything that has happened since...' On coming home she wrote, 'It was a beautiful sunrise after a dark and stormy night – but I knew as soon as perfect daylight was restored I should see all the old horror again.' Isabel's parents were both very elderly – her father was fifty-two when she was born and her mother forty, so she always knew that she was likely lose them while she herself was still quite young. The letter goes on with many crossings out, and suicide seems to be heavily on her mind.

Sometime after 1870, Isabel's letters cease and we don't have any of the letters that MEM may have written in response. However, by 1891 Isabel had moved to Hawkshurst in Kent and was living with J.A. Glazebrook, listed as her 'partner', and female. They are both 'teachers' and have two teenage girls as pupils. Perhaps Isabel had found her true self at last with J.A. Glazebrook, even though polite society saw marriage as the only respectable option for young girls of good family.

Marriage was a subject obviously much discussed between the friends. In one letter Annie Rising described matrimony as 'a chilling idea'. Whether or not she overcame the feeling is not known as it has proved impossible to trace her. Rachel, Kate and Isabel seem to have agreed with her – none of them married. But Nellie, Polly, Julie and Mary all did what was expected of them and married young. Julie was the first to find herself a husband; in 1866 she became the second wife of the brewer, Charley Bullard. Nellie followed a year later. Her husband was Edward Saunders who was in the army and the couple spent much of their married life in India; her letters to Polly are densely written on flimsy paper. MEM herself married in 1871, and Mary Lee married Alfred Cooke Self, 'gentleman', in London in March 1874. However, as a girl, Mary had been interested in Polly's brother, George, and Mrs Rackham's letters suggest that the interest continued after her marriage. 'Mrs Self' would walk along Ipswich Road and hover outside the gate to Town Close House in the hope of seeing George in the garden. However, she did not trouble him for long. Mary died in 1876, soon after the birth of her first child, a little girl, and a year later, Alfred remarried.

Little is known about what Polly and her friends did together out of school hours. In the 1860s the rules about young women being chaperoned were quite strict and evening outings at least would have required the presence of one of their brothers. Their letters to each other are full of descriptions of books they have read, quotations, poetry and recommendations of things to read, and Kate Nicholls' letters to Polly are full of questions like 'Are you going to the concert on Wednesday?' and 'Did you enjoy the opera?' They were intelligent young women who valued their education; they would have been aware that they were much more fortunate than their mothers had been in that respect. Everyone in the group seems to have valued Polly Rackham's friendship and eagerly awaited her letters, and what comes through very clearly is that she was a very erratic correspondent. In letter after letter her friends complain that she has not replied to them, and in fact few of the friendships seem to have lasted very long. She always seems to have preferred male friends.

There is another collection of letters which MEM kept tied up with pink ribbon. They were letters from the young men who had courted her – Tom Dixon Smith from Bungay, Edward Bassey (Ted), David Sayer (Dave), two brothers, John Hilling Barnard and Alfred Barnard - and Fairman Mann. Again through their use of language we can hear their voices – young men desperate to appear as sophisticated adults in one sentence, and exposing their juvenile doubts in the next. Only Fairman, who was a good deal older than the rest, writes in a more restrained and mature way. What do not seem to have survived are the poems they wrote her. In 1900, as a woman of fifty-two, MEM wrote to her nephew about them. 'When I was young I received many poems from the appreciative youth of the district. Some of these effusions I have still, and some of the quite early ones which produced only a red shame that anyone should pretend to be in love with me I have, alas! destroyed. I remember one of these beginning "Pretty Polly Rackham, fresh and fair and plump, Into your affections I should like to jump" which was a perfect torture to me because my brother had an inconvenient knack of quoting it to my shrinking ear on any occasion.' Being the only girl in a house full of brothers must sometimes have been very difficult!

But by the late 1860s she was growing up. Polly was not a beauty, but she was young, attractive, clever, and amusing company. Her parents expected her to marry and seem to have allowed her a good deal of freedom to play the field, and her brothers were now useful chaperones rather than an embarrassment. Having grown up with so many boys she was confident in the company of young men - and she enjoyed playing the coquette.

The first of her suitors was Tom Dixon Smith and he seems to have taken an interest in her while she was still at school. There is only one letter from him, written in a flamboyant copperplate and saying very little, but there are occasional coy references to 'Tom' in some of her girlfriends' letters. Another early admirer was David Sayer who had been at school with her brother, Willie, and would also have known her since she was a schoolgirl. He was obviously intelligent and lively, but his letters are too verbose and in his attempt to sound grown-up he comes over as very patronising.

'Dear Pops,
My dear child I was extremely pleased at receiving so charming and delightful epistle from an old friend. I suppose I may class you with my friends as I believe you were the first of the female tribe....'

... but then he ends rather nervously, 'If there are any objections to my writing to you show this to no one.' Ted Bassey tried hard to impress her as well, but one of his letters ends 'I have no news. I am dull. Please write soon.' A dull boyfriend was unlikely to hold Polly Rackham's attention for long – though no doubt her parents would have thought him a good catch. His family were ship-owners and coal merchants in Yarmouth.

Alfred Barnard, the son of a local ironmonger, also fancied his chances with Polly Rackham. He even sent her a live salamander by train from Oxford! 'Tis a charming creature docile and intelligent ... It should be kept in a fern case and feeds on insects and fire-moss or grass,' he wrote, and went on to describe, tongue-in-cheek, how to 'give him fire'. Legend had it that salamanders lived in fire. History does not relate what Polly thought of the gift – or how long it survived. Alfred's friendship with Polly continued long after her marriage. In 1883 he contacted her about publicising her first novel, *The Parish of Hilby*. 'I have just seen Stafford of the Chronicle,' he wrote, 'and he will give the book a swinging notice from what he tells me.'

But it was Alfred's elder brother, John Hilling Barnard, usually called 'Hilling', who was the most besotted with Polly. To begin with he is cringing towards her. 'I hope you will not be angry with me for writing as I cannot help it...' ran one of his early letters, 'PS. Please excuse all blunders.' While most of the young men soon gave up in their quest for the vivacious Polly Rackham, Hilling Barnard did not. He was completely in love, and in awe of her.

30

Hilling was the heir to an established Norwich firm of general and furnishing ironmongers which also had show-rooms in London; had Polly wished to marry him it would have been a very good match. The initial attraction between them seems to have been a common love of literature, and the romantic Barnard had a sensitivity and passion for words that matched Polly's own. An early letter, sent with a loan of a book, is written on superior writing paper decorated with an embossed German scene and is entirely in verse, though written out as prose. It is a neat and humorous résumé of the novel and the product of considerable time and effort in an attempt to charm her. In 1869 he sent her a copy of *Lucille* writing a fairly scathing note that the author 'forgot in his preface to state that most of the plot, every thought and expression was taken verbatim from an older writer.' By November of that year he was answering conundrums and playing word games in correspondence with her, they were obviously close, though he must have known that there were other suitors on the scene. However, from the beginning of 1870 his letters change in their tone, intimacy and vigour. Someone had come between them, and that someone was Fairman Mann. This letter, from January 28th 1870, marks the beginning of the end of their relationship:

'Mr John Hilling Barnard begs to return Miss Rackham's scarf which she so kindly lent him and to thank her for the loan. He has noticed a small hole in the scarf and also an inkblot neither of these must be laid to his charge. They are old offenders ... Mr John Barnard fears that Miss Rackham's hope of peace has poor foundation ...'

Hilling must have realised that Fairman Mann was a serious contender for Polly's affections, though it is hard to see why she was so attracted to him. He was ten years older than her and not from Norwich. The Mann family were farmers and entrepreneurs in the hamlet of Rockland St Andrew; at one stage they ran a drapery-cum-grocery business there and it could be that they bought from the Rackham warehouse in Norwich. Fairman came up regularly for the Norwich Saturday cattle market and seems to have been introduced to the Rackham family early in 1870 as this letter shows.

27th March 1870 Sunday morning
My dear Miss Rackham,
...What an awful fool I made of myself last evening in attempting to rush away from the station because your father was there. Why I did this I can't

for the life of me explain. I really begin to think I am a 'funny' sort of fellow. What think you?
I should <u>wonderfully</u> like to have MER's reply

31st March 1870
....You don't mean your father actually saw me? It makes my fingers tingle to think of it. Now I don't intend to reply to your brother in writing but verbally on Saturday. I fancy I can talk a little better than I can write. You will say 'Both are bad enough'. Fact admitted...

Fairman, too, seems to have been in awe of Polly's ability with words and a pen but he was mature enough to know his own worth. He was an intense, single-minded suitor and he persevered with her. He was well-educated but not literary; at thirty-three he was well-built, attractive, a sporting man yet comfortable enough in the city, a true English country gentleman, probably more 'manly' than her swaggering 'city-swell' brothers and her more artistic and thoughtful suitors. Polly's family liked him, and perhaps she found him more confident and grown-up than young men of her own age.

He wrote very frequently.

April 20th 1870
My dear Miss Rackham
I send the third number of 'The Vicar of Bulhampton'. What can it matter where I get these numbers? Why ask? I wish to send them to you. You also know the intense pleasure it gives me to give you even the very smallest gratification. This is not 'talk' but a fact ...My powers of perception with you are nearly worthless.

They met almost every weekend and became increasingly intimate though, with rivals about, Fairman could never be certain of her affection. Consciously or otherwise, Polly Rackham was playing her admirers off against each other while she considered her options. However, by June 1870 it seems that she felt she had to make a choice: John Hilling Barnard or Fairman Mann? We already know her decision - but Fairman was aware he had a rival and could not be sure which of them she would choose. His letter of Sunday June 12th is cryptic and almost illegible and indicates his agitation and lack of belief in his ability to snare for himself the lovely Polly Rackham,

'...for I cannot determine to my own satisfaction which is the favoured one. I some-how think it is a 'dead heat' the consequences will then be to cast lots,

the losing one to drown or shoot himself. Had I to decide, I should have no hesitation but plump for H?'

But he was wrong. That evening Polly Rackham agreed to be his wife. Fairman's letter marking their engagement was restrained to say the least. He was not a man given to extravagant displays of emotion.

17th of June 1870
My dear Miss 'Mary Elizabeth'
This is to thank you for your extreme kindness and thoughtfulness in complying with my wishes on Tuesday last …
Ever yours truly
Fairman J Mann.

By contrast, Hilling Barnard was distraught and could not contain his grief and disappointment.

In the summer of 1870 Fairman was clearly very much in love with Polly. He extended his weekends with her, then caught the late train back, but he had a farm to run and there are hints that she really had no idea what this entailed. It was going to come as a more of a shock than either of them foresaw. In July 1870 they still had much to learn about each other as they settled down to wait a respectable time before they actually got married. They wrote to each other every few days:

13th July 1870, 2p.m.
I find everything all right here. I am just starting to Rockland to be on a tour of inspection and hope to continue fortunate. Had anything of importance occurred during my absence I should never forgive myself. Please write….This is if you wish and will not find it irksome to do so…a long letter what <u>you think of all</u> I told you yesterday.
Ever yours
FJM
PS You are the coolest and least susceptible girl I ever knew. Alas, so hard!

15th July 1870
You are very good and kind to write. I am so grateful. I admire your courage with your brother [Willie the solicitor? Or Harry?] I never could understand why he should be so autocratic to you and your good mamma… George tells me that your father told him to ask me to stay over Sunday. I wish I could do so. <u>You know</u> I do wish this. But I must have to resist

33

pleasures. How hard it is I know this is an uninteresting letter but I feel better assured,
Ever yours totally
FJM

17th July 1870
Just awake. Have been sleeping nearly all day to make up the deficiencies of last week. What an unsatisfactory way of spending a Sunday. Oh how I wish you were here. I do...I must go round my farms at Rockland, Ellingham and Attleboro'. You say I don't work. Isn't this work?
Your Fairman
Tell me if your father's £1000 is right of heritage?

The only farm Fairman actually owned was Mill Farm, in Shropham, and he was only the tenant of Church Farm, where he lived. These 'farms' may have been farm lands that he rented. The £1,000 seems to be Polly's marriage settlement.

A little later, when Fairman was obviously trying to get Polly to visit Shropham, we get an interesting glimpse of life at her home when Fairman came courting. Her mother and brother Willie would not leave them alone.

'Won't you pay your promised visit? Can you resist this attraction?...I promise you...the sole and entire use of my celebrated sofa during the best of the day, and in the evening you can come just across my meadow to the 'Grove' where there will be no fear of interruption from big brother or from mamma calling 'Polly'! Speaking for myself I do like secluded places where I can be romantic...Shall this intense delight be yours?'

Fairman's courtship letters also show that, besotted as he obviously was by her, he recognised that Polly Rackham had hurt Hilling deeply. He was also concerned about another young man who had suddenly appeared on the scene, Albert Kincaid. He was a teacher and came from Dublin, no doubt he had the gift of the blarney and romantic good looks – Fairman nicknamed him 'Adonis' – and despite her engagement Polly seems to have encouraged young Mr Kincaid. Years later, MEM's granddaughter remembered hearing about the teacher that her grandmother had wanted to marry but the family forbade it, so MEM seems to have been genuinely attracted to Albert and must at least have considered breaking off her engagement to Fairman. She obviously continued to remember him. In her photograph collection

34

there is a photo of a rather portly middle-aged man with a moustache labelled 'Albert Kincaid' (though not in MEM's writing), and in *Milly Strong*, her first ever novel (never published), there is a character called 'Kinsaid'. It seems Fairman had good reason to be jealous, but his letter of remonstrance is very cautious.

'I think I saw him, Kincaid, being your escort to the theatre this week. Allow me to ask you not to flirt too much. Perhaps the young man may be an exception... Bear in mind one admirer is now pining his life away...in the South of England, in fact I fear his friends feared his mind would go had he remained longer in Norwich.'

This must be a reference to John Hilling Barnard. A year later Hilling was still wretched. Polly collected verses and mementoes in her autograph album and she had asked Barnard to contribute to it. His self-esteem was at its lowest ebb and he simply could not think of anything appropriate to contribute.

12th June 1871
Dear Miss Rackham,
I have been looking at myself from various points of view and I am shocked to find that I am not nearly half as good as I was. There was a day when I should not have allowed a day to pass by and leave a lady's letter unanswered but that day has passed...my thoughts for the past month have been entirely devoted to your album. I have had album on the brain. My mind in fact has been full of it and I fear if I don't write something soon I shall bust and I feel thoroughly discontented with myself and everyone else and without a kindred spirit in the world and the world a wilderness to me...but I'll send your book back probably this week. Knowing you are fond of dance music ...etc I send you a merry little jig hoping you will learn to dance it.
Good bye. Please remember me kindly to Mrs Rackham
I am dear Miss Rackham,
Yours, very respectfully,
J Hilling Barnard

26th July 1871
Dear Miss Rackham.
'I send you back your book'. [This phrase was culled from a book on wedding etiquette.] *A general want of confidence in everything I do which I feel to be growing on me has prevented me from writing anything of my own...'*

The long letter goes on to describe his sleepless nights, general apathy and listlessness, and his total wretchedness at not being able to contribute anything sparkling or original to her autograph book for her to remember him by. He is obviously desperately unhappy at having lost her and does not know what to do. He signs off

'...you may be disgusted for a moment but I – I shall think I have made an everlasting fool of myself in your eyes.
Trusting that I have not and that you will not be hard on my dream,
I am, my dear Miss Rackham yours very truly,
J Hilling Barnard.'

Polly Rackham c. 1870
This portrait may mark her twenty-first birthday in August 1869. Her hairstyle is elaborate; she wears hair ornaments and large dangling earrings. The effect is of a young woman trying to seem mature beyond her years.

Poor Hilling was rejected, but not completely forgotten. Years later MEM used Barnard and his lost love in a novel entitled *Moonlight,* where youthful misunderstandings lead to the breakdown of a relationship. No doubt she was distressed to hear from her mother some time later that Barnard had been seen in a drunken state in the street proclaiming loudly that he had missed a prize in Polly. Willie was with him and told him fiercely the next morning to hold his tongue and never to mention her name again. In another letter, about a year after her marriage, Willie told her of a chance meeting he had had with Barnard and commented on his very excited and peculiar behaviour. Barnard was obviously still suffering deeply. He had, Willie wrote, begun to talk about Polly saying, 'Ah, that is all a thing of the past – won't bear thinking about. No, I never mention her – Fairman had a bargain....' Two years later Polly learnt of Barnard's wedding from her mother in a newspaper cutting that she stuck in Fairman's scrapbook. 'The marriage is announced of John Hilling Barnard to Alice Maud Horsey from Ringmer, Sussex, on February 6th 1973 in London.' It is to be hoped she made him happy.

Fairman was a farmer but he was not a country bumpkin. His scrapbook, which he started in 1872 shortly after their marriage, gives us some idea of the sort of man he was and what his interests were other than agriculture – though the book does contain many articles on farming, disease in cattle and various modern methods of control. There are many pages devoted to the court case that he fought over shooting rights. He kept cuttings of poems, about archaeological digs, on philosophical thoughts. There are odd quotations: 'a monster there is in this world, an idle man...', 'A Dandy is a chap who would be a woman if he could but as he can't he does all he can to show the world he is not a man.' He loved puzzles, particularly code puzzles. He kept curious proverbs, and poems in dialect. There are lots of cuttings about court cases with sketches printed that show the defendants and juries. There are news items which he found interesting: the death of Siamese twins in a London hospital, the visit of the Prince of Wales to Norwich, a letter detailing the weather on Christmas day every year from 1827 to 1872 - and in 1875 this gem; 'A performance of an educated flea is attracting much attention in Berlin.' He copied out poems, including one by an E. Rackham, he wrote out recipes, he cut out medical articles: 'On catching a cold alcohol is recommended.' He kept reviews of plays that had been performed all over the country and cut out pictures of willow pattern plates. It is not the scrapbook of an intellectual, but of a highly intelligent man with an eclectic range of interests.

However, even before the wedding there were indications that life in Shropham was going to be rather dull for city-bred Polly. Her brother George was nineteen in 1870 but seems to have been very immature. Unlike his brothers, he was not sent to Wymondham but to a Mr

Cavell at Warham, near Wells-next-the-Sea. Presumably his parents felt he would not cope with boarding school life and needed one-to-one tuition. He appears to have been an amiable if lightweight character, but Fairman invited him to stay – perhaps he was there to act as chaperone if Polly visited before the wedding. His early boyish letters to Polly always showed them to be on good terms and the tone barely changed as he grew up. However, the contents of a letter written in July 1870 throw an interesting light on life with the Manns in Shropham and might have given her cause to reconsider her choice. He had been to Mr Bolton Mann's, Fairman's uncle's, for dinner. 'Very grand. It was very slow. No one spoke except Fairman. Not more than three words spoken. Mr Sims-Reeve was there but left early so no time to get funny. He is very funny after lots of wine. Fairman went to sleep after dinner and Mr Mann had to kick him ...'

And this was the life for which Polly Rackham was leaving Norwich! Gone would be her adoring suitors and her lively girl-friends. She and Fairman were to marry in September 1871, and no doubt her family were delighted; he was a responsible man, the tenant of a sizeable farm and other farm lands, the sort of estate her father had always dreamt of, and in 1871 his prospects looked good. In Shropham she would be expected to be a serious and responsible wife, not a giddy and clever young woman. She would soon find that, as she would later scribble in one of her many notebooks, 'Marriage is a picturesque gateway to a common place estate.'

Church Farm, Shropham,
where Fairman and MEM lived from 1871-1877

Chapter 3. Norwich to Shropham 1871-1881

On September 28th, 1871 pretty, talented, flirtatious Polly Rackham passed through that picturesque gateway and became Mrs Fairman Joseph Mann, mistress of Church Farm and a person of some importance in the little village of Shropham. She was just twenty-three.

We know very little about the wedding other than that it took place at Holy Trinity Church in Norwich and the vicar who officiated was the Reverend Rust. In 1871 weddings were not the over-blown, astronomically expensive affairs they are today and there are no details of what the bride wore or who was there. MEM's bridesmaid was her school friend, Mary Lee, who also helped Mrs Rackham make the wedding cake, and then parcel it up and send it out. The wedding breakfast was probably also home-made, held at Town Close House and provided by Mrs Rackham and the cook. We do not know where the couple honeymooned or for how long, but soon enough they were back in Shropham.

The Mann family were farmers. At the time of Fairman's marriage his father was also running a local inn, the White Hart in Rockland St Andrew – probably a rather smaller establishment than the present pub that bears that name. His grandfather, Joseph Mann, and his Uncle John had taken the tenancy of Manor Farm (then called City Farm) in Shropham back in 1809. Fairman's father would have spent part of his childhood there and was probably still living at home when the present house was built in 1822. By 1871 Fairman's elder brother, John Eagling Mann, farmed 370 acres in Rockland and two of his sisters had married two brothers, James and William Warner, who had large farms in Scarning.

So Fairman Joseph Mann was a countryman born and bred and farming was in his blood. He had taken the tenancy of Church Farm in 1862, and it was to the comfortable red-brick farmhouse with its tall chimneys, Tudor-style windows and low-beamed ceilings, that he brought his young bride. He proudly inscribed his name and the date of the wedding at eye level in one of the bricks on the garden side of the house, a custom the family seem to have invented to record the major milestones of their lives. Over the years, bricks in the walls of

Fairman's homes would be used to record the names and birth dates of all his four children. But though they were farming folk, living in small villages, the Manns were not country bumpkins. Fairman was well-educated, intelligent and public-spirited. For example, in his commonplace book he records that he won the Spelling Bee in Attleborough in 1878 but immediately gave the first prize of twenty shillings (£1) back to the committee to be re-awarded.

Shropham as MEM would have known it.
It is a straggling village without a proper centre.

MEM wrote in her memoir that her own father had always hankered after life in the countryside and he had probably imbued her with romantic notions of what such a life would be like. She soon found the reality was much less idyllic. Shropham is a pleasant enough village, set in attractive but unremarkable countryside, but when the un-metalled country roads had turned to mud after days of rain, when the sky was leaden and a bitter wind blew from the east, it was bleak and depressing. Besides, she was a city girl who enjoyed going to the theatre and to concerts, attending lectures and borrowing books from libraries as well as meeting friends and going shopping. None of those activities were available to her in Shropham. The village is just twenty-one miles south-west of Norwich and today it takes a little over half an hour to drive there, but in MEM's day a trip to the city was a major excursion. First of all it required someone to be available to drive her the three miles to the Eccles Road station and to collect her on her return – two round trips of six miles because the pony and trap could not be left all day at the station. Today the journey by train takes approximately thirty minutes but it was probably slower in MEM's day. She then had to make her way from the station to her home on the other side of town or into the city centre. It was not a trip she could make often.

Shropham is sparsely populated and very scattered and in 1871 there were few neighbours with whom the Manns could socialise as equals. The Budds at the Hall were seldom in residence – George Budd was a solicitor in London – and relations were not friendly because Fairman was constantly at loggerheads with him about shooting rights. That left the Manns' kinsfolk at Manor Farm, George Bolton Mann and his daughter, Edith; William Robbins the vicar and his family of daughters; William Smyth Thorpe, vicar of Breccles, who lived at The Villa; John Barker at Grange Farm and old Miss Mary Young at Ivy Cottage as the only other gentry in the village. Of these, only Edith Mann – whom Polly did not much like – and some of the vicar's tribe of daughters were near her in age. She must have been very lonely in those early years. There were other families like the Salters in Attleborough and their relatives at Scarning whom they visited occasionally, but those visits entailed journeys of several miles over rutted roads in the pony and trap and Fairman was seldom free to accompany her.

Most of the remaining inhabitants of the village were farm workers: labourers, shepherds and 'teamsmen' and a few who worked at the local brickworks. There were a couple of smallholders, a miller, a carpenter, two shoemakers, a plumber and glazier who was married to the schoolmistress, two washerwomen and three women who took in dressmaking. Sophia Lusher on Villa Road ran a small general shop with her daughter, and their near neighbour, Mary Ann Barrett, sought to eke out her labourer husband's wage in the same way. William Warren ran a grocers-cum-drapers and George Allen kept the White Horse public house. William Brame was a butcher and George Gregory combined blacksmithing with keeping the village's other inn, appropriately named the Three Horseshoes. The family at the Hall employed a gamekeeper and coachman and the more genteel

41

inhabitants of the larger houses had gardeners and servants. Twenty-one villagers admitted to the census enumerator that they were paupers. Sixty-seven year old Susan Dexter was on parish relief because she had to look after her son who had broken his back; couples like old James and Dinah Plain had grown too feeble to earn a wage; there were elderly widows, feckless families and grandmothers like Elizabeth Thursoe struggling to support orphaned grandchildren. Polly Mann would have known them all, along with the thirty or so inter-related village families: the Betts and the Nobbs, the Burtons, the Barnards and the Barretts, the Lawrences and the Chaneys, the Grooms, the Allens, the Roses and the Musks. Readers of her novels will recognise many of the names, or versions of them, from her writing.

Shropham was a sleepy little place where very little happened. The local press records the births, marriages and deaths of the more prosperous inhabitants, frequent sales of timber and fat lambs, and a surprising amount of petty crime. Drunken brawls were common and occasionally they resulted in prosecutions. In March 1875, for example, George Musk refused to leave the Three Horseshoes public house and the landlord, George Gregory, attempted to remove him by force. In the ensuing scuffle George Gregory's pocket watch was damaged. The penalties were swingeing. George Musk was fined five shillings and sixteen shillings costs; George Gregory was fined a pound and eighteen shillings costs – huge sums in a village where the average weekly wage was eleven shillings. Maybe George Gregory was already a known troublemaker for in 1878 he was before the magistrates again, this time charged with the much more serious offence of getting £13 15s. from the Hockham Rangers' branch of the Ancient Order of Foresters under false pretences. He was fined £10 (reduced from £20 on the grounds that he had a wife and family to support) and ordered to repay the money – though how he was expected to do this is far from clear. In September 1881, Everett Eke, who had taken over the Three Horseshoes from Gregory, was fined £2 for assaulting Stephen Corley outside the pub. Eke was another serial offender, appearing before the magistrates half a dozen times in a decade.

Some crimes seem to have been borne of resentment. In November 1875 James Fincham's dislike of the gentry boiled over and he blocked the road to Rockland and damaged the brougham belonging to the Reverend Hemsworth, rector of Bacton and a member of the Hemsworth family of Shropham Hall. Fincham was a drover; maybe he disliked the rector, maybe the gentry in their fancy carriages were constantly in his way, or maybe he had just tired of tugging his forelock. Whatever the reason, it was an expensive gesture; he was fined a total of £2 5s.and ordered to pay 15s.6d. in costs.

Other crimes were the result of poverty and overwork. In 1882 George Burlingham and William Copeman (one of Fairman's labourers) were fined 5s. apiece for not sending their children to school. William had three school-age children and two toddlers – maybe his wife was too harassed to get the children out of a morning. George was a widower with four sons; he, his sixteen year old and the thirteen year old twins were all farm workers and their days would have started at first light – there was probably no-one at home to see that eight year old George went to school. But the real force of the law was reserved for poachers. In January 1870, seventy-eight year old Robert Dye from nearby Shipdham killed two pheasants to feed himself and his wife. It cost him £3 9s. – an impossible sum for a couple their age to find. MEM and her friends would have been aware of all these misdemeanours; there was little enough to talk about and the gentry gossiped as much as the villagers.

Fairman was never a magistrate but he was well aware of the difficulties the village poor faced. For much of his time in Shropham he was an active member of the Board of Guardians for Wayland Union, he was a churchwarden and, until he resigned in the 1890s, a manager of the village school which he had helped set up. In 1870 the school had between sixty and seventy pupils and in March that year the parish advertised for a schoolmistress. She had to be married and under forty and her salary would be £30 p.a. plus the children's pennies, which would add up to about another £10 a year. Few people wanted the job and the following month they advertised again, this time with a salary of £35 and an upper age limit of 45. The young woman they appointed was Sarah Ann Roberts from Coltishall; she was twenty-five, married to a plumber, and she must already have been pregnant with her second child when she took the post. She did not stay long, and by 1880 she had been replaced by Mrs Dack who would prove to be equally unsatisfactory.

As Fairman's wife, MEM became the unofficial lady of the manor, and she and Fairman threw themselves into improving the cultural life of the village. The village held an annual Flower Show and MEM was on the Flower Show Committee alongside the Reverend Robbins, the Reverend Thorpe, Miss Robbins and Miss Agnes Robbins. Mr Robbins was vicar of Shropham and the Misses Robbins were his daughters. There was a band from Harling in 1875 and Mrs Fairman Mann's flower arrangements were 'especially noticed'. She and Fairman and the Reverend Robbins were the prime movers in setting up a Working Men's Reading and Coffee Room in the village which was to be open every evening from 7 – 10 p.m. 'with a liberal supply of newspapers and magazines', and there would be games to play as well. Perhaps the Manns and other village gentry hoped to persuade the labourers to go somewhere other than the pub after work; the woman of the village had no such luxury. By 1879 MEM was not only helping to organise the Flower Show, where again her arrangements were much admired, but had introduced a handicraft section and given away the prizes. The evening ended, according to a local newspaper report that Fairman kept, 'in rural dancing until the light dimmed'.

MEM was also expected, like the vicar's wife and daughters and the other local 'quality' to visit the village poor and provide jugs of soup, jellies and cast-off clothing for the sick and needy. What she saw in the cheerless, comfortless cottages shocked her to the core. There was no shortage of poor people back home in Norwich but she had had little contact with them. In a small village everyone knew everyone else and the labourers' poverty could not be ignored. Times were hard, farmers struggled to make a profit as imports of grain from the new world depressed prices, and as labourers' wages fell and prices rose, whole families struggled to survive on 11s. a week. But it was not just money that they lacked; the villagers' lives were impoverished in every possible way. The census returns tell us that nearly everyone in Shropham in 1871 was born in the village, and those that weren't came mostly from the neighbouring villages of Larling and the Rocklands, so they could not envisage any other way of life than the

44

one they were living. They were uneducated, ignorant and super-stitious, they aspired to nothing and had no hope of better times to come; death was a blessing and a dead baby was a mouth that didn't have to be fed rather than a child to be mourned. But they were also courageous, resourceful and stoical, their sense of morality was pragmatic rather than conventional and among them there were some outstanding individuals. MEM's initial disgust gradually turned to admiration.

It was not just village poverty that she had to get used to. Polly was well-educated and well-read, but she knew very little about house-keeping. Someone presented her with a hard-backed exercise book as a wedding present. Her name was printed on a sticker pasted inside the front cover and it was intended to be used as a recipe book – Polly filled it with stories. Fairman seems to have been a kind and considerate husband, unlike the boorish Peter Howard in the novel she published in 1886, but some aspects of her heroine's early married life clearly mirrored Polly's own. Like young Millie Howard, Polly was a city girl, a merchant's daughter with a home full of brothers including an eight year old on whom the character of naughty Bert was most probably based. She also had several younger brothers, any one of whom could have been the model for Philip Harleigh, Millie's charming-but-useless brother who came to stay with the Howards. The contempt with which old Mrs Howard and 'Auntie' regarded the young girl who knew nothing of meals and budgets, and whose servants ran rings round her, may well have reflected MEM's relationship with her mother- and sister-in-law over in Rockland St Andrew.

MEM was certainly made to recognise her own shortcomings: in later years she recorded how she used to fear her husband's cousin, old George Bolton Mann, then the tenant of Manor Farm. The old gentleman would bow to her courteously when they met, but he always managed to imply that he thought it was perfectly ridiculous that he had to bow to such a young inexperienced girl.

Fairman was preoccupied with his farm, and for the early part of their marriage much of his energy seems to have gone into fighting a court case about shooting rights on tenants' farms. Landowners had the right to preserve hares and rabbits because they were 'game', and they also had the right to shoot over their tenants' land, often doing considerable damage in the process. Hares and rabbits did an immense amount of harm to crops and so tenant farmers and labourers were entitled to hunt and kill them, but they were not allowed to set traps, ostensibly because the traps might catch game birds. The case rumbled on for a year and it ended up in London in the High Court in March 1872.

Fairman arrived in town on the 20th March and wrote home from his hotel – Maxell's Exeter Hotel in the Strand – to say that he had had a safe journey with 'no adventures to tell' except that somehow he had left his portmanteau behind. He addresses MEM as 'My very dear wife' and tells her how much he is missing her. 'I would a thousand times rather be at home with my dear little wife … You know why I actually dread going to bed. What a thing custom is. You know, dear old Pops, what my thoughts will be.' He goes on more prosaically to tell her what he has ordered for dinner – veal chop and green peas - and signs himself 'Ever your most affectionate husband.'

She replied the next day, telling him how worried she was, how worried her father was and how she was dreading the telegram he had promised to send when the verdict was announced – but she still couldn't resist teasing him. 'I'm glad you love me and had green peas and didn't blow me up about the luggage,' she wrote, so it seems that she was in some way to blame for his bag being left behind. Delivery services were much more reliable than they are today, it would seem, and she paid sixpence to have the case sent on to him to be delivered in time for him to have a clean collar to wear in court. She missed him and tried to cheer him up. 'Even if we do lose this case there are worse misfortunes, and I will try to be good to you – now you are away I wish I was always good to you. You must take a deal of notice when you come home please, and love me awful.' She was in the early months of her first pregnancy and no doubt she did miss Fairman, but she obviously recognised even then that she was not the easiest of people to live with.

Fairman must have asked her to let him know how things were going on the farm and her reply, in the same letter, betrays her ignorance of most things agricultural. 'I have been round the farm,' she told him, 'as far as I know how.' The men had told her all was well, and she reported that 'two ewes have calved' (!) and that his favourite bullock seemed well but wouldn't come to her to have its back scratched as it did to him. The weather was awful with snow and rain, Copeman was putting up railings, Solomon was working in the garden, and the butcher hadn't brought any meat, so when the cold beef was finished she supposed they would starve!

The verdict, when it came, was unsatisfactory. The case was dismissed and all the accused were acquitted, but Fairman was not content to let matters lie. He wrote a very long, detailed and erudite letter to the *Standard*, stating his case and telling of the huge expense and trouble it had caused him and of the dreadful situation that the present laws had created. He pointed out that many smaller tenant farmers would not have had the money or the education to enable them to fight as he had. His landlord, he explained, did not shoot, and had allowed him to put up barriers against the rabbits, but the landlord also had the right to let his land out to shooting parties for a considerable sum and the barriers were in their way. In November 1870 he had brought a case against the gamekeeper, William Lines, for damaging his 'rabbit trap bank'. He had been successful, but the problem was ongoing. Fairman was adamant that the law needed to be changed.

An article in the *Mark Lane Express* stated that in 1873 Fairman Mann had been called to London to give evidence before the Game Laws' Commission since he had been successful in the case brought against him. His statement began: 'I live at Church farm Shropham, my occupation having commenced in 1862. I have a twenty-one year lease and my farm consists of 400 acres. I pay a rent of £605 [a year] that being an advance of 5/- an acre paid by the previous tenant...after two years the Hall and shooting rights were sublet to Mr Budd ...' He explained that under Mr Budd the amount of game had increased enormously and he estimated that the damage that had been caused in one sixty-four acre field had cost him £150. Other tenant farmers in the area, some with much smaller farms, were suffering badly too. Mr Budd was not a local man, and he had hired the hall, gardens, park and all the lands and cottages and gardens that went with it, for a mere £200 a year. Fairman suggested that, having no knowledge of farming, and not living locally, Mr Budd neither knew nor cared how much trouble he was causing. 'We should not expect to find the same consideration and good feeling on the part of the shooting tenant which might have characterised relations between the latter and his own landlord,' he said tactfully. The rest of his statement shows that over the past few years he had suffered very considerable losses and brought several unsuccessful actions against Budd.

The hearing went on and on and was eventually adjourned. Fairman saved many pages of newspaper cuttings and attended many more meetings of committees – and there are lengthy reports rating the value of rabbit meat against that of lamb or mutton, and the value of wool against meat and so on. Unfortunately most of his press cuttings are undated so we cannot be sure about the sequence of events. It must have been an intensely frustrating period and the case took up a huge amount of Fairman's time. The Ground Game Act was eventually passed in 1880 by a substantial majority in the House (to loud cheers) and welcomed by a 'multitudinous majority across the country.' Fairman had shown himself a man to be reckoned with. However, the case had absorbed eight years of his time and a good deal of energy, and he was considerably poorer in pocket at the end of it.

As well as coping with the farm and a husband with an obsession, MEM was learning to manage her home. In this she had the advice and support of her mother. Mrs Rackham visited often and was only too happy to help her daughter, though it is clear she often despaired of MEM's kindness to the servants. 'I hope that Fairman will prevent you from giving her a good character' she wrote when MEM was about to sack an unsatisfactory cook. Old Mrs Rackham was a fussy, managing little woman, like Millie Howard's mother in *Mrs Peter Howard,* MEM's semi-autobiographical novel of 1886.

'Nothing dreamt of in Mrs Harleigh's philosophy would refuse to be affected by management. And she had cause to put faith in its wonder-working power – she had effected so much by management. She had managed her husband and her sons, after a method creditable to herself and perhaps pleasant to them. She had managed the marriage of her only daughter, and was about to induct her into her new duties and manner of life, to arrange for her matters domestic, financial, social, before returning to the scene of her own private labours ...She was a small woman of fifty years

and upright as a dart, with bright dark eyes shining in her thin and eager face, with alertness and decision showing in her every movement ... [but t]here was a hardness and a briskness and general unsympathetic aspect about her which the most indifferent did not fail to feel.'

MEM's mother was small and bright-eyed, though surviving photographs suggest she was plump and comfortable-looking rather than slim and upright, but like Mrs Harleigh *'... she had victoriously subdued her husband, a man of great tenderness of heart and very little backbone; her sons, whose varying dispositions she did not comprehend or even guess at; her daughter, with more brains than herself, and a nature as unknown to her as it was entirely alien to her own.'*

It is not a flattering portrait but it does seem to have been quite an accurate one.

Mrs Rackham, MEM's mother

Mrs Rackham wrote to her daughter almost every day when they were apart. Her pen often ran away with her – one long letter deals almost entirely with her difficulties in purchasing a bunch of grapes! She wrote at length about illness and death and the terrible train crash at Thorpe St Andrew in September 1874 provided subject matter for several letters. The Rackhams knew some of the people who were killed and injured and Mrs Rackham affected to be completely traumatised by the horror of the event, but that did not stop her going to view the crash site and describing it in graphic detail. Other letters were filled with family news, gossip about friends and neighbours, goings-on at 'The Warehouse', the family business, and her worries about 'the Boys' – MEM's brothers.

The boys certainly gave their mother plenty to worry about. Willie, the eldest, became a solicitor and in time was very successful, he won a prestigious Law Society prize when he was still in his early twenties and later became a partner in the firm of Coaks and Co in Banks Plain. Willie Rackham was well known in the town for his flamboyant ways – 'With his grey bowler hat well on one side, his cigarette, cane and "peg-top" trousers, he passed outside the office as a flaneur, or man about town …' a journalist wrote some years after his death, adding that he was nonetheless well-respected for his

Willie – William Simon Rackham
1846-93, MEM's elder brother

competence and his discretion; 'he was a sound lawyer and conveyancer, and worked very hard, while his brother lawyers often had reason to admire his ability.'

Early in the 1870s Mrs Rackham wrote to her 'dear Polly' complaining about Willie's flamboyant streak and in particular about his expenditure of the vast sum of five guineas on gold monogrammed stationery. A few years later there was even greater cause for alarm. Willie had proposed to Fanny Elizabeth Newman, one of the young ladies who worked at Chamberlins, the department store in which the Rackhams had recently been junior partners. Department stores employed educated girls with lady-like manners, and Willie's Fanny came from a respectable family in Lowestoft; her father was a shoemaker whose business employed eleven workers. However, a family that allowed a daughter to work in a shop could never be respectable enough for the Rackhams. Willie and Fanny married in 1878, but though Mrs Rackham's letters continued to report Willie's visits and sayings in some detail, Fanny was never mentioned.

Years later MEM would put Willie and Fanny's marriage to literary use. In an unpublished novel, *Mattie, a Portrait*, she wrote of the marriage of a promising young lawyer, Randal Saddlebow, to Mattie Simms, the girl at Tibbles' shop from which he bought his socks. Mattie is a big girl, dark haired, brown skinned and handsome, but she is also clumsy and completely unaware of the ways of polite society. MEM wrings much entertainment from the Saddlebows' horror at the marriage and Mattie's social faux pas, but eventually concludes that she was a good and loyal wife. Mattie's father is a cobbler, as was Fanny's; Randal's father dies of cancer, as did William Rackham; the family live at 'Mile End' which sounds rather like 'Town Close' and there are numerous other parallels – but of course we do not know whether Fanny was really anything like Mattie or whether MEM just took a situation with a potential for embarrassment and used it to comic effect. She does not seem to have had much contact with Willie after she married; there are no letters and he does not feature in any of her correspondence until she reports his funeral. Then her comment is revealing – 'If only he had not taken that false turn at the beginning what a career his might have been!' In the novel Mattie commits suicide to allow Randal to be with his partner's young daughter with whom he has fallen in love. Fanny died suddenly of 'Morbus cordis' – medical jargon for 'cause unknown, probably a heart attack' – and Willie married a much younger woman barely a year later. No doubt it was a perfectly innocent set of circumstances – but perhaps it gave MEM the idea for *Mattie*.

Harry and George, the next two brothers in line after Willie, worked with their father at the warehouse, though neither they nor he seem to have had a great deal of business acumen. William Rackham's early success seems to have been largely due to his partners' drive and ability; once the partnerships were dissolved things began to go downhill. In several of her novels MEM writes of a dreamy, loving, impractical father who is particularly close to his only daughter. One such was Mr Harleigh in *Mrs Peter Howard* looking 'with that meek expression habitual to him, over the top of his book into space, with the same dreamy look in his pale blue eyes that his daughter had in her black ones.' Another was Mr Cummin in *The Eglamore Portraits*. Mrs Cummin was spiteful in a way that Mrs Harleigh was not: 'You have wrought with your tongue and your temper more harm in my life than if you had been a downright wicked and vicious woman,' he tells her towards the end of the novel. 'He had been without ambition, loving his book, his pipe, his garden and the society of his little girl. It was her tongue which had lashed him to effort …' One can never be certain how closely MEM's characters are based on members of her own family, but in her memoir she recorded how fond she was of her father, in a letter she described how the person she hated most in the world was her mother's youngest brother, Tom, who she believed had harmed her father's business, and as an old woman 'the day of my dearest father's death' was a date she continued to mark in her diary. It therefore seems likely that characters like Mr Harleigh and Mr Cummins, together with loving, popular, almost-destitute Dickie Birch in *A Winter's Tale* and Mr Burne, overshadowed by his extrovert wife and six 'unmanaged' daughters from *In Summer Shade* were based in part on William Rackham.

MEM's brother Harry, to judge by his photographs, was probably not the marrying kind, a dapper young man with a spindly moustache, a neat centre parting, a sensitive face and a rather quizzical expression. He was an accomplished draftsman as a letter he sent to his father in 1868 shows. Harry was in charge of the family firm whilst his father was at Horning Ferry on a fishing trip. He wrote to his father giving him an update on the business; on the envelope is a very good pen and ink sketch of a man fishing – presumably intended as a portrait. He also had a sense of humour. In July 1872 he wrote to MEM about an infestation of rats. 'Just as well you married and got out of Town Close House, as I am sure we shall wake up one morning to find ourselves devoured by Rats. They made such a noise in my room last night that they waked me up. As soon as I discovered what the noise was I dared not go to sleep again so got out to light a candle. I had barely put my bare feet down on the floor when one of them (the rats not the feet) ran over them. You know what an awful horror I have of them … the first thing I saw was a very fine specimen of a jack rat running along the top of the foot of my bed …'

Harry and George Rackham, two of MEM's younger brothers

George, the third brother, the one who stayed with Fairman in the period leading up to MEM's marriage, seems to have remained rather weak and immature. In 1878 he married Edith Mary Salter, daughter of a farmer in Shropham – MEM probably introduced them. George and Edith honeymooned in London and George wrote a pathetic letter home to his big sister saying how frightening they both found the city and how they dared not venture out of their hotel for fear of getting lost. He sounded entirely serious. A little while after their return to Norwich Mrs Rackham confided in Polly that George had recently been in trouble with Edith. She thought he had walked the family dog too far and the animal had had to be given a hot bath before George could have his dinner!

Next in the family came the twins, Frank and John, born in 1855. When MEM married they were still at school in Wymondham, but within a couple of years they had returned home and they too started work in the family business. Eddie (Edward Clement), the youngest of the family by some years, was born in 1863 when MEM was fifteen. He was the apple of his mother's eye and she fondly told her daughter how clever he was, how caring, how she once

Eddie Clement Rackham, (1863-97)
MEM's youngest brother

found him crying over a particularly affecting novel and he begged her not to tell his father and brothers he had been 'blubbing'. Victorian men might despise tears but to Eddie's doting mother they were a charming proof of his sensitivity. But Eddie was not to delight his mother for long. 'I fear [he] is perfectly unscrupulous where money is concerned' she confided to her daughter when Polly happened to mention that her little brother had borrowed 10s. The teenage Eddie, it appears, was borrowing numerous small sums of money from different people, frequenting dubious public houses and making unsuitable friends. 'Do not tell Fairman,' she cautioned her daughter, 'he will only make a laugh of it with Eddie.' Eddie never seems to have gone away to school and at no point in his life did he get a proper job. His elder brother, John, seems to have been equally feckless; of the younger boys, Frank was the most competent one, and he chose to become a farmer.

In 1877, the tenancy of Manor Farm in Shropham became available. It had been Fairman's grandfather's farm and the tenancy had passed to his Uncle John. John Mann was twice married but had no children of his own, so on his death in 1845 he transferred the farm to his stepson, George Bolton, on condition that he adopt the surname 'Mann'.

The twins, John (1855-98) and Frank, centre (1855-1931) and Eddie Rackham (standing), MEM's brothers. Her children called them the 'wicked uncles'.

George Bolton Mann was only fifty-five in 1877 but he was a widower and his only surviving child was a daughter, Edith. Fairman was anxious to move into his grandfather's old farm and George Bolton Mann was quite ready to retire. Rather surprisingly, twenty-two year old Frank Rackham then opted to take on the tenancy of Church Farm which Fairman had vacated. He had absolutely no experience of farming, but presumably Fairman was willing to teach him and Frank was anxious to learn, so the farm prospered, at least for a while. The arrival of an eligible young bachelor in the neighbourhood caused considerable excitement and the theme of MEM's first published novel, '*The Parish of Hilby*' is almost certainly a description of the effect Frank's arrival had in Shropham. The novel came out in 1883, the year Frank ceased to flutter hearts in the village by marrying Harriette Warner, MEM's niece-by-marriage, the daughter of James Warner and Fairman's sister, Harriet.

While her brothers struggled to establish themselves, Polly Mann was learning to manage her household and having babies. Her son, Fairman Rackham Mann, always called 'Rack', was born in 1872, a year after the wedding. MEM idolised her son, 'he beats all the other babies in England' she wrote proudly to Fairman while she and the baby were spending time at Town Close House, and she told him all about how smart 'Baby' looked in his new hat and the admiring glances she got when she took him out in his spanking new perambulator.

Rack c.1873, MEM's only son

He was the first grandchild in the Rackham household and his grandmother adored him. He spent a good deal of time at Town Close House 'surrounded by uncles and dogs' as his proud grandmother told MEM. He was a happy, docile child, delighted to play with the 'genteel toy' his uncles made for him from an inflated ox bladder on a stick. He ate his meals, slept, smiled and was quite unmoved by separation from his mother. 'I go see Mummy another day' he would tell his delighted 'Gran'. For her part she took great delight in dressing him up. 'I have just turned your son out a great swell in a white dress trimmed with red,' she told her daughter, 'he looks splendidly and he knows it.' But she was a practical grandmother too, the children were her responsibility, not the servants,

55

and she kept her daughter informed of their every movement. One day little Rack had been in the Town Close garden with his uncle George and came running up to her. 'Grannie, George has not got a piece of paper,' he said. 'So,' wrote Mrs Rackham, 'I leave it to you to imagine what took place by the gooseberry bushes!'

A bare two years later MEM gave birth to her second child, Mary Berthalina, named after her paternal grandmother and known to everyone as 'Bertie'. Bertie was a very different proposition from her good-natured brother. She was a feisty child, stubborn, self-willed and highly intelligent and she was clearly not her grandmother's favourite. In one long letter, written when Bertie was a toddler and staying at Town Close House, Mrs Rackham described how one after another the entire family had tried to persuade little Bertie to say 'thank you'. Her uncles were reduced to fury, one of them even threatened to hit the child, and the little girl was kept in her room for several hours – all to no avail.

Bertie may have been staying at Town Close House because her mother was about to give birth again. Margery Poppie Mann was born in 1876 – 'a dear, sweet child' according to her grandmother, a good little girl whose 'hair is never awry'. Unlike Bertie, Margery was neat and even as a toddler kept herself clean so she could wear smart dresses with white collars and cuffs. She has on 'her green of course with Cuffs' wrote Mrs Rackham during one of Margery's visits, 'a clean tie and a sash improvised from a red handkerchief – her hair, too, is lovely and she is contentedly looking in the glass and admiring herself.' She was an unselfish little girl too, and when she was given some grapes insisted that she keep some back for 'Baby'. 'Baby' was MEM's youngest child, Dolly (Dorothy Warner Mann) born in 1878. If Dolly ever stayed at Town Close House, no letters survive to record her grandmother's impressions of her.

MEM loved her children and she worshipped her only son, but she was not necessarily the wisest of mothers. Into middle age, Rack remembered and resented how she had once dressed him up in his sister's clothes and held him up in the window for all his father's labourers to see. He was old enough to be profoundly humiliated and it is difficult to know whether it was done as a joke or a punishment or to toughen him up. MEM was well aware that her brothers were weak men – 'the wicked uncles' as her children learnt to call them – and she feared that her docile, loving little boy might be like them. His cousin Madge recalled various unkind tricks she would play on him to teach him resilience – like putting him out of the trap when they were out for a drive and asking him to pick flowers for her, then driving off without him. Her fears that he took after the Rackham menfolk were dispelled when he was barely six years old. Sitting nursing baby Dolly on her knee one day, a spark from the fire set MEM's flannel apron alight. Cheap flannel is highly flammable but it was used for nursing aprons because it was warm and comforting. Little Rack beat the fire out with his bare hands, saving both his mother and his baby sister. At last MEM felt able to say, 'Now I know my son is not a coward!'

MEM was fond of children, especially cute, cuddly babies, and from time to time she reminisced about her own children's babyhood. In one letter to her nephew she recalled how an old servant taught Rack and Bertie some of the words of a mummers' play and how they used to act it out. 'Here come I, the Turkey Snipe' one of them would say, and invite the other to meet them at something (MEM couldn't remember the name) bridge. 'At something bridge if I'm alive, I'll meet you there at half past five,' would come the answer. The pair would then fight a duel with sticks 'and both babes would fall prone on the dining room carpet. Your elucidating remarks on this only fragment known to us we find highly entertaining,' wrote MEM. Her nephew was interested in old traditions and had just learnt that the words 'turkey snipe' were a corruption of 'Turkish knight.'

Bertie and Dolly were strong-minded if difficult little girls but their mother seems to have preferred them to Margery. Their cousin Madge recalled how MEM would greet little Margery's appearance with a cheerful 'Here comes the idiot' and in a letter when Margery was seventeen her mother described her as 'a rather virginal idiot' recovering herself quickly by adding 'but a very sweet and dear one.' Margery does not seem to have been as quick-witted or as academic as her siblings and took to herself the role of family drudge. A story that she wrote when she was probably about fourteen, in a school exercise book with illustrations by Rack, has a spelling mistake on almost every line.

By the late 1870s MEM's father was unwell and her brother George was married. Mrs Rackham may have taken little notice of Fanny Rackham, Willie's wife, but George's Edith was another matter. Both daughters-in-law were childless, but Edith expected her husband's mother to dance attendance on her; Mrs Rackham's letters to MEM explain her difficulty in balancing Edith's needs against those of the rest of the family.

In September 1880 the family faced a major crisis. In a brief note scrawled in a very shaky hand, old Mrs Rackham broke the bad news to her daughter: William Rackham had cancer. The Rackham boys hardly ever wrote to their sister – their mother was the conduit through which all the family news passed – but this situation was different. George dashed off a tragic letter to Polly in his scrawling handwriting on what was probably once a sheet of cheap vellum but is now like a brittle piece of folded plastic the colour of brown wrapping paper. Harry followed it with a much more carefully written and considered missive, describing his conversation with Dr Williams and his father's likely prognosis. Dr Williams, like all doctors imparting bad news, had tried to make the best of the situation. The case was terminal, admittedly, but there was a new drug, developed in Cyprus, that slowed down the growth of tumours. Treatment for cancer had improved in recent years, they need not fear that their father would suffer as their mother's father had done, he would fade quietly away, there was no need to worry ... He also gives us an interesting insight into his parents' relationship: 'the missus is behaving herself but sometimes the cloven hoof peeps out,' he wrote. It would seem Mrs Rackham, like Mrs Cummin and Mrs Harleigh in her daughter's novels, had not always been the most forbearing of wives.

Another panicky letter arrived at Shropham from Mrs Rackham when she had had time to absorb the news. What was to be done about her husband's dogs which were going to live longer than he would? How could she stop him drinking whisky which she was sure was not good for him? Then Mr Rackham wrote to his daughter himself, a calm, reassuring letter, re-iterating the story about the new drug from Cyprus, assuring her that the doctor had told him to drink his whisky if it helped him sleep and comforting her by telling her he was not in pain but that he had noticed himself becoming very crotchety with the staff at the warehouse so he had decided to give up work there completely. There were more letters from Mrs Rackham asking for some of 'those eggs he is so fond of', a hopeful one saying her husband had been told he could live for five years and one about the funeral. It is clear that money was a problem; they were discussing how cheap a funeral he could have and how feckless, jobless 'Eddie weighs heavily on his mind.' From surviving letters and photos there is some suggestion that Eddie was rather backward, if not actually mentally handicapped. No doubt the next few months passed in something of a blur – and from the biographer's point of view it is a largely undocumented period. All we know is that William Simon Rackham died on the 19th of March, 1881.

After the funeral Mrs Rackham went to Shropham to stay with Fairman and MEM while Eddie went to stay with Frank. Harry, presumably with some help from George, John and Willie, was left to close up Town Close House, pay the servants off and dispose of most of the contents. Mrs Rackham then took a house in Attleborough to be near her daughter, son-in-law and grandchildren and her son Frank and his family. John and Eddie moved in with her; no doubt she hoped the two hapless young men would get up to less mischief in a quiet country town than among the fleshpots of Norwich. The house was not at all what she had been used to, a grey stone semi-detached villa which she grandly named 'The Pines' in honour of a rather scruffy pine tree in the tiny front garden. There was land at the back, however, sufficient to support a carriage horse and her flock of three dozen chickens. It was convenient too, part of a newish development along Connaught Road and just a couple of minutes' walk from the town centre and the church.

Harry and George stayed in town to try to keep the family business afloat. Neither of them was a natural business man and times were changing. Norwich was no longer a centre of the cloth trade as it had been when their father and grandfather were young men. In those days most of the fabrics the Rackhams sold were manufactured locally and the manufacturers, wholesalers and retailers all knew each other, belonged to the same clubs, frequented the same pubs and married each others' sisters. Stock could be collected by the Rackhams' drivers in one of their own wagons and brought back to the warehouse within a matter of hours. By the 1880s and 90s much of their stock would have come from Manchester or Bradford and imported fabrics came in through London, so buying from manufacturers was a much more time-consuming and expensive business than it had been earlier in the century. There was also more competition. The coming of the railways meant that commercial travellers working for individual firms could tour the country with samples, allowing drapers to order their stock direct from factories in the north and elsewhere. This was preferable for the manufacturers as they no longer had to establish relationships with warehousemen from every major town in the country – and it meant that there was no longer the need for local warehouses to buy up fabrics at prices that were inevitably going to be uncompetitive. Goods could be shipped by rail to the nearest station and collected by the drapers themselves. Even when a commercial traveller did not visit, shopkeepers could receive brochures and circulars by post. Developments in printing and the introduction of a reduced postage rate for circulars made it increasingly easy for such materials to be produced. Retailing was changing too; town shops were becoming larger and more specialised and it was only old-fashioned shops and little village stores that still relied on firms like Rackhams, and they, of course, only bought very small quantities. It was inevitable that the business would decline and neither Harry nor George had the initiative to find ways of adapting their business to move with the times.

MEM had always been a reader, and correspondents thanked her for her 'long chatty letters' so she seems to have enjoyed writing and may originally have written stories to amuse herself and her friends and to pass the time in the long winter evenings in Shropham. Indeed, in a letter to her husband's nephew Tom Ordish in 1893 she wrote 'I should never have attempted to do more than pester my friends with long letters if it had not been for you.' Her first stories seem to have been published in the 1870s; in one letter her mother tells her how much she and Eddie enjoyed *Bel. Gale* and that it was 'so much less depressing' than her previous story. However, she also urged Polly to ask her father not to tell people that she had had it published 'otherwise all Norwich will hear about it…' Mrs Rackham could not see that that would matter – but Polly herself had apparently made a particular point of keeping her success a secret. Most of Mrs Rackham's letters are undated – references to 'Tuesday' or 'Sunday evening' are all there is to go on – so we cannot be precise about when this letter was sent but it was obviously before William Rackham became ill. We have been unable to trace these early stories and it may be that they were published under a pseudonym – amongst MEM's papers in Norfolk Record Office there are four unpublished novels labelled 'by M.S. Manton'. But before very long she was writing and publishing under her own name. The most important chapter in her life had begun.

Chapter 4. A published author 1881-1891

Fairman Joseph Mann with MEM and their four children c.1878

While most of the Rackham sons were struggling after their father's death, their sister Polly was thriving. By the early 1880s she had more time to herself. She had a reliable cook and a housemaid to manage the house, a nursemaid for the smallest child and there was a dairymaid to milk Fairman's herd of red poll cattle and turn the milk into butter. Rack was sent away to Mr Jessop's school in Norwich in 1877 while his grandmother was still living at Town Close House. She was deputed to check up on him and the early reports were not encouraging. Five-year-old Rack was shy, tearful and unhappy when she visited him, desperate to go home and unable to make friends. 'All I want to tell Mother is that I am so miserable,' he explained to his grandmother, 'and that everyone deceived me – they said I should like it – but every hour I hate it worse.' Part of the problem was that he couldn't write well enough to send letters home and he couldn't read well enough to decipher the ones his mother sent him. Mrs Rackham was upset and confessed that she hadn't eaten or slept since seeing him, but nonetheless she urged her daughter to leave him to settle down. 'He is such a Baby and so little able, from the sort of life he has led, to fight his own battles,' she wrote, going on to describe how one of the other boys had taken the shilling little Rack had been given and refused to give it back.

But within a few weeks the news was better, the little boy was making friends and if not exactly happy, he was resigned to his fate. 'I have the best possible news – I have just been to see the child and found him quite an altered creature – he seems really reconciled and said he did not mind it nearly so much now,' she told MEM. She seemed to believe that he was being well-treated, though her description doesn't sound as if he was receiving much help in looking after himself. 'I wish you could have seen him when he rushed into the room – he was very cold, his hair cut very short and he had braced his trowsers up until they were scarce knicks – both his boots were unlaced part of the way and both the laces dragging after him – I never saw such a young object.' Nor were his teachers particularly kind to him. Some correspondence survives from the end of the year; Rack had obviously complained to his parents about how one of the masters treated him, and Mr Jessop was anxious to reassure them that the complaints were unjustified and that Mr Briscoe, who had been with them for fifteen years, was 'a popular fellow'. Mr Briscoe went out to Shropham to explain himself to the Manns and this was followed by another letter from Augustus Jessop hoping that they were not planning to withdraw their boy from his school. The adults' version of events prevailed, and five-year old Rack stayed where he was – and one hopes Mr Briscoe treated him more gently from then on. 'What little boy is happy in his first term at school,' MEM would later write, rather callously, in *There was a Widow*.

Boarding schools were draconian places but there are occasional glimpses of the lighter side of life. On one occasion Rack reported that he had bought a tame rabbit for 1d. and sold it for 2s.6d. 'that is good proffit.' A few of his later letters home survive, and in amongst the tales of cricket matches won and lost we get an idea of how discipline was meted out. He thought it 'awfully hard', for example, that one of his schoolmates, a boy called Press, had been caned for some minor misdemeanour minutes before he was given the news that his mother had died. Rack did not report being beaten himself (perhaps the earlier episode with Mr Briscoe had taught him it would be pointless) but he did admit 'I have been cept in every day this term and last term' for not being able to learn his Latin.

Once out of the nursery, the little girls were educated at home by a governess. In 1884 this was Kate Allen. That year she forwarded a letter to MEM and Fairman who were on holiday in Yarmouth, penned by little Margery who was then about eight. A note on the back signed 'KA' confirms that Margery had written the mis-spelt incoherent scrawl all by herself, and the governess commented, rather spitefully, that 'I fear my father's words "this child is a disgrace to you" are true.' Kate Allen's father was the Mann's neighbour, Dr Allen. A year later, when the Manns were away in London, Miss Allen told them that the little girls were having a lovely time sleeping all together in their parents' big bed but that she had resisted their invitations to her to join them. Having heard Bertie saying the bed was full of bread crumbs and cheese rinds she had decided she would be more comfortable in the privacy of her own room.

But the following year Kate Allen's relationship with the Manns turned sour. One of the other servants reported to MEM that Kate had been sitting up late at night and 'getting up to no good' with Fairman. Miss Allen was forced to write a letter in her own defence. She insisted that there was nothing in the accusation; she thought no more of being with Fairman than she would have of being with her own grandfather, she had been sitting up late to finish a jersey she was knitting, Fairman had kept her company, he was a 'pure-minded' man and liked to talk, and she was a good listener, even though he was rather 'prosy'. She would never have spent time alone with him if she had thought it would give rise to gossip – and so on and so on. It is a curious little episode and one wonders whether MEM genuinely believed her husband had dallied with the governess or whether it was an excuse to get rid of a woman she disliked. It perhaps also shows that poor Fairman was lonely because MEM was so busy with her writing and her young children that she had little time for him. They were drifting apart.

Kate Allen was given notice to leave but MEM was not anxious to publicise the real reason for her dismissal. 'She neglected the children when I was away from home,' she wrote. 'At least that will do as well for a reason as another as it is not always convenient to give the true one', which seems rather unfair to poor Miss Allen. On 30th September, 1886, MEM advertised for a replacement in the *London Standard:*

'A governess wanted, at once: a young lady competent to teach music, singing, French and drawing with good

English to three little girls from 9 to 12 years old, highest references required, a comfortable home but not a high salary given …'

They had seventy-four replies all 'so apparently suitable that I am perfectly bewildered and don't know how to choose.' The governess MEM appointed in 1886, or soon after, seems to have been Miss Edwards whom the family later remembered with affection. In the *Cedar Star* written in 1898, MEM described a family rather like her own, consisting of Betty, Peter, Emily and Jan. The story starts with the children, led by Betty, a strong-minded, stubborn little girl, obviously based on Bertie, being appallingly rude and disobedient to their governess with her 'mud-coloured hair' and 'mud-coloured neck.' The governess handed in her notice; she was one in a long line of governesses the children had managed to drive away. Did this reflect MEM's experience with her own children back in Shropham?

It seems that MEM recognised Bertie's talent for drawing early. In a letter home from school in May 1886 Rack asks 'Has Bertie been to Miss Worthington's to learn drawing yet? I don't suppose she will like it.' It's not clear why twelve year old Bertie would have disliked it – perhaps Miss Worthington had a reputation for strictness. Within months she was winning prizes for her painting but, according to her mother, it was the only thing she was any good at.

Bertie was also the family spokesperson when it came to writing to their parents and food usually featured prominently in her epistles – though she may not have told the unvarnished truth. In 1884 the letter that accompanied Kate Allen's note was all about how they were having 'cocoa and rabbit pie' for breakfast and 'cocoa and radishes' for tea – possibly not the most balanced of diets. Writing home from Attleborough in 1888 when she was staying with her grandmother, food was again her major topic of news. It was raining; there was nothing to do, but for dinner they had had turbot, soles, lamb, pork, stewed plums, blancmange and les oeufs en neige. Dolly was off to stay with 'Bunk' (Uncle Frank at Church Farm' and they all sent love to 'Fuff' as she called Fairman.

In or around 1889 Dolly gave a recitation at a 'grand Concert' in the Corn Hall at Attleborough. 'She looked very childish and pretty in her festive attire standing up among the azaleas and lilies on the platform,' ran the press report. 'On all hands last night people said "the child is a genius" – the "genius" being perfectly indifferent to everything but the "set" of her first silk frock and the question as to how she should spend the shilling her father had promised her as a reward for her success.' Dolly was eleven and no doubt enjoyed the opportunity to show off.

All three girls spent a few terms at boarding school as young teenagers. Bertie was at Edmundsbury near Ipswich. She was scathing about the size of the grounds; 'the garden is scarcely bigger than our lawn at home and when all forty of us are outside we are crammed like sardines!' This meant that playing tennis, which she loved, was all but impossible. However, she enjoyed the company and got into trouble. 'I had a pillow fight with Connie and Lilian (the two new girls) and as I was throwing the pillow at them it went into a basin full of water ...' The penalty in a girls' school was a fine that went into the 'mishonery box.'

Dolly and Margery went to school at Surrey House in Norwich and hated it. The school was run by the three Miss Clarkes who seem to have taken over Mrs Dunnett's old premises. It is in her letters home from school that we first begin to catch a glimpse of the less-than-attractive child that Dolly seems to have been. 'About being happy at school,' ran one missive, 'I wish you to learn once and for all (that is à la Miss Clarke) that I shall <u>never</u> be happy at school, <u>never</u>.' Dolly struggled to look after herself; 'My nails look awful because I have to cut them myself,' and making her own bed was a problem. 'You have to give yourself clean sheets and pillow cases and all that and I get in such a muddle.' Nonetheless she had lots of friends – in another letter she demands that her mother send her photographs because all her friends want one of her. The girls seem to have had quite a lot of freedom and in one letter she relates how Horace Jack, a young man whose family were friends of the Manns, took her to hear the organ in the Cathedral – 'simply glorious' – ordered a book by Dean Garnier for her as a Valentine's Day present, and sent her back to school with pounds of preserved fruit. Fearing the girls would make themselves sick, Miss Clarke forbade her to take it into the dormitory – 'Old Beast, I do so loathe her,' grumbled Dolly. But best of all, Mr Jack had mistaken her for her elder sister. 'Tell Bertie that he thought <u>I</u> <u>was Bertie</u>,' crowed Dolly, 'and ask her if she doesn't feel flattered.'

She describes her behaviour at a school dance. In what looks almost like a deliberate attempt to get herself expelled, she described how, at the dance, she had waltzed the length of the room by herself with a large slice of cake in one hand and a lump of toffee in the other singing loudly, to the tune of 'There is a Happy Land', 'There is a boarding school, far, far away, where they have turnip tops four times a day.' She gave all her teachers nicknames like 'Snub-nose'; they were all horrible and she pleaded homesickness. Years later, her school friend, Winifred Auld, recalled how Dolly spent her time drawing graveyards and sketching her own tombstone which was to bear the legend 'When I am dead, my dearest, Sing no sad songs for me'. That taste for melodrama and self-pity would stay with her for the rest of her life. She was generally acknowledged to be the prettiest of the three sisters and, as the youngest, was rather spoilt.

Home-loving Margery does not seem to have spent so long at the school but she was certainly there in 1893 when she was sixteen, and it sounds as if she had not been there long. 'I really try awfully hard with my lessons,' she wrote, 'Miss Clarke says my writing is improving already.' It is a long, sensible letter, written on lined paper in a slightly childish, but very neat, hand. She had enjoyed a trip to Ringland but the countryside wasn't as nice as Shropham. The coach driver had teased her about marrying Lord Stafford when she was a little older and she and her best friend, Nellie, had enjoyed themselves enormously. She'd also been to hear a ladies' band but the pieces had all been very similar and she'd been bored, especially as she and Nellie had found themselves sitting next to Miss Clarke so hadn't been able to stuff themselves with sweets and look at the dresses the ladies in the audience were wearing as they had planned. She was careful of her mother's feelings, but in a letter to Bertie, probably written at the same time, she described the big school room as the room she 'hated most in all the world' and admitted 'Whenever the lucky day arrives when I leave school I will never look at a lesson book again because lessons have been the very curse of my existence.' But she was still able to share with Bertie her amusement that their little sister had a very obvious crush on Miss Rose Clarke.

Both girls make much of missing their family, but MEM visited them most Wednesdays and they both went to see their Aunt Fanny, Willie's wife, once a week. She was childless and seems to have made a fuss of them, giving them jars of jam and marmalade, washing Dolly's hair and giving her honey and vinegar for her cough and having them both to lunch. They both describe her as an angel – though admittedly Margery spelt it 'angle'.

Margery may not have been much of a scholar but her adult letters are well written; as an old lady she told her niece, Diana, about the stories she used to write, and in an exercise book full of family poems there are some quite clever ones by Margery:

A knot for your breast,
No not for your best,
Not when you go to town
But for a country gown.
A simple posy you have got.
Wear it, and forget me not

is a typical example. Another, written in the 1924, is about an old tablecloth which they had had for fourteen years. It begins:

So oft I've laid it at your feet
In winter days and summer heat …

It was typical of Margery to be able to see poetry in everyday things. Sadly, MEM never seems to have valued her second daughter as much as she did Bertie and Dolly.

With the children off her hands for at least part of the time, MEM could devote herself to her writing. No doubt, like all first time authors, she was delighted to find herself in print when her first novel, *The Parish of Hilby*, was published in 1883. She later described writing it with 'the rest of them laughing and talking … the only one [of my books] I have ever written without conscious and more or less painful effort.' It appeared under her married name, Mrs Fairman Mann, (not Mary E. Mann which was the professional name she used thereafter) and was published in London by the firm of Elliot Stock, an old established firm that was enjoying something of a resurgence around the turn of the century. We do not know how she fixed on Stock but it seems very likely that the negotiations were undertaken on her behalf by her husband's nephew, Thomas Fairman Ordish. Stock's list was eclectic, but they specialised in works about history and antiquity in which Tom was interested and on which he had already written extensively.

He was the son of Fairman Mann's eldest sister, Sarah. In 1853, when Fairman was still a boy, she had married a London stationer, Thomas Ordish, and moved with him to Fulham. A letter survives that Sarah sent to MEM in the early days of her marriage to Fairman, written in the careful copperplate of one who does not write many letters, regretting that they had been unable to meet, saying how she wished her brother was a better correspondent and pointing out that though they lived in London she was 'only a penny or halfpenny stamp away'. However, that is one of just two surviving letters from her – the

68

second congratulated MEM on Rack's birth – so we do not know whether Sarah and MEM ever really got to know each other. Thomas and Sarah Ordish had six children and Thomas Fairman was their second child, born in 1855. No doubt all six visited their Norfolk relatives, but young Tom seems to have struck up a particular friendship with his Uncle Fairman's young wife who was only a few years older than he was. They were interested in the same things – history, literature, art and the theatre and, living in London, Tom was able to amuse MEM with news of the latest happenings in the world of the arts.

Thomas Fairman Ordish (1855-1924), MEM's nephew by marriage

Both Tom and his elder brother became civil servants and joined the Board of Trade. Tom spent nearly all his working life as a clerk in the Patents Office, but like MEM he had literary ambitions. He was a self-taught academic and was well ahead of MEM in the publishing stakes; his first articles *Fact and Faith* and *Skeptomania* appeared in *The New Monthly Magazine* in 1876 when he was just twenty-one. In all he published over seventy articles on a range of topics, and two books, *Shakespeare's London* and *Early London Theatres,* in the 1890s. Allan Gomme was one of his colleagues and Tom became a friend of Allan's father, George Laurence Gomme, whose background was similar in many ways to his own. They both came from comfortable but comparatively humble backgrounds, and from large families. Both were highly intellectual but needed to earn their own livings from an early age and so were denied the opportunity of the university education from which they would both so clearly have benefited.

Laurence Gomme's day job was with the Fulham Board of Works and later with the Metropolitan Board of Works, but in his spare time he was a historian and folklorist, publishing copiously, particularly on the history and antiquities of London. He it was who persuaded the LCC to take up the blue plaque scheme to commemorate the homes of the famous. He was one of the founders of the Victoria County History project and a founding member of the Folklore Society. He was knighted in 1911. Tom Ordish held him in great esteem and they collaborated on at least one publication, a catalogue of the Camden Library. It may well have been Gomme who persuaded Tom to take an interest in folklore and vernacular theatre; the Ordish collection of over six hundred plays that resulted is now in the library of University College, London. In her letters MEM makes frequent flippant references to 'the great Gomme' and rhymes the names Tom and Gomme, but she was outraged to receive a letter in the late 1880s from Laurence Gomme suggesting that he, rather than Tom Ordish, take over the management of her career. She hardly seems to have appreciated just how fortunate she was to have two such men take an interest in her.

Tom Ordish married in 1880. His wife was Ada Lamacraft, daughter of a London stationer who was a family friend; Tom's elder brother, William, married one of Ada's cousins. It was not a happy marriage. Ada was some years older than Tom and seems to have suffered from some form of mental illness: she spent a period in an asylum and a good deal of time being looked after by families in the country. When Bertie went to London she described her first impressions of Ada in a letter home. 'Ada is a nightmare and is positively hideous,' she wrote. 'She is very fat with a badly shaped head from which the hair is raked back into a small greasy knot. Her face is crimson, her eyes blue, watery and imbecile. She has a few broken stumps of black teeth which stick out and over which her loose wet mouth refuses to close ... She cannot walk straight but moves about with a sort of shambling trot. When she sits down all the top of her appears to sink into her immense corporation ... She very seldom speaks but when she does her conversation is sensible enough.' Even allowing for Bertie's habitual exaggeration and unkindness it is a chilling picture. Ada's family were not in the least supportive of her or of Tom. 'They are all as cold and passionless as fish,' wrote MEM when Tom complained, 'and would be serving the cause of humanity better on the table with lobster sauce ... I abominate them and always did.' It is hard to see why Tom ever married the woman. MEM tried to persuade him that Ada was better off being cared for away from home, but whenever her condition improved Tom felt obliged to have her back. The strain must have been immense. Ada outlived both Tom and MEM and died in 1930, aged eighty.

The couple had one child, a daughter, Eliza Lydia, known throughout her childhood as 'Lily'. She was the delight of Tom's life and features regularly in his letters. He worries endlessly about her schooling, her work, her health and her relationship with him. From about 1885 to 1900 Tom and MEM seem to have written to each other every few weeks. He kept all her letters and on his death they were returned to the Manns. MEM seems to have kept nearly every letter she ever received, Tom's amongst them. It is on this correspondence, which continued sporadically until Tom's death in 1924, that much of this biography is based.

The letters are fascinating. They shared ideas, theories, news of what they were reading and, most importantly, of what they were trying to write and why. 'You and I are not successes ... but we won't be failures to each other,' wrote MEM. ' "You write because you must write" said someone to me one day and that is true of me and true therefore much more of you.' She tells Tom about her family, her emotions and her irritation with Fairman, and sends news of the Mann and Warner relations, particularly 'Leila'. Leila or Lila Lamacraft was a relative of Ada's and was the second wife of Fairman's much older brother, John Eagling Mann. They had a large family, whom MEM seems to have avoided as much as possible.

Tom was a scholar and an intellectual with wide-ranging interests, and as the correspondence progresses one can sense MEM striving to keep up with him. 'You have never applied the talent that is in you to one particular purpose,' she told him, 'you have not kept yourself to one alone of the many walks in the art that you and I love. You have strayed over them all because you have a ... facility in each.' To begin with, she was the one encouraging the 'dull, shy, imaginative boy' to write, but by 1892 it is she who defers to his literary opinion, is constantly grateful for the magazines and papers he sends and freely explains her finances, her trouble with publishers, and her frustration at being isolated from the literary world. His letters are beautifully written, erudite and full of philosophical insights, he shares his concerns over Ada and Lily but seldom gives much away about his own feelings – for which MEM regularly takes him to task. Her own letters are full of long rambling descriptions of her state of mind and her various fantasies.

She seems to have got considerably more out of the relationship in a practical sense than Tom did, for by the early 1890s he was conducting negotiations with her agent, seeing publishers on her behalf, handling copyright issues, writing to the Norfolk papers to persuade them to review her work, persuading W.H. Smith to stock her books and even, in 1893, corresponding with Mr Salter, the Mann's friend in Attleborough, about how best she should invest £1,700. Part of this was money she had earned, but at least half of it was her inheritance from her mother. For a time MEM seems to have reimbursed him for his services by having her royalties paid into his account.

Without Tom's tireless efforts she would have published far less. For his part, Tom hero-worshipped her. Years later, in August 1910, by which time their correspondence was relatively infrequent, he confessed 'Your success has been a great support to me. It has probably done more than most earthly things to keep me true to myself; for your friendship and belief in me in times past I offer you my heartfelt thanks'. A few years earlier, in February 1906, he had told her, 'I have a lock and key bookcase and it is my desire to fill it with all your books in all editions'. It sounds a slightly unhealthy ambition to the 21st century reader, but the truth was she provided him with a safe outlet for his feelings. He could write to her about topics that interested him, he could confide in her his worries about Lily and his unhappiness with Ada, but he does seem to have been careful that they should not actually meet very often. Maybe he did not trust himself in her presence, maybe he feared that in the flesh his idol would prove to have feet of clay, maybe he had no real liking for visiting the country. In letter after letter MEM begged him to come to Shropham – for Christmas, for Easter, for a holiday in the summer, and of course 'dear Lily' was always welcome to visit too, whenever she wished. However, as far as can be ascertained, Lily only went to Shropham once, in 1889 when she was quite a little girl. Unfortunately, during that visit Dolly managed to spook Bertie's pony and got kicked in the mouth. Lily was shipped off to Church Farm to stay with Frank and Hattie's brood while MEM tended to the invalid – which seems rather unfair as Hattie had four children of her own under the age of five and was in the early stages of her fifth pregnancy. Eleven year old Dolly had had a nasty accident but was not in any danger, and Margery and Bertie were thirteen and fifteen respectively – surely they could have helped look after their six year old visitor? The visit was never repeated. Perhaps Tom felt that MEM had neglected Lily, or perhaps the Mann children had been unkind – years later Bertie would write to a friend about 'old "Tunty" Ordish and his frightful daughter – <u>what</u> was her name?'

Bertie had a spiteful pen, she seldom wrote kindly of anyone and she loved to give people nicknames that no one else used. In fact, Tom was good to them all. Month after month he sent them art and literary magazines from London at no inconsiderable cost to himself. When Rack was a medical student in London in 1891-2 he lived with the Ordishes, no doubt much more cheaply than he could have got digs elsewhere, and years later, when Margery was ill in a London isolation hospital, lonely, bored and complaining about the hard chairs and the thick mugs in which the patients' tea was served, he sent her newspapers to read, a cushion, and her own china cup and saucer to drink from. Even MEM's brother Harry seems to have spent some time in London with the Ordishes.

We do not know how much MEM was paid for *The Parish of Hilby*, though we do know she turned down an offer of £12 from the *Family Herald* to serialise it. Only later did money really become an issue. To begin with she was more concerned with getting into print and what the critics thought. 'We have seldom read a more gracefully written idyll, odorous of English rural life and thoroughly true to nature ...' cooed the *Bristol Mercury* on March 24th 1883, but it was one of the few papers to notice it. This is unfortunate for it is a fine piece of work. MEM was writing about what she knew, a version of what had very probably happened to her brother Frank when he arrived in Shropham as a young man of twenty-two, an eligible bachelor with the manners of a town-bred gentleman and as the tenant of a tolerably large farm. An analysis of the Shropham census shows that there were twenty-two men of marriageable age in the village when he arrived – none of them particularly eligible. Small wonder then that 'James Massey', as Frank is called in the novel, is immediately seen as a most desirable catch. MEM is particularly good on the petty snobberies and the infinite gradations of social status in a small village. Polly Freeman, the pretty, rather vulgar daughter of an old-fashioned farming family, recently 'finished' in London but still only half-understanding the rules of polite taste and with no-one in her family to guide her, is contrasted nicely with the saintly Helen, the vicar's sister-in-law. She is beautiful, ladylike, well-bred, rather stand-offish, but a vast improvement on her ineffectual brother-in-law, the Reverend Pearson, and Anna, her ghastly, pious sister who writes short stories about temperance and distributes them throughout the village. Polly Freeman sets her cap at Massey as soon as he arrives and the descriptions of them in her father's house are very amusing. She traps Massey into an engagement from which he eventually escapes to marry Helen. Polly then marries her flamboyant London cousin, Arthur Gosling.

MEM had a low opinion of the local clergy and their wives which resurfaced in novel after novel. It did not make her popular. 'The vicar's family has immediately turned the cold shoulder upon me' she reported to Tom Ordish in 1884 'and another neighbouring clergyman openly says the Vicar of Hilby is intended for himself!' She had obviously touched several nerves.

The novel also gave her the opportunity to air another of her pet hates – socialism. Helen persuades James Massey to take on the labourer, Tom Moore, a notorious trouble-maker and drunkard, because he has agreed to sign the pledge and work hard. Advised by Mr Freeman, Massey refuses to raise his labourers' wages at harvest time and, led by Tom Moore, they go on strike. Tom is an unpleasant character and the only one of the men to derive any benefit from the action: he became a worker for the trade union while the other men sank deeper into debt and their wives and families suffered even worse privations than when they were at work. MEM understood how difficult it was for labourers' families to manage on the pittance the men earned, but paradoxically, she could never approve of their attempts to get better wages. She was also influenced by her hatred of Joseph Arch, 'the arch humbug' as she called him, the labourer and Primitive Methodist preacher who founded the National Agricultural Labourers' Union in 1872; he was elected MP for North-west Norfolk in 1885, and it is on him that the character of Tom Moore is based. Arch came from Warwickshire but spent much of his political career in Norfolk. The farmers saw him as a hypocrite and a dangerous agitator. MEM was a farmer's wife - she saw the agricultural depression from her husband's perspective and she stood by her class. 'I am horribly vexed to find that Arch is returned today for parliament,' she told Tom in December 1885. 'We all so earnestly desired him to be kicked out ... he is the self-called "labourers' friend" who calmly takes the scant shillings from the labourer's pocket to line his own'. This was deeply unjust. Joseph Arch was first elected to parliament in 1880. It was an extraordinary achievement for a working man and he took pride in appearing in the House in his countryman's salt-and-pepper tweed suit and billycock hat, to the chagrin of his fellow MPs. There is no suggestion that he ever used the labourers' Union contributions for his own ends, indeed there are meticulous accounts to show he did not. However, the NALU tried to do more than it could afford to, and when wages were raised in 1874 many labourers left the Union because they felt it had achieved its purpose – so income fell. The result was a good deal of juggling of money between the Sick Fund and the Union and there were accusations of malpractice which Joseph Arch's opponents, farmers like Fairman, seized on to discredit him.

Naturally, MEM was proud of her first novel and for a few years in her letters to Tom, Manor Farm is always described as 'Hilby Farm' and Ivy Cottage, where she was anxious he should stay with Lily, was 'Hilby Cottage'. She was also surprised, and no doubt delighted, to receive fan mail like the letter from Katherine Wrigley who was 'so charmed' with the book that she had read it aloud to her 'young (male) farm servant'. It would be the first of many such letters.

Manor Farm, Shropham. Fairman and MEM lived here 1877 to 1913

Tom Ordish may have persuaded Elliot Stock to publish MEM's first novel and may have interceded with other publishers on her behalf, but she was still aware of the trials and tribulations that beset authors in search of a publisher – and authors who had found one. Miriam Elgard, a character in *One Another's Burdens* (1890), is a novelist. She has tried without success to find a publisher and almost

75

given up, but then one day she finds herself reading a really badly written novel and wonders who on earth would publish such trash. If they could publish this rubbish, perhaps they might take her novel? 'Once more she had packed up the much-travelled manuscript and despatched it again to try its chances. And on this occasion, to her very great surprise, her mind being attuned to disappointment, the result appeared to be favourable.' She then found that 'the obliging publisher proposed an arrangement by which he himself was to be secured from risk, but Mrs Elgard in her gratitude to him would not let her mind dwell on this particular'; besides he assured her that it was quite normal, just a matter of form. The novel duly came out and was comparatively well reviewed. True, one reviewer accused her of over-using a rather vulgar slang expression – though when she searched her text she found she had not used it at all. Another accused her of being 'too faithful' to George Eliot, while yet another assured readers that that lady would have been flattered by the comparison. Then there was the reviewer who always had something unpleasant to say and swore that he'd rather spend time on a treadmill than read anything else she had written. When Miriam queried whether the book had been advertised, because it was not selling well, the publisher assured her it had, in their own publication 'of which, by the way, Miriam had never heard.' Miriam sees her book in a bookshop window, week after week, and eventually goes in and purchases the copy herself. All of this has the ring of bitter experience; indeed, in a letter to Tom many years later MEM described Elliot Stock as 'my old enemy and publisher'.

MEM's writing career began at a time when the fiction publishing industry was in a state of flux. Up to the 1880s, the three-volume novel had been the norm. These usually sold at 10s. 6d. per volume or 31s. 6d. for the set, an enormous price which few readers were able to afford for something as ephemeral as a story. The majority of novels, therefore, were sold to circulating libraries which meant that demand was relatively low. Consequently, publishers produced fiction in limited runs – 1,000 was the usual number – hence the high price. Other novels started life as serials in magazines or newspapers and were subsequently re-published in book form, usually priced at 6s. By the 1880s this had come to be the preferred form and price for novels, whether previously serialised or not; but in 1894 a consortium of libraries dealt this pricing structure a blow by refusing to purchase any works of fiction for more than 4s. a volume. It was not an unreasonable stance; improvements in methods of reproducing illustrations and in printing technology generally were making it possible for publishers to produce 1s. and even 6d. editions of novels. This was good news for readers – but not for writers. MEM's work appeared in all these forms: three volume novels, 6s. novels and 1s. 6d. editions.

Of course, finding a publisher to take one's manuscript was only the first hurdle to be crossed. The critics' reactions to the finished book were important, but it was even more important that the publisher advertise the new work as widely as possible. They usually used quotations from favourable reviews in their advertisements, but one of MEM's complaints about almost all the firms she worked with was that they often didn't do this, or at least didn't do it often enough. Even books that had had glowing reviews were not, in her view, publicised sufficiently widely, and that meant sales would be poor.

There were three ways in which an author made money out of a book: the down payment, royalties and, sometimes, the sale of rights. At the start of MEM's career the down payment was usually around £40; at its height she got £300. This down payment was all-important because the ongoing royalties were often pitiful. To take an example of one of MEM's books for which we happen to have records: *Susannah*, first published by H. Henry and Co. in 1895, was re-published by Methuen in 1903. That year the royalties, at 10%, amounted to just 9s. 9d., even though the book was published as a 6s. volume, suggesting that just sixteen or seventeen copies were sold. The following year the royalties were 15s. 4d. from the sales of an estimated twenty-five copies. On 1s. editions of books the royalties were just 2d. a volume; on 6d. editions they were 1d. or a halfpenny. For library copies there was a one-off payment of 3d. The royalties on American editions were more generous as publishers there served a much wider market. Again the surviving information is patchy, but as an example, in October 1911, Mr Paget of George H. Doran in New York bought the American rights of *There was a Widow*. The royalties were to be 10% up to 5,000 copies sold, 15% up to 20,000 and 20% on any sales thereafter. From time to time a second firm would buy the 'rights' to a book from the original publisher to enable them to re-publish it under their own imprint, and the author would then get an additional payment from the new firm. This was usually quite small – around £15 to £25 – but most of MEM's books were republished at least once in her lifetime. Additional payments were made to the author when the rights were sold abroad.

Publishers offered complicated contracts: so much down, so much more as increasing numbers of books were sold, so much in royalties depending on the cost of the edition and so on. MEM was totally inexperienced, seldom visited her publishers in person and, as a woman, was at risk of being taken advantage of. Tom Ordish knew the literary world better than she did, but he was not a novelist and neither were his friends. He was prejudiced against certain firms and was fiercely protective of MEM's reputation, and he may not always have acted entirely wisely on her behalf. Similarly, her first agent, Hanneford Bennett, seems to have been too polite and gentlemanly to have secured her the best deals available, though Mr Watt, who replaced him in about 1902, was much more ruthless. MEM's letters to Tom Ordish contain a litany of complaints, some reasonable, some not, about the various firms she worked with.

Success had not come immediately. Among MEM's papers in Norwich are the drafts of a number of unpublished novels, and in some cases it is possible to guess the date when they were written. *Milly Strong*, *Good for Nothing*, *It is Housekeeper* and *Kate the Shrew* are all written under the pseudonym M. S. Manton. By the time she published her first book MEM had abandoned that name and was writing as 'Mrs Fairman Mann', so we can reasonably deduce that these works predate 1883. *Milly Strong* opens with a death bed scene. A young mother lies dying, her husband is desperate and tortured, there are seven small children and a stout-hearted governess, the eponymous 'Milly'. It is melodramatic, sentimental and full of purple prose, but the second chapter, which deals with the effects of the agricultural depression, is interesting. 'The agricultural depression about which we hear so much and probably think so little was something more than a phrase ... to the inhabitants of Battersby Green and the region round about. It meant the throwing of farms out of cultivation, of men and families out of work; it meant the breaking up of the old squire in heart as well as fortune, the loss about the place of familiar honoured faces and kind helpful hands; the shutting up of cottage homes, emigration, pauperism – starvation.'

Good for Nothing is another tragic story, a tale of misunderstandings and friendships destroyed. *It is Housekeeper* is incomplete, but it is the story of a young man who employs a housekeeper to help look after his elderly mother. The old lady is senile and her mind drifts between the present and the past when her son was a baby. *Kate the Shrew* is a first attempt at the theme that MEM re-used in *Mrs Peter Howard* and *The Eglamore Portraits* – a disappointing marriage poisoned by an interfering mother-in-law. By page three, the young bridegroom, Mr Gorton, sees that his marriage 'had proved the signal for the dispersion of a good many illusions, and his anticipations in the matter of this homecoming were not destined to be fulfilled.' MEM tried and failed to get *Kate* published by the *Family Herald* – the manuscript bears their imprint on the back – but of the four Manton manuscripts it is the most assured and formed the basis for MEM's second published work.

Three years after *Parish of Hilby*, MEM published her second and third novels, *Mrs Peter Howard* and *Confessions of a Coward and a Coquette*. In *Mrs Peter Howard* she was again writing about what she knew and Millie Howard's experiences as the city-bred merchant's daughter, married to a farmer in a small, isolated village where she is a complete outsider, are clearly more than a nod to MEM's own experience. The church bells rang as Peter Howard brought his new bride home from honeymoon – we know that the church bells tolled in the same way for MEM and Fairman, though we have no way of knowing whether it was pouring with rain (as it was in the novel) or whether, like Millie, MEM found the sound melancholy. Millie's husband is too absorbed in his farm and his stock to pay her the attention she needs; the servants despise her; her in-laws are shocked by her lack of housewifely skills; only her husband's father (perhaps modelled on George Bolton Mann) and the dashing but untrustworthy Captain Gressley (hopefully an invention!) treat her with sympathy.

To modern readers it is an unremarkable tale, but the critics in 1886 felt they had to sound notes of caution. 'In "Mrs Peter Howard" is observed a distinct progress on the author's previous works …' admitted the *Morning Post's* literary critic, but added, 'The author's sex and her inexperience may be guessed from this very one-sided view of the obligations of matrimony as affecting women … it is to be regretted that a more healthy tone does not reign in this tale …' It is equally easy to guess the sex and experience of the *Morning Post's* literary correspondent! The *Pall Mall Gazette* was kinder. 'To George Eliot's quiet earnestness in study she adds an amount of downright malignity, which may be unholy but is remarkably amusing … At her best she is so good that we cannot name her equal among modern writers in her own peculiar line …'

The other novel which came out in 1886 was *Confessions of a Coward and a Coquette*. Here MEM departs from writing about what she knows to produce a convoluted love story of an orphaned girl who, more or less inexplicably, chooses to take a room in a spooky deserted farmhouse with a family straight out of a Hammer House of Horror production. She is befriended by a fellow lodger, Mr Carlyle; there is a black sheep criminal brother, a gruesome suicide, a fire in a barn and an ignorant maid servant, 'Giner', who speaks broad Norfolk and, against all expectations, turns out to be a useful person to have around in a crisis. Finally, there is Drummond Martin, the taciturn-but-worthy son whom the heroine eventually marries. It is a page-turner, quite well-written – MEM was incapable of writing really badly even when her material was unworthy of her – but it has little else to recommend it. Quite rightly, most of the critics ignored it completely. It seems likely that this was a novel MEM had written some time previously and reworked at her agent's request; it is closer in feel to *Milly Strong* than to any of her other work, though the subject matter is quite different.

It was published by Ward Downey. There was a correspondence with them which she reported to Tom Ordish in some bewilderment. She had sent them the manuscript two weeks previously and had had no reply. 'I do not at all understand the etiquette of such matters ... to the uninitiated it looks very much like rudeness.' She clearly did not realise how long it would take a publisher's reader to decipher her appalling handwriting. They agreed to publish, but MEM was concerned about the terms. '... they send me an agreement to sign which is an undertaking on their part to pay £20 <u>3 months after publication.</u> ... Now is that definition enough? ... To gain time till I heard your opinion I have written saying I should like to have some definite date for publication fixed before I signed the agreement.' Tom seems to have persuaded her to accept their terms and the novel was published successfully.

She was still trying to pretend that she was not a serious writer. 'If I <u>meant</u> to do anything with my pen I would have my certain hours on which there must be no intrusions,' she told Tom, 'but people never dream I require any privacy for myself. I cannot bring myself to believe that what I do is worth making a fuss about ...' She was being deliberately disingenuous; in reality MEM had quite a high opinion of herself. It is easy to understand why Fairman so disliked her attempts at humility – 'of all my moods,' she told Tom, 'he dislikes most my being humble.'

At this stage she was not tied to any particular publisher. *Mrs Peter Howard* was published by Smith Elder, the firm whose claim to fame was the discovery of Charlotte Bronte and the publication of *Jane Eyre*.

R. Bentley and Co. would take her next; old Mr Bentley felt she had potential and was clearly rather taken with young Mrs Mann. The next book was *Lost Estate*, published in 1889. It is set in a country village and the hero is young Peter Merry, the vicar's ward, his housekeeper's son. Fussy little Mrs Merry who hoped to marry the vicar but could never get him to notice her, kind, other-worldly Reverend Budsworth, a good man but not one whom his parishioners could love, his ungainly son, Archie, a modern curate with a strong social conscience, bad tempered old Harry Barber at the Grange, a gentleman who has forgotten how to be gentlemanly, and pretty, silly, sexy Sally Pack who is no better than she ought to be and abandons her illegitimate baby to freeze to death on a cold winter's night, are all more or less believable. It is also just about credible that the ill-tempered old man would take a shine to young Peter and make him his heir. Much less so is Mariana, the woman with the terrible-but-unspoken past whom Harry Barber marries, and the possibility that young, handsome, lively Peter would ever have fallen in love with her, however temporarily. That the dying man should rouse himself from his bed to catch them in their one and only embrace, and then recover sufficiently to send for his lawyer to change his will to disinherit Peter, beggars belief. The plot is clumsy but MEM is back in the world she knows, with characters based on real people – Peter is almost certainly one of her younger brothers – even if at this stage she is making them behave in an improbably melodramatic manner.

Good is rewarded and evil punished in ways that should have pleased Victorian sensibilities, but the critic at *The Graphic* was horrified. Mrs Mann 'has bestowed good work upon as disagreeable, indeed repulsive, a plot as can be imagined. A complication of moral disease finds denouement in an actual operation for tracheotomy, under circumstances which, however heroic in fact, are anything but suitable for fiction ...' Needless to say, Peter Merry, who had trained as a doctor, performed the tracheotomy to save the little boy who inherited the estate that should have been his. Peter then contracted diphtheria and died as a result. The critics did admit that the depiction of the characters was excellent but that had only 'rendered their moral degradation the more painful'. *Vanity Fair* was equally critical, considering that MEM must be a very wicked person to have 'such an extraordinary knowledge of the character of a thoroughly bad woman.' There were numerous other negative criticisms and MEM wrote angry defensive letters seeking Tom's reassurance. Even before the book was published, Mr Bentley (the publisher) had had her in to his office to discuss softening the character of Mariana so as not to shock the readers. MEM was outraged. 'To make just an ordinary milk and water woman do her work would be manifestly absurd,' she complained.

The offer for this novel was £40 down plus another £35 if they sold more than 500 copies. She thought it a poor offer and so did Tom but she accepted it. 'I knew it was no use to haggle for better terms with him because he would just have thrown up the book and no-one else would have taken it,' she said. She was not yet well enough known to be choosy, though she did make it clear to Mr Bentley that she thought the terms 'ridiculously inadequate'. Tom was indignant that she had accepted so little, but at this stage she was more anxious to be published than to make money – 'the book will fare as well as if it had been fairly paid for and no-one but you & I & the courteous old skinflint Richard B will ever know it was valued so very cheap. And if I dared I should like again to allude to the fact that probably the princely sum I shall obtain for it is all it is worth.'

One Another's Burdens followed a year later, again published by Bentley and on the same terms, despite MEM's protestations. It was well received. 'Mrs Mann's village stories are refreshingly clever' approved *The Morning Post*. 'In point of conception, of character drawing, and of directness and clearness in the telling, the story is good throughout' agreed the *Academy*. MEM was back on village soil, writing about life as it might have been lived in Shropham. She was also angry. In *Parish of Hilby* she had written critically about the vicar, and vicars and their wives are often presented unsympathetically in her books. In *One Another's Burdens* she takes this to a whole new level. Simon Elgard, the newly-appointed vicar of East Gramlingham, is the villain of the piece, too lazy to carry his grand schemes through, too poor to help his parishioners, too inept to write the sermons he preaches so beautifully and too selfish to see how his philandering wrecks lives. He is eventually horsewhipped by the husband of one young woman he has favoured, burnt in effigy by his parishioners and chased by some local youths to his death under the wheels of a stagecoach. His hopelessly idealistic young wife is left humiliated, disillusioned and penniless. MEM is no more complimentary about his elderly predecessor; 'that cold white hand of his had never come into contact with his humble parishioners, except in bestowing its final grip of encouragement and farewell on their death beds.' Elgard's successor gets equally short shrift, but MEM's real venom is reserved for his bossy wife, who was delighted 'to be mistress of a parish at last; to be where she could interfere with affairs to her heart's content, without the fear of interference from any superior power; while she having, alas! no curate of her own to worry and no curate's wife to snub could yet look down from a safe eminence on that defenceless race; where she could be inquisitor, ruler, despot all in one.' Simon Elgard, MEM told Tom, was based on a popular clergyman she had known as a child, who was much loved by all the ladies in the parish including her own mother. He made a great fuss of her too, kissing and petting her; then he married a widow with daughters. His affectionate behaviour to these girls overstepped the bounds of propriety and he was disgraced and unfrocked.

By 1890 MEM's own marriage was becoming increasingly miserable and in the same novel she is deeply critical of the institution as a whole – even a honeymoon is described as that 'joyful feast of overthrown illusions'! The Strong girls, Miriam and Libbie, are the product of a bullying violent father who has reduced his wife to a state of total inertia. Miriam's marriage to Simon is a disaster; Dora Harrison, Simon's victim, marries a jealous, possessive, hot-headed husband. The couple do not live together during the course of the novel and though they are reunited at the end the reader is left to conjecture just how happy their relationship is likely to be. MEM takes several swipes at men, like Edwin Strong, who do not believe women should have opinions, and there are several tongue-in-cheek comments on women's irrationality. For good measure, she introduces another of her hate figures. Thomas Cheek, the tailor, is a radical socialist, a trouble- maker and general rabble-rouser – 'It was, of course, part of his creed to acknowledge no superior. He did not touch his hat nor condescend to any title of respect in addressing those (temporarily) above him in the social scale.' As the wife of an employer of men she had little sympathy with socialism or trades unions, despite being able to see more clearly than most the evils that they were trying to eradicate. Finally, as we have already seen, she uses *One Another's Burdens* as a vehicle for attacking publishers and critics through Miriam Elgard's literary ambitions.

By the end of 1890 MEM had published five novels in eight years while running a home, bringing up her children and taking part in village affairs, and she was also anxious to display her credentials as a farmer's wife to Tom Ordish in London. In one letter she recounts how they had had to call the police because someone had poisoned the turkey chicks she had raised; she was sure it was 'Ben' one of the labourers, because she had scolded his children for throwing stones at the fowls and breaking a duck's leg. The only 'Ben' in Shropham in 1891 was Benjamin Groom, a farm labourer who lived in one of the cottages attached to Manor Farm and presumably worked for Fairman. He had two little boys, Frederick and Ernest, who were probably the culprits. MEM was clearly distressed by the loss of the chicks. 'I was awfully sorry as I had grown fond of the little things, and when one remembers the constant care they had been for months – then to see them lying in a heap dead, it grieved me very much.' She was particularly angry with the police, 'the local blunderer' and 'the thick headed fools', who were convinced that the arsenic the men used as sheep dip had somehow poisoned the ground under the turkey pen, even though she could prove that it had not done so. They were facetious when she mentioned also having had four chickens stolen and meat from the pickling pot going missing, and were clearly unwilling to act against anyone in the village.

In another letter she told Tom how she went to the village school to hear the 'little wretches read for an hour'. The inspectors' reports often described Shropham school as 'unsatisfactory'. In 1880 the managers, of whom Fairman was secretary and treasurer, appointed a 'qualified' mistress, Mrs Dack, which suggests that the previous teachers had been untrained, even though formal training courses for National School teachers had been running since the 1840s. By 1880 schooling was free, so the teacher's salary was no longer augmented by the children's pennies; instead the government made a grant to the school, but the size of that grant was dependent on the inspectors' reports. In November they appointed Miss Laughlin as assistant mistress at £8 a year, but things didn't improve and the inspectors' report in 1883 was still disappointing. After yet another unsatisfactory report in 1887 there was talk of firing Mrs Dack, but it was agreed to give her another year to improve things. If the next government grant was less than £35 she was to resign. It was, but somehow Mrs Dack was allowed to stay on 'more for her personal and moral worth than for her teaching capabilities' as the minutes recorded. In a small village, sacking even the most incompetent of employees was fraught with difficulty.

In an attempt to improve standards the vicar agreed to visit more often and MEM began to go in regularly each Friday to teach reading

Shropham School photograph c. 1900

and dictation. From January 1888, Bertie seems to have helped too – she would then have been nearly fourteen. MEM had taken all three girls to visit the school back in June 1887; such visits were thought to be good for children, a way of making well-to-do children grateful for their good fortune and of showing villagers' children how a well-brought-up child behaved. By 1890, Dolly had taken Bertie's place at the school – Bertie was never willing to do things she didn't enjoy and MEM never seems to have been able to manage her. The reports continued unsatisfactory: attendance was poor, the children were dull and inattentive, they couldn't do sums, their writing was hopeless, and the poor little infants were all badly behaved. In 1891 things were so bad the government even threatened to withhold Shropham's grant altogether. Then, as now, a good head teacher made all the difference. Blanche Dack died of diphtheria in 1892 and was replaced by Mrs Eastlaugh who found 'the children in a very BACKWARD state in all subjects' when she arrived. But within three years she had turned the school round completely, and in 1895 the inspectors' report was outstanding. Fairman at last felt able to resign from the school board.

As well as the practical help they gave, the Manns also distributed oranges and nuts to all the children each year when the school broke up in December – probably the only Christmas presents many of them would have had. Some years they also held the annual school treat at Manor Farm.

MEM was also on the flower show committee and in August 1886 she wrote to Tom about a meeting she was going to. 'In a quiet way I enjoy myself at these assemblies with their fuss and their pretence. I have had to call this solemn conclave because one unfortunate wretch with a wife and children and ten shillings a week for fortune took a prize of two shillings with rhubarb from a neighbour's garden. I need not state that my sympathy will be entirely with the culprit, but the church, powerfully represented, will be too much for me and the fraudulent prizetakers will doubtless be done to death.' It was an incident worthy of *Tales of Dulditch*.

A church bazaar in Shropham c. 1897
The figure on the right is one of the Mann girls

MEM's was a record to be proud of, but from time to time her self-confidence seems to have wavered. 'I shall not attempt another book – where is the use?' she told Tom Ordish in March 1888, 'I know that <u>parts</u> of the last book were very good but I couldn't get anyone to read it'. His reply is revealing, '... you lack faith, and honestly speaking, I don't wonder at it when I read the atmosphere of thought, ideas and mood you are surrounded by. The flower of your genius would bloom better amid downright poverty, with a few rays of hope, of loving belief in you ... Oh MEM!!! Don't sit down under that blighting mood!' There is a great deal more of the same and it would appear that Fairman was becoming cynical, depressive and an atheist and was not supporting MEM's ambition to write. The marriage that had begun with love and high spirits was becoming increasingly unhappy and the couple were drifting apart – small wonder that *One Another's Burdens* was such a bitter book. It would also seem that the atmosphere took its toll on MEM physically. She told Tom that she had lost two stones in weight, it didn't suit her, she said, 'but I love the melting process.'

In the 1880s and 90s it was becoming more and more difficult to make a living from farming. Even the Hemsworths at Shropham Hall seem to have recognised this; in March 1881 they made the magnanimous gesture of reducing all their tenants' rents by 10% for that year. However, the crisis would last much longer than a year. Imported grain and meat from America kept prices low, and nationwide, farmers struggled to make a living. The more enterprising countrymen migrated to the towns in search of work or headed to the colonies leaving their older, duller counterparts behind. Fairman was an assiduous record keeper; in his den at the back of the house he kept decades' worth of farm records pinned to his walls, yellowing and crisping in the smoke-filled room. 'To see Mr Mann in his office or 'den' at the rear of the Manor House was altogether a charming experience. There amidst a medley of heterogeneous agricultural publications and miscellanies of all kinds he was ever ready to welcome his friends and impart some of the valuable knowledge he had gained by long experience...' enthused his obituary writer. MEM took a rather more jaundiced view.

In earlier years he had been a great experimenter with farming methods. A letter to the local press in 1878 describes how he had cured rickets in his sheep by altering their diet. In June 1888 he sent a detailed account of the benefits of selling washed fleeces against unwashed ones to the local paper – he had kept careful records and found that he got 3½d more per fleece for washed ones. From time to time he sent off statistics to the press. In 1887 he reported to the *Morning Post* that his wheat harvest that year was the second worst he had experienced in twenty-five years of farming (1870 was the worst) because of the drought conditions. Prices for English wheat that year were at an all-time low and the harvest of all types of grain in America was very good. But an article in a Norfolk paper on June 18th 1889 hinted at just how bad things were becoming. Fairman's herd of red poll cattle, a Norfolk breed noted for both milk and beef, was his pride and joy. By 20th century standards his herd was tiny – just seven milch cows, or six-and-a-half as he told the paper because one cow 'Mother Mary' was such a poor milker. His records showed in meticulous detail that he had made 1,759 and a quarter pounds of butter for sale that year, at an average price of 1s. 3d. a pound, and this had made him £107 3s. 9d. or, if he added the value of the milk, butter and cream consumed by the household and the skim milk fed to the new born lambs in spring, an average of £22 13s. per cow. Against that, the turnips, hay and cattle cake he fed the herd between May and October added up to £13 per cow per year, so his beloved herd brought him just £67 11s. a year in profit. Fairman had good reason to be depressed and demoralised.

Set against the failure of his farm, his wife's growing success must have grated. Rackham, his only son, showed no signs of wanting to farm and was about to go off and train as a surgeon. Fairman was fifty-three in 1890 and had worked hard all his life; he must have begun to wonder whether any of it had been worthwhile. It is not surprising that he grew cynical. He became increasingly morose, spent more and more time ensconced in his 'den' – and began to drink heavily.

Chapter 5. Writing for money 1891-1901

The Mann family albums from the 1890s and early 1900s are full of photos of tea on the lawn and groups of laughing young people in punts on the little lake, the ladies of the party in billowing cotton dresses, the men casual and relaxed. There are photos of pretty daughters and family pets – dogs, ponies and Poddles the parrot. Relying on the photos alone one would be left with a vision of a country idyll peopled by a happy, united family enjoying an endless golden summer. The reality was much darker – the family had major money worries and the head of the household was drinking himself to death.

Entertaining in the garden at Manor Farm c. 1900

Living in a grand house, eating their own meat, vegetables, butter and eggs and baking with flour milled from their own wheat, the financial problem was not immediately apparent, but out of the dwindling income from the farm there was £600 a year to find for rent, house servants and farm labourers to pay, coal, lamp oil and tea and sugar to be bought. On top of that, there were Rack's hospital fees and living expenses to pay, as well as his books and medical equipment to buy. Bertie was anxious to become an artist and had enrolled at the Slade – not for her the cheaper courses at the local School of Art in

Bertie harvesting, mid 1890s
This is a posed photograph, wearing artistic dress; her white pinafore and frilly bonnet
would not have stayed clean for long had she really been working in the harvest field

Norwich. Between 1896 and 1902 she lived in a London boarding
house at a rent of around £5 12s. a month and struggled to get work as
an illustrator. The occasional commission came her way, but never
enough to cover her expenses. Dolly and Margery were still at their
hated boarding school in the early 1890s and their fees, too, had to be
paid. MEM's hobby now needed to make money.

The Mann family c. 1895
Bertie and Dolly stand wearing artistic dress (very outré for Shropham). Margery is
more conventionally dressed, gazing at her father who looks uncomfortable. Rack is
smoking and MEM sits looking away from her family, and the dog is centre stage – a
very odd grouping.

Over in Norwich, Harry and George Rackham gave up the unequal struggle to keep their father's business afloat and in 1891 they closed the warehouse. Harry got temporary employment with the County Council. Aged forty, and with absolutely no experience, George took the extraordinary decision to become a farmer and took the tenancy of a farm at Sprowston, three miles north of Norwich. Tenancies were cheap because there was no money in farming and no-one wanted them – perhaps he was misled into thinking he had a bargain. Perhaps his wife, a farmer's daughter, hankered after life in the country, perhaps he had helped his brother and brother-in-law on their farms from time to time and thought he knew enough to set out on his own – we have no way of knowing. The venture was not a success, and within a few years George had changed direction and become the proprietor of the Bell Inn at Methwold. Harry was even less lucky and was soon out of work altogether. At that point he seems to have got a job with the L.C.C. and moved to London and it sounds as if he stayed with the Ordishes for a while. Rack was already lodging with them and was unimpressed by his uncle's arrival. 'Rack thinks Harry is a fool,' MEM wrote sadly. 'As a matter of fact, quite established by themselves, none of my unfortunate brothers are brilliant – but I don't think Harry quite a fool by nature. He used to be able to appreciate good things and to have sense and a certain amount of tact. But he has lived all his life in a narrow clique of which, unfortunately for himself, he was about the most shining specimen and I suppose he has flattened down to what he is. And want of success is not improving to all natures, only the best.' Rack was young and intolerant but one suspects that his judgement was not entirely inaccurate.

In 1892, old Mrs Rackham, MEM's mother, died, leaving a careful will in which her every possession was allocated to one of her children or grandchildren, down to the bust of Apollo that went to Willie, the stuffed trout that formed part of George's share and the red Bohemian glass vase that Frank inherited. MEM got the lion's share of her mother's belongings plus two bequests, one of £700 and one of £500 'held in trust by Mr Kirk' – presumably the residue of some sort of marriage settlement. She also seems to have inherited all the family photos and letters, though these were not listed in the will, and she kept them carefully through several changes of address, with the result that Eddie's childhood letters to his parents, notices of the deaths of family friends and letters congratulating Mrs Rackham on Willie's success in his exams are now intermingled with MEM's own multifarious collection of papers.

Under the will the Rackham sons got just £100 apiece on top of their share of the proceeds from the sale of their mother's remaining effects. Few of them lived long enough to enjoy it. Harry was the first to die, in 1895, but strangely MEM kept no funeral notice or letters of condolence relating to his death. Two of the younger boys used their legacies to head for the colonies: John to South Africa, Eddie to Canada. Young men who had no experience of making a living were unlikely to be able to make their fortunes. Eddie died of galloping consumption brought on by cold and hunger (he'd written to MEM telling her he could not afford to eat) in a Winnipeg hospital in December 1897. She was grief-stricken. 'I loved Eddie so' she confided in a letter to Tom; for all his faults, Eddie was still her baby brother. John ended up as a waiter at Jumpers Deep Boarding House in Johannesburg and died there in September 1898. George Rackham died in 1900 of pneumonia, at the inn in Methwold, leaving his widow, Edith, penniless. For a while she eked out a living as a dressmaker in Norwich, then she took a post as housekeeper to a London piano maker. Fanny Rackham, Willie's wife, died, probably of a heart attack, in July 1900 and, with almost indecent haste, Willie remarried the following year. His second wife was Katherine ('Kate') Gardiner from Great Yarmouth, a farmer's daughter fifteen years his junior, but the marriage did not last long for Willie died in 1903. MEM was quite surprised by the eulogies he received from his brother lawyers. 'I always knew he was a very clever man,' she wrote, 'but have been so out of touch with him that I did not realise how high a place he took in the esteem of others.' In just eleven years she had lost her mother, a sister-in-law and five of her six brothers; of the once prosperous middle-class family from Town Close House scarcely a trace remained.

Throughout the decade MEM's own children continued to be a worry and an expense. As early as the mid-1880s, when Dolly had flu, MEM wrote to Tom fearing it would be a long while before she was better because 'her robust appearance is misleading,' and Dolly does seem to have suffered from a lot of nervous illness. Some rather curious correspondence in 1896 shows that Dolly spent some time with a specialist in London at 3, Endersleigh Gardens. The name on the letter is illegible and it seems that by the time it was written Dolly was recovering. The specialist did not think 'your dear child is either ill or depressed now. She was much distressed whilst the painful circum-stances were taking place but her brother's timely visit and the assurance of the safety of the other have I think quite tranquilised her. I was also glad she told me the story which she did most freely and frankly – in fact she has behaved admirably throughout and given me the highest opinion of her courage and self-control...I enclose a receipt for your cheque.' There is nothing in MEM's correspondence of the period to enlighten us further about the 'painful circumstances', and it is unlikely that Rack, when he visited, had much sympathy with his little sister's histrionics. When Dolly was again ill some years later, his advice to his mother about her treatment was brusque and un-sympathetic and he clearly thought she was a hypochondriac. What we can be sure of is that Dolly's treatment did not come cheap.

Once he had qualified as a doctor Rack was anxious to travel. In a letter in February 1898 MEM asked Tom if he knew anyone who could help Rack obtain a post that interested him at a hospital in Cairo – her faith in Tom's ability to act as fixer for the Mann family was unbounded. A few years earlier she had asked his help to get her eight year old nephew, Simon, a place at Christ's Hospital school. Rack did not get the post and opted to join the navy instead. The second Boer War broke out in 1899 and, to MEM's relief, her son was not posted to

Rack in uniform – he joined the navy in 1898-9

Africa, even though Rack himself would love to have been at the scene of the fighting. Tom was anti-war and sent MEM a press cutting which supported his view. MEM replied proudly that the villagers in Shropham were excited and patriotic; 'even in Dulditch the love of country and the pride of race and the national determination to "beat the lot-of-em" wherever they may be is strong'. For MEM, a war many thousands of miles away was an exhilarating prospect. She and Tom seldom agreed about political matters. 'These are the sort of things I should like to write about,' she continued, 'but my agent continually demands <u>cheerful</u> stories …'

By 1900, as the casualties mounted, she became more despondent but still could not bring herself to condemn the war, and admitted the

93

whole family pored eagerly over the paper as soon as it arrived each day; 'not very lively reading for us,' she complained at the beginning of 1900, 'but the little fat Belgians roll about with ecstasy ...' She was outraged by a 'letter I saw from Mrs Andreas' German nephew in which the little reptile says "The English are getting a whipping. I wish I were there to help with giving it."' Mrs Andreas was a Belgian friend of old Mrs Rackham's who came to visit, became ill, and stayed at Manor Farm for weeks. MEM still saw England as the greatest nation on earth and was unable to appreciate that the rest of the world did not share that view. Fairman was less sentimentally patriotic than his wife and daughters. He 'comes in and grumbles that supper has been kept waiting, and grumbles that the generals don't know what they are doing, and grumbles that the nation is one of fools and that the government for many years deserves hanging, and so we settle down to cold chicken and resignation,' MEM complained.

MEM with Alfred Munnings and James Hooper at Shropham c. 1900

Fame brought visitors and MEM loved to entertain. Probably their most famous visitor of this period was the painter, Alfred Munnings, or 'Muggins' as Bertie irreverently called him. They must have met through MEM's childhood friend, Kate Nichols, herself an artist and founder of the 'Woodpecker Club', an art society in Norwich to which Alfred Munnings, MEM and Bertie all belonged. He was something of an eccentric, often oddly dressed, and his manners were not of the best. On one of his visits, according to Bertie, he could not be bothered to conceal the fact that he would rather have been at home painting! She described him in one diary entry as looking like a 'pierrot turned horse dealer' and in another as 'the half-tamed one.' The day after the King's death, when everyone else was wearing mourning, Munnings chose to sport a cinnamon coloured riding coat, grey trousers, green waistcoat, blue tie and vivid violet-blue socks. However, when he was in a good mood, he was entertaining company and he did do several paintings for the Manns of their pet dogs – mother and daughters were obsessively fond of their animals – and there are numerous surviving letters from him to MEM embellished with little pen and ink cartoons. He got on well with Bertie too, and on one of his visits to the theatre in London he acquired a whole batch of autographs for her collection: Max Cowper, Gough, Dion Clayton Calthrop 'and the wriggly name on the right is Edgar Wilson'.

Portrait of 'Troy', one of the Mann's dogs, by Alfred Munnings

Through Munnings, MEM was introduced to his friends, Thomas Case the poet ('very young, very grave and rather shy' according to Bertie) and James Hooper, a Norwich antiquarian, who wrote occasional pompous, self-aggrandising letters to MEM which failed to impress her. It is obvious from Munnings' correspondence that they both regarded Mr Hooper as something of a joke. Bertie's diaries make it clear that the three of them, but especially Munnings, were regular visitors. When his three-volume autobiography was published in 1950-1, Bertie and Margery were then old ladies and they became quite excited, expecting there to be lots of references to the happy times he had spent with them at Shropham. They were disappointed. For all their years of friendship, the Mann family received only one mention, and that to Fairman's herd of red polls which, co-incidentally, Munnings' brother also bred!

Another regular visitor in the 1890s and 1900s was Miss Warvalzi (Bertie's spelling and probably inaccurate), a Russian aristocrat who often stayed at Ivy Cottage with a companion. She was exceedingly well connected: her family estates had been given to her great-grandfather by Catherine the Great and her father was a cousin of Talleyrand. MEM liked her; 'she is a nice, sweet, natural, gay little person'. Miss Warvalzi dressed very fashionably and flamboyantly in high heels and silk dresses; Bertie described her appearance in Shropham as being 'as out of place as an orchid in a cornfield'! Nonetheless, the friendship lasted and when Miss Warvalzi settled in Bournemouth one or other of the family visited her most years.

Shropham Church

Eighteen ninety-eight saw the installation of the *Nativity* window in Shropham church in memory of the Reverend William Robbins, his wife and nine daughters. It was designed in the Arts and Crafts style by Mary Lowndes, the first woman to work full-time as a stained glass artist, and forms a wonderful patch of glowing colour in an otherwise rather sombre little church. The angels at the top and the one standing behind Mary are all in red, the Holy Family and their visitors are brightly dressed, seated in a clearing in a wood of gnarled, twisted trees, and the bottom section of the window shows the star in the sky and the angels appearing, all in the muted colours of a starlit night. We do not know what MEM thought of the window, though she must have been at the unveiling – she had known the Robbins family well for many years – and the installation must have been one of the most significant events of the decade in sleepy little Shropham. Perhaps it was too modern for her taste, perhaps she thought it an incongruous addition to a mediaeval church; or perhaps she disapproved of Miss Lowndes who was a keen supporter of the London Society for Women's Suffrage, a movement with which MEM had little sympathy. Nonetheless, it is strange that she makes no mention of it at all.

Perhaps she was just too busy writing. MEM's literary output in the 1890s was prodigious – ten novels and numerous short stories. Fairman may have retreated into the background, her birth family, with the exception of Frank and Hattie who were still at Church Farm with their growing brood of children, were leaving her one by one, but her own career was successful and sometimes happy. She still found Shropham stultifyingly boring, especially in the long winter evenings when the family were thrown on their own resources – 'I believe we have immense vitality,' she wrote to Tom in 1894, 'or we should literally perish of dulness.'

By the 1890s she was employing a typist – Miss Messer in Surbiton who charged 1d. per hundred words, or £3 for typing a 72,000 word novel. This was not an inconsiderable expense but, given MEM's idiosyncratic handwriting, must have made life more bearable for her publishers' readers. Poor Miss Messer was often working under pressure. A note on one manuscript says, 'I am in rather a hurry for this, if you can will you do it quickly?'; on another, 'Can you let me have this by Christmas?' MEM once told Tom it took her about two months to produce a fair hand-written copy of one of her novels once she had completed the original text, so a typist must have been a boon.

Inevitably, quantity led to a decline in quality. Of the numerous novels MEM published in the 1890s – *A Winter's Tale, Perdita, In Summer Shade, Susannah, There Once was a Prince, Cedar Star, Moonlight* and *Out in Life's Rain* – probably the two outstanding works are *When Arnold Comes Home* and *The Patten Experiment* which were published in 1896 and 1899 respectively.

When Arnold Comes Home is unusual in that it is written from the perspective of the child narrator. That did not, as some critics seemed to think, mean it was a children's book, far from it; it was intended to make adults think about the casual cruelty they sometimes unwittingly mete out to small children. The central character is six-year old Philip Margetson. His father has recently died, his mother has little money and other small children to care for, so little Philip is sent to live with his father's sister, Aunt Marion, and her three almost-adult children, Scott, Hester and Ruth. He is a timid, shy little boy, easily reduced to tears, and besotted with his collection of stuffed toys – the monkey family, Old Father, Uncle Monkey, Sister, Cousin and Baby, 'resembling nothing in natural history. They had been originally covered in soft white fur which was now, however, in a ragged and mangy condition. They had red eyes of glass, and a couple of rows of white beads for teeth. They had long tails, and stiff and jointless arms, and legs terminating in bits of fringed white kid to represent toes and fingers.' His cousins, especially Scott, tease and humiliate him mercilessly and threaten the monkeys with cremation if they are brought into the house. When asked what 'cremation' means, poor little Philip stutters that 'It was done in seven days!' The girls are charged with educating him and neither understands how to teach a small child, how hard he finds it to control a pen or how much they frighten him. He is scared and miserable all the time.

One day he encounters a 'tramp' who tells him his name is Jim and who is kind to him. Philip brings Jim water and food and, unbeknown to the rest of the family, lets him sleep in the summer house with the monkey family. Jim calls Philip his 'little matey' and tells him he is 'faithful and true'. Then the house is apparently burgled, the police are called, Philip admits to knowledge of the 'tramp', and Jim is arrested. The burglary turns out to be Scott playing a joke and Jim turns out to be Philip's Uncle Arnold, his mother's brother, who has been in Africa and who, Philip has been led to believe, will solve all his mother's money problems when he comes home with the fortune he has made. Only Jim/Arnold has no money; he has drunk and gambled it all away and ruined his health in the process, and Philip never learns the truth about his identity. Arnold is re-united with his sister only to die in her arms. Meanwhile, Scott finds that Delia, the love of his life will have nothing to do with him while he is tormenting the little boy; Philip runs away and everyone realises how fond they really are of him. The dénouement is necessarily contrived, but some of the child's reactions – dressing up in his toy suit of armour with 'his helmet and breastplate shining above his scarlet pinafore' to feel brave enough to go and see if the tramp is really dead, for example, and his hopeless misery when he simply cannot do his lessons – are recognisable to anyone who remembers what it was like to be a child. Philip quickly forgets Jim/Arnold and the story ends, after a day at the zoo with Delia, with him saying, 'D'ye know, I think we'd better be going home now ... I should like to tell my mamie about the ephelants; and Baby Monkey is such a little thing, it's prob'ly time the poor boy was put to bed.' MEM was extremely good at beginnings and endings.

Following Tom's advice, MEM kept assuring him as she wrote 'the child story' that she was 'trying to keep to the humdrum' – and the story is the better for it. Her personal taste was for melodrama and plenty of it, though she did not say so in as many words, but she was trying to 'positively tie myself down with cords' and she was grateful for his help. 'I wish I could help you as you have always helped me,' she told him, 'I should have given up trying to do anything a long time ago if it wasn't for you.'

There once was a Prince, which was published the same year, also has a child protagonist, little Lolly Rolfe, with her brave, ailing mother, abusive, violent stepfather and lazy, worthless brother. The 'prince' is Edward Richmond, a recovering invalid staying with family in the neighbourhood, who eventually rescues the girl, sends her to a London boarding school while he goes abroad and then comes back when she is grown up and about to become a governess in Paris. It is left to the reader's imagination as to whether or not Lolly ever marries her 'prince'. MEM writes knowledgeably of the isolation of a family of which a village disapproves; even when everyone knows the wife and children are being ill-treated no-one feels it is their business to interfere. There is a sympathetic portrait of an old gipsy couple who befriend Lolly's brother and horrendous descriptions of hunger and family brutality and indifference. It seems likely that MEM knew a family like the Rolfes in Shropham.

Both these books were published by H. Henry and Co. They were not the easiest of firms to deal with. In February 1893 MEM told Tom '[They] have sent the books (there is one for you of course) but – alas! not the cheque. Fairman is not nervous about it and does not desire me at present to bother them.' She was clearly more worried than he was. The book in question was *In Summer Shade*, which was the first book they published for her. Somehow they also managed to defraud her of the rights to the book, and the cheque, when it came, was for £50 when she had been expecting £150. Despite this, she stayed with the firm and the second book they published for her was *Susannah* in 1895. That year there was some correspondence about a published interview. 'Emphatically No,' MEM told Tom. 'I suppose it is the fault of the interviewers that all the interviewed are made to present themselves in such a guise of smug snobbishness ... But I have always thought if the chance came to me I should not give myself away after that fashion. I am sure you would not like to see me laying bare the secrets of my heart? How you would squirm when you read of me gracious and smiling and extending my hand and taking the public to my bosom, and telling her how I first came to turn my attention to literature and which I consider my <u>finest work</u>.' The refusal was probably a tactical mistake on MEM's part ; more exposure might have led to increased sales.

Tom was equally unsuccessful when he tried to get Bertie an interview to do some illustrative work for the firm. Bertie point blank refused to go and Tom was both offended and embarrassed. MEM's excusing of her daughter does not ring quite true. 'As to Bertie I am utterly angry with her for not having the "wit" to seize the moment's gift and go off with you to Henry and Co,' she wrote. 'She suffers largely from what is the ruin of all my family ... a sheepish inclination to hang back when the period is ripe for pushing forward ... She is painfully shy and afraid of people and not sure of herself ... She knew she was behaving foolishly and had to brazen it out.' Nothing else that we know about Bertie suggests she was ever shy or unsure – quite the reverse.

One of Bertie's illustrations for *There once was a Prince*, **1895, with curiously inappropriate framing.**

By 1897 MEM was wearying of Henry and Co. and their inadequate offers and was exploring other avenues. 'I beg you don't make any more preparations on my account,' she told Tom. 'I wrote to Mr Simon and I enclose his very polite and kind reply. It has occurred to me would there be any use in trying to get Tauchnitz to take Susannah? What do you think? And should I communicate with Hutchinson about the advance copy of Cedar Star for Tauchnitz … I should like to see Susannah in Dutch!' Tauchnitz dealt with the Continental rights of almost all her books. 'I don't know why you are infuriated with me about Warner and Co.' she went on. 'I have the story on my hands and have to send it somewhere. I see by the talk in The Author that Ward and Lock and Warner and Co bring out …similar books and I thought they were the proper people to apply to. Can you suggest another firm? because the ms is all ready. So long as someone will give me a few pounds for it I don't care where it goes …' In the end neither firm took her work – Tom had his way. 'About Fisher Unwin,' she continued, 'you must be <u>ill</u> to be cross about that! … Why didn't you say "don't"?'

Hutchinson and Fisher Unwin published a book apiece for her in both 1898 and 1899 – (*Cedar Star* and *Out in Life's Rain*, and *Moonlight* and *The Patten Experiment,* respectively). They were both comparatively new firms, founded in 1882 and 1887, and were probably still feeling their way. She was outraged because in mid-March 1898 'Mr Fisher Unwin' was asking her to make changes to *Moonlight*. 'The split infinitives can be hunted up,' she told him, 'the "and whiches" blotted out, but to alter the whole character of my heroine, to make her into an up-to-date psychological study instead of the child of impulse … is rather a large order, surely!' She went on to tell Tom that 'the vulgar lawyer' in *Moonlight* was based on her brother

100

Willie, and that the threatened suicide was an episode that actually happened. A couple of days later she again wrote to Tom for advice about more changes Fisher Unwin wanted her to make; 'you are better able to form a cool judgement than poor MEM who is rather for the minute in a temper,' and she asked whether he could find out who the three readers were who had criticised her work. She described the theme and the suggested changes, 'and all that I am coolly told to alter and the Fisher man will write me further, you perceive, in a day or two and will kindly give me further advice as to doctoring up my story to his standard!' Fisher Unwin seems to have climbed down in the face of her opposition to his suggestions; she signed the agreement and agreed to give him first refusal of her next work.

In some ways she was cannier than Tom who tended to be very defensive of her work. 'Besides,' she wrote, justifying herself, 'he will give Moonlight a better show for the sake of the one which comes after.' It did, however, make her appreciate her previous publisher more. 'Do you remember how sweetly old Mr Bentley asked me to alter a few things in the first ms I took to him?' she asked Tom, '"I think it is possible," he said "that this lady may achieve fame; and I am desirous that she give herself every chance." Different this from Fisher's brutal frankness as to the reason he interests himself and his talk of "our standard"!!' Sadly, the charming Mr Bentley's firm closed down in 1895.

Tauchnitz was also unhelpful. 'Isn't it strange that Baron Tauchnitz takes no notice of my second application to him? He is a rude old pig of a baron and I wish I had not wasted a copy of C.S. on him,' she wrote in March. But two months later her agent, Mr Bennett, sold the rights of Cedar Star to Tauchnitz for £15 of which MEM received £13 10s.

The Patten Experiment, which came out in October 1899, published by Fisher Unwin, is probably MEM's most important work. Unlike most novelists who tried to plead the cause of the poor, MEM's approach is half-humorous, but unfortunately most of the reviewers do not seem to have seen beyond the comedy. The Sheffield Independent hailed it as 'deliciously entertaining' and the literary critic of the London Standard wrote that 'It is a long time since we came across anything so fresh and excellent a bit of comedy as this'. 'The Patten Experiment is a clever and charming piece,' opined the Pall Mall Gazette on December 14th, 'and only a very clever writer could make so much that is interesting of such unpromising material'. The London Daily Mail saw it as 'a

101

delightful book. It is written in a limpid style, with a happy blend of gaiety and poignant realism. The many unforeseen touches of character and incident mark it with the stamp of first hand observation. The central idea is felicitous.' That felicitous idea may well have come from MEM's newly acquired son-in-law, Charles Edward Bolton Hewitt, who married Dolly Mann in 1897. MEM thought very highly of him. 'There is not an atom of paltriness or feebleness in all his great frame,' she told Tom.

The theme of *The Patten Experiment* is simple; an idealistic young clergyman, the Reverend Eustace Patten, his brother, his wife and her four sisters decide to see whether it is possible to live on 11s. a week – the standard labouring wage. Mr Boyan, the girls' father, is adamant that his labourers are well-treated. 'My men have no cares, no responsibilities. Every fortnight as pay-day comes round they receive a fortnight's wage; whether they've earned it or no they get it, whether I can afford it or no I pay them.' But Eustace has his doubts, 'You and I think we shall be in a tight place with a living bringing in two hundred and fifty,' he tells Rica, his wife. She and her sisters are clueless as to the value of money and most of the housekeeping falls to Rosamund, one of the younger girls who has no knowledge of cooking or cleaning but is at least willing to try; Rica spends most of the week in bed with a headache. The dumplings are inedible, the joint runs out by Monday, Rosamund is forced to disobey Eustace and buy on credit from the shop and, to cap it all, Tony, Eustace's brother, poaches rabbits for them to eat and is caught and prosecuted. MEM points up the kindness of village women, the ineptitude of well-brought-up young ladies struggling to light fires, cook simple meals and wash up, and the weakness of apparently fit young middle-class men when set to do the work of field labourers.

Charles Hewitt as a master at Marlborough College

Charles Hewitt was a serious, thoughtful man, a master at Marlborough School and would later be ordained. It is just possible he was the model – without the sandy hair or the freckled skin that turned bright red in the unforgiving heat of the harvest field – for the Reverend Eustace. 'Every bone in his body ached, his hands had blistered upon the hoe; on the bridge of his nose and the back of his neck and the outer edges of his ears he got his wife to dredge flour, no other cooling remedy being at hand.' There is plenty of comedy in this and in descriptions of the inedible meals, of Rosamund covered in soot with a lump of whiting in her hair from the flaking wall above the cooker and of the ghastly vicar's wife peddling her tracts and berating Rosamund for not being in service. The experiment comes to an abrupt end when one of the little girls gets measles and it is clear that the Reverend Eustace is becoming seriously unwell. 'About two days more of want of food and unaccustomed work under such a sun will about finish him. Serves him right!' announces the doctor unsympathetically. 'What right had he with his physique, and a wife with no more staying power than a chicken, to engage in such a prank?'

But the critics all seem to have missed what was clear to MEM – that for some men with Eustace's physique, field labour was not a 'prank' but the only way of life open to them. She knew that labourers' wives performed miracles of household management on a daily basis, that the ones who also managed to keep their houses clean and their children in school and out of mischief were little short of heroines, and that husbands who worked uncomplainingly and didn't drink all their wages displayed courage and fortitude that their 'betters' could not match. The twist in the tail that MEM was so good at providing came with a final swipe at the Reverend Eustace. Once installed in his parish and apparently forgetful of what the experiment had actually shown, he would regale his parishioners with little homilies; 'It seems hard, I grant you ... And an outsider will not understand how a man, his wife and children, can live in decency on the wage you receive. It sounds impossible. But it can be done, I know ... for I've done it!'

MEM was furious about the lack of publicity Fisher Unwin gave the book. 'The Patten Experiment was simply <u>lost</u>. Not a single use of the <u>extraordinarily</u> laudatory notices. Dozens of them. I have done with Mr Fisher Unwin.' But she hadn't; two years later he published two more of her books – *Among the Syringas* which first came out as a serial, and *The Mating of a Dove.* They too caused problems. The critics were rude about *Syringas,* largely because they felt it did not serialise well. It might, of course, have been better reviewed if Fisher Unwin had remembered to include the first chapter. And MEM was unhappy about the payment method. 'What does "£50 to accrue mean?" ' she asked Tom.

However, her fan, Alfred Munnings, was delighted with *The Patten Experiment*. 'It's a wonderful book!!' he wrote in a letter to MEM, 'And many people who read it will not see half the perfection of it although everybody <u>must</u> like it.' 'Never was a novel with a purpose more thoroughly readable' agreed the *New Age*'s critic, but most of MEM's readers were probably happy to accept the sop that she threw in towards the end, the doctor's explanation that 'It's only through the *habit* of semi-starvation that the system accommodates itself to the condition.' Had more of her readers taken note of what she was really saying, this novel had the potential to change attitudes and lives.

Out in Life's Rain came out in 1899, the same year as *The Patten Experiment* and it also seems to have been based in Shropham. A little girl is collected from the 'Wragland' Union workhouse – Shropham was in Wayland Union – and fostered with a village family. The mother with whom she is placed has two toddlers of her own and an older stepson and the boy and the little orphan are neglected and ill treated. The girl is taken in by the Vicar's wife and brought up as a lady, but then goes off with her real father who promises to make a singer of her. In fact she ends up singing for pennies to crowds at the seaside and is eventually rescued by 'the boy Step' who was her foster brother in her first placement. MEM considered *Out in Life's Rain* to be 'the worst thing I have ever written and goody goody besides' and not worth the £50 Hutchinson paid for it.

However, her treatment of workhouse life in *Out in Life's Rain* is interesting. Was MEM perhaps a lady visitor at the workhouse? Certainly she visited occasionally; on October 6th, 1904, for example, Bertie recorded in her diary that she drove her mother to a meeting at the workhouse. Bertie's diary entries are erratic and she was much more concerned with her own doings than with those of her family, so it is unlikely that this was MEM's only visit to the 'big white house' at Rockland All Saints. Did she place children with foster families in Shropham? The scene in the workhouse with a kindly matron, set in a comfortable room with a roaring fire, has the ring of authenticity in that it belies most descriptions of Victorian workhouses, as does the neat, respectable outfit in which Mercy is despatched to her new home. She 'was in new garments from top to toe. A new little dark blue dress worn beneath a new white pinafore pulled up into a frill about her neck; new black ribbed stockings with stout boots; and, on her close-cropped hair, a white sailor-hat, many sizes too large for her, and which was generally hanging ... by the elastic beneath her chin, at the back of her neck.'

In a short story entitled *A Thankful People* MEM gives an equally positive picture of the workhouse. It is the day of the harvest festival at the 'Infirmary (We never call it the workhouse now unless we forget).' The inmates file in, the old cripple, the girl with chronic rheumatism who is brought in on a chair, senile old Martha Bell who tells everyone 'I'm a goin' to Heaven', Anne Boddy who has no teeth but fancies an apple dumpling – and so on. The matron is kind, shushing Martha and promising the crippled girl she shall have some of the beautiful flowers for her very own. They sing *Now Thank We All Our God* and the parson looks round at his congregation 'whose sowing has borne such scanty fruit' and realises with relief that among them there is 'no ... suspicion that such a service in such a place might from any point of view be considered a mockery.'

It is not known where *A Thankful People* was published. Most of the short stories survive in manuscript form, sometimes typed, sometimes hand written, sometimes as page proofs, and apart from odd references in letters to Tom Ordish we do not always know when, where or even whether they were published. What we do know is that they seldom earned MEM more than a few pounds apiece. She wrote for women's magazines, among them the *Family Herald*, a story magazine that cost twopence an issue, 'that high-class and irreproach-able magazine!' as MEM described it scornfully. The stories she sent them were often pot-boilers, love stories with a sting in the tail. She wrote for other magazines too, *The Daily Mail Supplement*, the *Girls' Own Paper*, *The Lady's World*, *Woman at Home*, *Storyteller*, and many others, and occasionally Bertie would be 'The Lady' commissioned to do the illustrations.

Later, MEM collected together what she considered to be the best of her short stories and published them as books: the collection of Dulditch stories in 1902, *A Sheaf of Corn* in 1908, *Bound Together* in 1910, *Men and Dreams* in 1912, *Through the Window* in 1913 and *The Pedlar's Pack* in 1918. The quality of the stories is variable but the plotting is often clever: the mistaken identities in *K.B., Forty-five* and *The Brown Overcoat,* for example, or the schoolboy's manipulation of his susceptible cousin in *Easy as Kissing*. Others are more obvious, like the play on a mother's suspicious mind and love of her son in *A Doubting Heart,* or the re-working of a contemporary urban myth in *The Five Pound Note*. Some are gruesome murder stories, like *Old Abel,* the kindly shoemaker who kills his discontented wife, and *HMS Fairy,* the name on the sailor hat worn by little illegitimate Dicky whose loving mother pushes him down a well so that she can marry the fiancé who knows nothing of the child's existence. Many feature clever, manipulative wives, as in *My Cousin Violet's Husband, It Answered* or *A Family Party*. Social class is a theme in the short stories as well as in the novels; *In a Tea-shop* is a prime example. MEM implies that it is dishonourable for any lady to earn her own living. The bankrupt lawyer's daughter is urged by her aunt not to 'mention the tea-shop, even before your cousins, dear,' and this reticence loses the girl her chance of a good marriage. She hides from the young man who comes courting her because she is ashamed of her work; he marries her colleague because he grows tired of waiting. There are fanciful stories about people, often children, who 'see' the dead; *As 'Twas Told to Me, The Little White Dog* and *Miss Alpe's Headache* are of this genre. MEM told Tom that the *Little White Dog* was her family ghost – her father had seen it and she saw it herself at Manor Farm the day her brother Harry died.

There are other stories that embody people, or things, in MEM's own life. *Mrs Varley's Parrot,* for example, is just as embarrassing as her own Poddles could be. A number have heroines called 'Bertie' or 'Bertholina'. *To Bertha in Bombay* is one such. Others, like *Sister Helen* or *The Private Ward* draw on Margery's experiences as a nurse. Some give MEM a platform for her own thoughts: she voices her hatred of shooting game birds through the tender-hearted little girl in *Queen of the Pheasants*, and the careless shooting of Missington in *Blazing Away at the Birds*, for example. This last may have been prompted by an incident in November 1912 when Dr Benjafield, one of their neighbours, managed to shoot another neighbour, Mr Heath, in the eye.

Self-portrait of Bertie, 1904 when she was an art student in London

Annie Kinross, the old music teacher in *Homecoming*, pressing her face against the window of her old home and finally being allowed in to sit by the fire is a version of MEM herself. In old age, MEM became equally nostalgic about places she had known as a child. The stories are really endless variations on a limited number of themes, but MEM had a powerful imagination and considerable skill as a writer.

Mills and Boon, then a rather more reputable firm than it is today, published the last three collections of MEM's short stories paying £100 a time, but they only ever published one of her novels (*Grandpapa's Granddaughter* in 1915). Her agent remonstrated with them about the low price they offered for it - £150. They replied that they were unwilling to take MEM's work because 'Mrs Mann writes such unpleasant books'!

Chapter 6. Books by the dozen, 1901-1910

Fortunately, MEM's readers did not all agree with Mills and Boon's analysis of her work. Throughout the first decade of the 20th century she continued to publish at an amazing rate – fourteen books in just ten years. It is from this period that most of the Dulditch stories, for which she is best known, date. She introduced us to the village in *The Patten Experiment* and in 1902 she brought out a first collection of short stories, *Fields of Dulditch*, which was followed in 1908 by *A Sheaf of Corn* which contains two more Dulditch stories interspersed with ones on other themes.

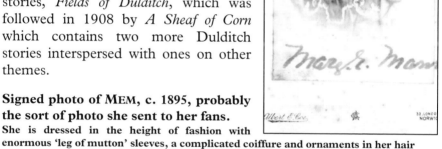

Signed photo of MEM, c. 1895, probably the sort of photo she sent to her fans.
She is dressed in the height of fashion with enormous 'leg of mutton' sleeves, a complicated coiffure and ornaments in her hair

The stories in these collections may well have been written earlier, and some of them were published elsewhere – *Our Mary*, for example, appeared in *Longman's Magazine* in 1898 – but it is not until the early 1900s that the village and its inhabitants really begin to come to life. The stories describe a world that was already vanishing; most of them hark back to the Shropham MEM knew as a young wife in the 1870s and 80s, when few adults could read and old superstitions held sway. *Rose at Honeypot* (1906) and *Astray in Arcady* (1910) are also about 'her' village. Seven more Dulditch stories appear in *Bound Together* and *Men and Dreams* (1910 and 1912) and a final eight were published in *Through the Window* in 1913. Of course, MEM had been writing about Shropham for years in different guises – as Hilby, Shenfield, Little Grissing, Oxmead, East Gramlingham and so on – but it was not until the late 1890s that she coined the name 'Dulditch' – dull as ditchwater – for which she is best remembered.

Outside her writing, her life continued much as it had for a decade or more. Her relationship with Fairman had not improved and his drinking was beginning to affect his health. In 1903 she wrote 'I verily believe he would be content to stay in his dirty little hole of an office, the blinds drawn, the stove roaring, he in a comatose condition, sunk deep in an armchair, for ever.' He had been ill and she was sure his ailments were largely imaginary, for three doctors could find nothing wrong with him. 'Fairman spends his whole life in his den, coming up for a few moments for meals without any appetite to eat them,' she told Tom a few months later. His 'constant cry' was 'we can't afford it' which she had to admit was probably true most of the time. However, he liked to keep warm and despite the price of coal, the fire in his den was always banked high. On no fewer than three occasions, MEM wrote despairingly, he had nearly set the room alight – probably because he was less than sober.

Companion portraits of MEM and Fairman c.1905

His daughter, Bertie, was less tolerant. Her 'dearest Fuff' was now simply 'Dad' on the few occasions on which she bothered to mention him in her diaries, and when she did it was usually because he was having 'a collapse' (April 1909), a 'work up' (Christmas 1909), was ill (May 1912) or hopelessly drunk (October 1912). On the latter occasion MEM was away in Marlborough with Dolly, and Bertie, to her disgust, had to help her father to bed. 'I have been having an awful time with Dad,' she wrote. 'All Thursday I knew he was drinking and had horrid doubts that I should be able to get him up to bed.' At about seven o'clock a crash resounded through the house and the servants came rushing to tell her Fairman had fallen flat on his face and couldn't get up. 'It all fills me with such horror,' she moaned. 'It is bad enough to be left with the responsibility of a sick man on one's shoulders, but a sick man who is drunk as well is dreadful.'

The grim reality of farming life in a bad year was captured in MEM's 1893 novel, *In Summer Shade*. 'By now the black and shrunken swaths of hay were gathered into stacks in the Ashfield's Yard, the lambs, lamed by the constant wet, hobbled about the meadows on their knees, dragging their stiffened hindquarters after them. The turnips were seen to be stunted, the corn very scant and to show signs of blight.' The theme is taken up again in *The Smallholder,* a story published in 1913. Job has a small farm and cannot make it pay. He even envies his own impoverished workers. 'Tain't their prop'ty,' Job said, thinking of the convivial party left behind. 'Whativer come they git their wage. As for me, I ha' struggled. I am dead beat. These here floods ha' finished me. My heart's broke.' If these descriptions were based on what MEM had seen at Manor Farm – and they almost certainly were – Fairman had every reason to be depressed.

With Dolly married, Bertie spending as much time as she could in London and Rack working away, MEM had more time on her hands but it was not worry-free. When Rack announced his intention of joining the navy in 1898, it made his mother 'horribly nervous'. Within a few years her fears began to be realised. From as early as 1904 there were rumours of impending war with Russia and MEM was beside herself with anxiety, convinced that her beloved Rack would be killed with the first shot that was fired. Bertie lost patience with her, 'I have at last given over fighting these anticipatory horrors,' she wrote in her diary that October, 'and now agree with her – she really seems happier when I do,' – but a few weeks later when rumours of impending war were again circulating she expressed real concern. 'What will be done with Mother if it really comes off I do not know.' In Bertie's diaries her mother comes over as a terrible worrier, though MEM herself made light of her fears to Tom. By1910 it was the Germans rather than the Russians who were the potential enemy. 'They say when the Germans come they will land in Norfolk and walk victoriously over our degraded bodies on their triumphal way to London to burn down the National Gallery and the Shakespeare Memorial, among other things. Before this happens my only and dearly loved son will have been drowned like a rat in the bottom chamber of his ship in which they batten him down to attend to the wounded,' she wrote.

Charles and Dolly Hewitt with Mary and Leslie, MEM's grandchildren. Dolly married in 1897.

In 1898, a year after her marriage, Dolly gave birth to a baby daughter, Mary Dorothea, and two years later, in 1900, she had a second little girl, Margery Leslie, always known as 'Leslie'. MEM found herself spending more and more time in Marlborough helping Dolly. She was a doting grandmother and Bertie, who confessed to her diary that she did not like babies, grew exasperated. 'She talks of nothing but Mary and Leslie. I quite agree that they are nice and pretty children, but I confess I should like to talk of other matters occasionally. I wonder if Granny took the same deadly interest in us ...' Even Tom was invited to admire the little ones. 'We have discovered that my little Mary, Dolly's child thinks her father the Creator,' MEM wrote. 'She was heard informing someone "My Dadda made the stars and the flowers." In her tiny heart, I expect, she holds a little cheaply the Almighty, seeing him in everyday life.'

She loved her grandchildren, and as they grew up the girls adored her and sent her poems and letters begging her to visit. 'Make Nancy go her fastest trot to catch the fastest train' ran one from Mary. Nancy was Bertie's beloved pony who obviously doubled as a carriage horse. Another began 'Bring my Gran, O wind of the East ...' Poetry was in the family's blood and both girls wrote well from an early age. Mary was artistic, too; her poems were often embellished with little drawings and coloured capitals. The trip from Shropham to Marlborough took nine hours and was not one to be undertaken lightly, but MEM made it several times a year.

In October 1900, Margery, quiet, self-contained Margery, the farmer's daughter whose chief interest in life up to this point had been raising chickens and turkeys, decided that she wanted to do something more with her life and announced her ambition to train as a nurse. MEM was predictably scathing of this 'nursing experiment', not least because a premium would have to be paid for Margery's training at a London hospital. This would cost £50, which, to everyone's surprise, Fairman was willing to pay. However, he was less enthusiastic about paying

even more money for Bertie to do yet another course at the Slade; MEM supposed she would have to borrow the £100 that would cost. Margery duly went off to London, in floods of tears, homesick before she had even left the driveway. It was strangely quiet without any of the children at home, MEM admitted to Tom, but at least it gave her a chance to work.

Margery and Bertie at the door of Manor Farm c.1905

Soon, Frank and his family moved away too; he was struggling to make a living at Church Farm and by this point had eight children to support and the offer of a job as a farm bailiff on a guaranteed wage was too good to miss. Unfortunately, the promised job fell through, but not until he had already given up his tenancy, which meant that all the Rackhams came to live at Manor Farm for a while. Eventually he took a job in Enfield managing a sewage farm and the entire family moved to London. The older children were frequent visitors to Shropham, however, and as MEM got older she was grateful for the help of her brother or one of her nephews when she crossed London on her trips to and from Wiltshire.

With Margery away, MEM at last seems to have shown some appreciation of her second daughter, for in 1901 she published *The Mating of a Dove*, almost the only novel in which a character appears who is based on Margery. It is set in the wonderfully named Swilly Fen, a 'Heaven-forsaken, water-logged, mud-plastered hole,' and begins with one of MEM's best scenes, the Dove family looking through daughter Monica's collection of appalling wedding presents which MEM describes in all their old-fashioned, garish glory.

Monica has a village wedding, very like the one Charles Hewitt and Dolly Mann had had in August 1897. Dolly's wedding was reported in the press: 'The village was en fête for the occasion; arches, gay with evergreens, were erected, and bunting and decorative devices afforded evidence of the great popularity of the bride on the estate'. Margery and Bertie were bridesmaids along with two of Frank's daughters, and the following day Fairman and MEM entertained 150 villagers to dinner; the *Reading Mercury* described them as 'estate workers and their wives'. Monica Dove was rude and dismissive of the villagers' well-meaning attempts to decorate their village in her honour – one hopes Dolly was more tactful.

Amy Dove, like Margery, is overshadowed by an elder sister, Monica, and, like Margery, she is besotted with animals. Her constant companion is Little Billee (Wilhelmina) the goat, who is taken for walks, has her horns gilded to celebrate Monica's wedding and does untold damage when she jumps onto the table laden with the remains of Monica's wedding breakfast. 'Once established there, her ordinary calm deserted Little Billee, winding her crimson rope amongst dishes and glasses she leapt and leapt in the air. At every leap there was the sound of crashing glass and at every such sound came a scream from Mrs Dove who would have to pay for the damage ...'

Amy takes herself at her mother's evaluation; her family are unsympathetic towards her and 'Mumsie said it was because things did not hurt me so much as they hurt Monica and her. I have no imagination', and she only half-understands why her mother and sister despair of her. 'It is often what I don't do. I don't care, and I don't remember, and I have slovenly ways; and I can't enter a room as I should, or walk without draggling my skirts – oh, hundreds of things!' Sidelined by her mother in favour of beautiful, selfish Monica who marries the handsome, susceptible young clergyman, Michael Derrington Bell, Amy amuses herself, ignores convention in the matters of behaviour and dress and becomes very friendly with old Mrs Grand and her son George, the village carpenter. Amy and the young carpenter fall in love; he helps her make hutches for her rabbits, houses for her chickens and splints for their broken legs. She is naively innocent, more like a girl of fourteen than the twenty year-old she actually is, and sees nothing incongruous in the relationship.

The girls' mother dies and thereafter Monica forbids Amy's friendship with 'Grand' on the grounds that it reflects badly on her and her husband, the vicar. Monica's extravagance almost bankrupts her husband and her refusal to accept that his health is weak eventually kills him. The new doctor, Dr Lammb [sic], is attracted to poor, neglected Amy whom he sees as 'virginal' – the term, albeit followed by 'idiot', that MEM applied to Margery – and they become engaged. To begin with he dislikes Monica intensely, but after her husband dies he comes to respect her. As time goes by Amy's passion for her animals begins to get on his nerves and he falls in love with Monica and marries her instead – all of which Amy accepts with apparent indifference. It was George Grand she really loved, and he died fighting the Boers in South Africa, having enlisted because she told him their relationship had to end. His effects are returned to her, and they include her mother's wedding ring which Amy had given him as a present when he saved her life after a tobogganing accident. It was the only valuable thing she owned and she wore it on her ring finger for the rest of her life. Perhaps, at long last, MEM was beginning to appreciate her least demanding daughter.

MEM's girls soon came home. In February 1901 Margery contracted scarlet fever and was in Hither Green Fever Hospital. She was then sent to convalesce at Gore Farm Hospital near Dartford where she was thoroughly miserable and bored. Infection control meant that the patients had few visitors and all reading materials sent in from outside had to be burnt on site after they had been read, nor could she sew or knit because the work could not be taken out of the hospital as it might carry germs, and to make matters worse the place was thoroughly uncomfortable and full of crying children. Margery described it as 'worse than any workhouse.' She was there for several months and returned home to recuperate in early summer – and that was the end of her nursing career for several years. At the same time, over in Wiltshire, one of the grandchildren was having a serious operation on her ear. 'A specialist came down from London, there were three doctors, nurses and horrible preparations which nearly killed poor little Dolly ...' and during the operation special prayers were said in their church in Marlborough. MEM must have been desperately worried, but the operation was a success.

By 1904 Bertie was home again too, still trying to make a living from illustrations and writing; MEM seems to have devoted a good deal of time and energy to trying to further her career. She also had help from Alfred Munnings who always had a soft spot for Bertie. He put her in touch with Caley's, the Norwich firm that made chocolates and Christmas crackers, for whom he had worked himself before he became famous. They needed a regular supply of new images to decorate their boxes and Bertie continued to work for them for years. She was a forceful young woman and sometimes seems to have gone out of her way to irritate her mother – in 1908, for example, there was a scene because Bertie had had a fish tattooed on her arm. She was thirty-four and one might have expected her to know better. The tattooist was her brother's friend, Hugh Norris. Hugh had spent some time out east and had been elaborately tattooed while he was in Japan. Japanese tattoos were often works of art and apparently Bertie was very impressed by Hugh's.

In 1906 Margery volunteered to take over the housekeeping to leave MEM free to write. She also went back to breeding chickens and turkeys and by the time of the 1911 census her hobby had become a business; she described herself to the census enumerator as a 'poultry farmer'. Nora Chisholm in *Astray in Arcady* bred turkeys and MEM's description of her is probably based on Margery. 'Nan likes to watch Nora chop the nettles she mingles so freely with their food ... She likes to trot by Nora's side, chattering ... helping to carry the curd, the barley-meal, the custard, the black oats, with which clever Nora feeds her variously aged broods. Nora is a picture, standing beneath the apple trees in her green cotton frock, her shady rush hat trimmed with its wreath of red poppies. The little broods run screaming to her as she appears.' Turkey-breeding was quite a science. 'When the vieux papa of the families comes upon the scene, his parental attentions are sternly discouraged. 'What did you hang your father with?' Nora ironically inquires of him. 'Halter, halter, halter,' ... replies ... the gobbler.' When Margery went away, looking after the birds became Bertie's job and she hated it. In January 1910 Margery went to Bournemouth leaving her sister to look after the fowls. 'I detest tramping round in the mud after the wretches. Also Dad is in the midst of a 'work-up' and so things are not over pleasant,' grumbled Bertie. On another occasion she wrote 'I hate the very name of chickens.'

Like her mother and sister, Margery wrote stories, but MEM never bothered to try to get them published as she did with Bertie's. In later years Margery hinted to her niece, Diana, that she had once had a boyfriend, but the family apparently deemed him unsuitable; there was much teasing and mockery and the relationship came to nothing. One wonders if this happened before she went off to be a nurse. It is just possible that MEM based Amy Love's unsuitable romance with the village carpenter on Margery's failed relationship.

By contrast, when Bertie began an affair a few years later with her brother's (married) friend, MEM supported her. Hugh Leigh Norris – he of the tattoos – had been a student with Rackham and was a frequent visitor to Manor Farm. Like Rackham, Hugh went into the navy. He married Nina Dyson in 1903 and their only child, Helen Lavender, always known as 'Lavender' was born in 1905 in Portsmouth where both Rack and Hugh were stationed. In October

1908 the Norrises came to stay at Shropham. Bertie affected not to want them to come as they would not have anything to do, but after the visit she admitted to her diary that they seemed to have enjoyed themselves 'or rather Rack and Nina [did]. I wonder how it will all end. Oh, poor Hugh!' This is the first intimation that we have that relations with the Norrises were more than friendly. The affair was still going on in July, 1909. When Rack came home for a visit Bertie wrote in her diary that Hugh had a temporary posting to Oban and Nina and little Lavender were alone in their house a few miles outside Southsea, but that month her parents were staying with her 'hence my brother's return, no doubt!'

Bertie's drawing of her lover, Hugh Leigh Norris (1874-1916

However, Bertie was also becoming interested in Hugh. In April that year, she had spent some time in London with Hugh and Nina and one evening Nina had got tickets for Bertie and Hugh to go and see *Romeo and Juliet* while she and a Major Dobbs went off to 'do something else'! Within the year, Bertie's relationship with Hugh had blossomed. For the next few years they conducted an affair, albeit largely by post. Bertie would write to him on board his ship, but from time to time Nina would find out, there would be a grand scene, Hugh would be forbidden to

Nina Norris, Hugh's wife.

write any more and the correspondence would come to a stop. Nina admitted that she had married Hugh for convenience rather than love, but that did not stop her being jealously possessive. He would still write to MEM however, and messages and gifts would be passed on to Bertie, then, within weeks or months, he would ignore the ban and the letters would resume. Bertie's diary from 1910 onwards reads like that of a foolish love-struck schoolgirl, despite the fact that she was thirty-six. In the spring of 1911 Rack again invited the Norris family to Shropham. Bertie recorded in her diary that her parents would never refuse to entertain Rack's guests but they were both furious that the invitation had been issued – clearly by then they were aware that something was going on.

On July 5th 1911 Bertie wrote that she had just passed the happiest week of her life in Southsea with Hugh. She wrote a lyrical description of spending a whole afternoon sitting with him in front of a potato patch looking out over a turquoise and emerald sea under a clear blue sky. She was an artist; colour was important to her. She convinced herself that the relationship could not be and over the next few weeks her diary is peppered with entries such as 'He was and will always be – my adventure!' or 'Anyway, I have had my adventure, some people never have one at all,' and, more melodramatically, 'What will I do with the rest of my life?'

But against the odds the relationship flourished; before long it was common knowledge and even MEM seems to have accepted it with equanimity. He visited, there were trysts in London; MEM even wrote a story entitled *A Little Girl Called Lavender* for his daughter, the story of a brave little girl who goes off and has all sorts of adventures.

Lavender Norris, 1905-26, Hugh's daughter

Throughout the whole Norris affair MEM had carried on writing. She was getting old, she told Tom, reading was becoming difficult and she had to wear glasses. Fairman, too, was thinking of the future; in March 1909 he wrote to Rack about his will. He was only the tenant of Manor Farm but he owned Mill Farm, sixty-two acres of land and the cottages that went with it and a small property next door to Mill Farm called Ivy Cottage. Did Rack want to inherit them? He was anxious they should stay in the family; should they be entailed? Rack replied calmly. Yes, he would like to inherit the family land but he would not guarantee that he would never sell it though he did promise 'not to do so lightly.' He saw no point in an entail which in his view only made

Mill Farm

money for the lawyers who administered it, and pointed out that only Dolly had children 'so it will go to the husbands of the little Hewitts' unless he himself were to have a child. At that point Rack was in his late thirties and had no plans to marry; he was much more concerned that his father should make provision for Margery and Bertie. This both Fairman and MEM signally failed to do, and in old age their two unmarried daughters were condemned to lives of genteel poverty.

Ivy Cottage

Fairman became increasingly reclusive and depressed, the farm was failing and 1908 was the worst harvest on record. He drank ever more heavily to blot out his misery. 'His illnesses are entirely his own doing,' wrote MEM unsympathetically to Tom, 'but that is entre nous.' Sometimes her lack of understanding could be crass. Around this time three small children belonging to their farm workers got hold of some matches. That, one would have thought, would have been worrying enough, but the children actually managed to use them to set fire to two ricks of barley. The sheer danger completely passed MEM by – all she could say, describing the incident to Tom, was how terribly beautiful a sight the fire had been in the weak winter sunlight and how it had made her wish she could paint! She did admit that their insurance would cover the loss and that she was gratified that the parents of the children involved thrashed them soundly. At other times she found it politic to be more understanding. In an unpublished introduction to *Fields of Dulditch* she described Fairman as 'a man, well-to-do, kind and generous once; an excellent husband, father, master, farmer; getting now poorer in pocket, shorter in temper, year by year, a man who has struggled in a dogged, quiet fashion, but who is beaten and knows it, finding the knowledge bitter to a degree ...'

MEM was at last becoming well-known. This had its disadvantages as all sorts of people who fancied themselves as authors would come to see her for advice: Bertie described one who had written a truly dreadful novel set in prehistoric times that he insisted on reading aloud. In April 1904 MEM wrote to Tom about an author she had written to congratulate. He had sent her his second book 'by which I perceive to my infinite dismay that he is mad. The book is the work of a very clever brain deranged,' she wrote decisively. All attempts to put him off failed, however, and the entire family prepared for the visit rather cruelly by learning some of the crazier sentences from his book to drop into the conversation when he was with them! The example she quoted to Tom was 'Tom can stand much boiling.' On another occasion she talked about a visitor whose topics of conversation bored her to distraction. She got her own back by initiating an equally long boring conversation about – potatoes.

Fame also got her invited to literary dinners as a guest of honour – the Lyceum Journalists' dinner, the Dickens dinner, the Criterion dinner, the Mogul Literary Fund dinner, the Ladies Banquet at White Friars – though she seldom attended. And she wrote and wrote.

Fields of Dulditch was published by Digby Long in 1902. MEM was no happier with them than she had been with any of her other publishers. 'They harried me tremendously over the alterations that I wished to make in the ms. Even telegraphing me to send it at once ...' she wrote. Then for months she heard nothing. 'Mr Bennett agrees with me that we must try another publisher for my next venture if ever I make one.' There would in fact be many more Dulditch stories.

They were highly original and mostly dealt with real people and events, thinly disguised, but they are undoubtedly bleak. 'Perhaps in these times literature requires to be whetted with a little of what Ben Pitcher calls "a bad hussy" ' the literary reviewer of the *Dundee Courier* wrote disapprovingly in the New Year's Day edition of the paper in 1902; 'In this modern novel we get too many Bens and too much of the 'bad hussy' to be palatable, and we question if it can be recommended for the shelves of the home library.' But his was the only voice of dissent. MEM's fan, Alfred Munnings, could not have disagreed more, though perhaps he was biased by memories of happy times at Manor Farm. The stories, he told her, sparked his own memories of village men standing outside the pubs in their Sunday best with flowers in their hats, and of the old man who once told him how his grandfather used to distil gin in the barn. He told her how he had recently taken Mr Hooper to visit his local workhouse, the aptly named Humbleyard Union, and they had had the old ladies sing traditional folk songs to them – collecting folk songs and tales just as they were beginning to die out was an early 20th century preoccupation. MEM's village stories record something equally valuable.

The Dulditch stories can be divided into groups. There are ones like *Ben Pitcher's Elly* to which the *Dundee Courier* objected so strongly, that are stories of unrelieved cruelty and tragedy. 'Hair as golden as sunlit corn, a skin of roses ... eyes like the May-day sky ... Ben Pitcher's Elly.' The beautiful girl is the victim of abuse from childhood on, she gets pregnant, is rejected by the people who should have cared for her and eventually murders her illegitimate baby. She makes a dreadful choice, but the reader is in no doubt as to why she makes it and can even sympathise with her. Ben Pitcher is a loathsome character, as are the men of the Crouch family in *The Lost Housen* and the Jaggerds in *Rose at Honeypot*. There were many violent brutal men who took out their frustrations and resentments on their wives and children and who would have seen a daughter's unwanted pregnancy as an affront to their own fragile dignity. No doubt Shropham quite often saw men like Ben Pitcher viciously wielding brass-buckled army belts.

In 1898 one of them, Oliver Henry Hunt, a retired policeman and gamekeeper, found himself in court for overstepping the limits of what was deemed acceptable wife abuse. On March 12th he was charged with assaulting his wife and given the option of paying a fine of £1 5s. or spending seven days in prison, and was bound over for two years for the sum of £20. She was granted a legal separation and he was ordered to pay her 8s. a week maintenance for herself and their five children. In 1898 it was still perfectly legal for a man to beat his wife and domestic violence was commonplace – this must have been a particularly vicious attack for the magistrates to take it so seriously.

A notice that appeared in the local paper may have inspired MEM to write *Ella's Fortune*. John Barrett of Shropham had emigrated to Australia in 1856 and in February 1891 his sister placed an advertisement in an effort to contact him. At a period when few older village people could read and write, it was virtually impossible for families to keep in touch when a member emigrated, and when, if they returned, they might well be unrecognisable. In the story, baby Ella Dingle is fostered by a kindly couple who treat her as their own. Her mother is dead, but her father was a reasonably well-to-do chemist and is believed to have emigrated to join his brother. The family see advertisements in the *People's Friend*, like the one for John Barrett, and are persuaded to advertise for Joseph Dingle on the grounds that he must have made his fortune and will want to share it with Ella. As a result of the advertisement, a couple arrive in the village claiming to be Ella's aunt and uncle. She goes off with them and is never heard of again. The tale ends: 'It was as if the earth had opened and swallowed her. Better – far better – for her if it had.'

Other stories feature characters whom MEM liked and sympathised with, even as she held them up to gentle ridicule. Men like old Angel, desperately mourning 'Meery' his ungrateful, unlovely wife of many years' standing, comes into this category. His dictum that 'Them as ha' th' proputty is them as oughter rule. Tis for th' quality to ha' th' haughtiness, and for we to ha' th' manners' was a sentiment with which MEM would happily have agreed, however much she laughed at his velveteen coat, tall hat, huge green umbrella and pointless stories about his dead wife. The model for this story may have been old James Angel. His wife, Susan, died in 1887 and her tombstone in Shropham churchyard describes her as his 'beloved wife'. He died a year later and is described as her 'beloved husband'.

Another figure with whom MEM seemed to sympathise was Wolf Charlie, the simpleton who couldn't get a proper job. 'Yet such labour as is entrusted to him he does with unfailing industry and a dogged, dull persistence. When the vapours hang, white and ghost-like over the low-lying meadows, he stands all the day knee-deep in water "ditching": and he can always be trusted to "top and tail" the turnips.' And she wrote with grudging respect of the one-legged wife he found for himself in the workhouse and his willingness to take responsibility for her brood: 'And the children in some mysterious way seem to thrive on their half rations of bread, cunningly soaked in hot water to make the allowance appear more, their random dessert off hedge berries, wild apples and the fungus from the doorstep. They are ragged and they are filthy, it is true, but they are not particularly thin or pitiable looking; they inherit their mother's complexion of brick red; their hair, which one would not care too closely to inspect, seen from a safe distance is a luxuriant growth. Perhaps out of their potsherds, their bits of window glass, their "rubbage" heaps, and that most precious plaything, the especial property always of the youngest, a rusty key attached by a filthy string to the half of a pair of scissors, they get as much pleasure as happier-circumstanced children from a nursery overcrowded with toys.'

She also wrote almost affectionately of the *Gal La'rences*, two spinster sisters with an illegitimate child apiece. The women had worked hard all their lives to make a home for 'Biller' and 'Becker', they saw nothing improper or surprising when the two married and it gave them great pleasure to entertain their shared grandchildren. They had saved a little money and lived in modest comfort: 'To see the black handled knife and fork laid beside each willow-pattern plate, the white cup and saucer with the small blue flowers ... to admire the glass salt-cellar, the knitted mat adorning the plate which holds the loaf; to smell the wallflowers in their jar among the precious ornaments on the side-table; to catch glimpses through the open door of the neat little flower-borders, the buttercup meadows and blue fields of sky beyond ..' – these were the trappings of well-earned comfort and MEM approved whole-heartedly.

She was sympathetic too, to poor Queenie, the *Witch of Dulditch*, long time housekeeper to the eccentric, parsimonious Gentleman George, who marries the widowed Benjymun Squorl when his good-for-nothing wife dies, and transforms his home and his orchard by hard work and diligence. Queenie was the perfect housewife, industrious, resourceful and intelligent, but to the villagers her success was proof that she was a witch. She earned the title because she was the last person to see Benjymun's first wife alive. Mary Squorl 'jus' twirled her eyes on her, giv' a gulp – and were gone,' as Benjymun was happy to tell anyone who would listen. The villagers professed to fear Queenie, shunned her and eventually hounded her to commit suicide by drowning herself in the pond. They were unrepentant to the last. 'Tis well she chuse th'shaller water,' they said, 'sech as her 'ud never sink.'

MEM respected women like Queenie, and Dinah Brome, who, despite having an affair with her neighbour, Depper, goes in to look after Depper's wife in her last illness, cleans the house and makes the dying woman's final hours comfortable before, once again, taking weak, pathetic Depper into her bed. He knocks at her door the night after his wife has died, not being able to stand being alone in the house with her corpse, and begs Dinah to let him in. She does so, saying scornfully, 'You're a rum un ter call yerself a man and a husban'. MEM also acknowledges the hypocrisy that was rife in village life. Everyone knew what was going on, but that fact did 'not influence the demeanour of the shopkeeper towards her. There was a not a better payer in the village nor a more constant customer than Dinah Brome. In such circumstances Mrs Littleproud was not the woman to throw stones.' These women might not conform to middle class morality but they did their best with the hands they were dealt.

Many stories recognise the countryman's lack of sentiment and grim acceptance of life as it is. In *Levenses,* a father and his young son are deserted, left to pay off his wife's debts and nearly starve in the process. She returns at harvest time, full of apologies and explanations – there is no joyful reunion, just a recognition that having come back she may as well stay and take up where she left off – 'You kin stop and bring my fourses i' the arternune, if ye like,' the husband says. *A Gentleman at Large* features old 'Granfer' who almost weeps when he says good-bye to Albert and Gipsy, the two horses he has worked with for years; 'the eyes that had not shed tears when his two sons were killed were wet at the parting.'

Some stories are amusing. There is much humour in MEM's portrayal of *Our Mary,* the housekeeper at the Vicarage, for example, with her string of jilted suitors and her collection of layettes. She arrived 'an overgrown, freckle-faced, sandy-haired girl of sixteen, wearing her best frock of green merino trimmed with black braid, far above the tops of her heavy boots ...' and proceeded to organise and bully the vicar's family. She spoils the vicar's motherless baby daughter who grows up to love the housekeeper far more dearly than she loves her aunt. Mary refuses to go to church – a sackable offence for most vicarage servants – but spends a great deal of time poring over a huge, garishly-illustrated bible. 'So long as I ha' got 'em all theer, and kin see th' devil a temptin' o' Ave, and th'arth a-opinin' ter swaller Aburam I bain't a-goin' ter trouble no fudder about 'em,' she tells her embarrassed employer firmly, and he dare not remonstrate with her for fear she leaves.

MEM also pokes fun at the experience of little Herbert Shildrick, taken by charabanc to the coast but never seeing the sea because he goes off with a funeral party while his mother is in the pub. In *Medlars* an old farmer talks to a visitor from town who he addresses as 'Londoner.' There is a good deal of leg pulling. ' "What birds are those?" I asked "that show such a melting of soft yellow and green against the sky ..." ' 'Canaries' comes the answer. The medlars of the title are a box of the fruit the farmer sends to the squire to thank him for his gift of a brace of pheasants. The squire doesn't know what to do with them and makes a present of them to the doctor. He in his turn passes them to the shopkeeper, who gives them back to their original owner. He knew they would make their way back in due course because only his wife knows how to make medlar jam.

There is humour mixed with pathos in the story of *Dora o' th' Ringolets,* the selfish little girl with the beautiful hair, whose only thought as her mother lies dying is that she will never again be able to curl her ringlets. When the mother is dead, Dora sits by the death bed and snips the ringlets off with scissors, her own, practical way of mourning. When her poor father gets home from the fields and goes upstairs, he finds his daughter in his wife's bed where her body has been prepared by neighbours for her funeral. On moving his lamp he sees the glorious hair that his daughter has hacked off. 'I ha'n't got no one now to carl my ringolets,' the child sobbed, her voice rising in the scale of rebellious misery. 'My ringolets ain't no use to me no more. I ha' cut 'em off, mother she kin 'ave em. They aint no good ter me.' It is pure conjecture, but the model for this family may well have been the Wilsons of Shropham. William Wilson was a shepherd and the family lived next door to Church Farm, so MEM would have known them well. William and his wife, Eliza, had seven children, the eldest of whom was called Laura. MEM often used similar names when she based her characters on real people and Dora rhymes with Laura. The next children in line in the Wilson family were two boys; in the story Dora has a brother called Jim who is close to her in age. Eliza died in 1882 when she was thirty and Laura would have been ten, an age when a little girl might have been becoming conscious of her appearance.

Other stories are simply sad, like that of old *Billy Knock*, distraught at leaving the cottage in which he had lived for so many years and who dies on his way back to spend one last night there. The lyrically beautiful *Last Haysel* follows a similar theme: an old shepherd is on his deathbed, but wants to live to see the end of one last hay harvest. It is soon over and life is ebbing away from the old man. The story ends 'I'd ha' liked to ha' watched a longer job … I never thought he'd ha' carted it green … 'Tis my last haysell.'

Two rather more up-to-date Dulditch stories appear in *Through the Window*. They relate to the 1910 election and one is called *The Conservative Van*. The Conservative candidate, complete with a blackboard and a head full of statistics and rhetoric, tries to convince the villagers that they should vote for him. Most of the men do not understand a word he is saying but in any event they would not have voted for him. They have their own barrack room politician, as ignorant as they are but one of their own, and it is this man, the Radical Cutty Twiss 'who has the ear of Dulditch.' *The Sunday After* explores what happened when the voting was over: 'the class hatred which goes decently veiled at other times' began to subside and MEM reports a conversation between two men who have taken opposing

124

stands on the issue of tariff reform which neither of them understands. One asks the other what it is. He replies that he doesn't know the ins and outs but thinks 'it's something to do with the "runnin" of these here trams and cars and wehicles i' th' Lon'on streets ...'

MEM and her daughters couldn't vote; votes for women were not introduced until 1918 and then only for women over thirty. Not until 1928 did women get the vote at twenty-one. MEM professed to be uninterested in politics though she and the girls had to hang the Shropham schoolroom with flags several times in the run-up to the election for the candidates' meetings. In 1910 Fairman voted for the Unionist party – Bertie describes driving him to the polling station in a gig decorated with Unionist rosettes and streamers. This was an unusual outing for him for by this period he was almost a recluse, seldom leaving his den. However, MEM admitted, 'he takes the deadliest interest in politics – far more than he does in his farm or the affairs of his family.' The Conservatives and right wing Liberal Unionists were in power as a coalition 'Unionist' government from 1895 to 1905, and in 1912 the two parties merged completely to form a single 'Unionist' party, so in 1910 Fairman was effectively voting Conservative. Tom Ordish was a Liberal, a fact that made MEM rather uncomfortable because she respected Tom's intellect. 'It is because I am so ignorant in these matters I suppose, that it seems such a matter of marvel to me that any <u>decent</u> man can be found to join the opposite side who are fighting for the destruction of their class and the downfall their country,' she wrote. 'But in our letters we will call a truce ...' 'So strange to think you are working for one thing and I for its diametrical opposite,' she wrote a few days later. 'You for the downfall of your country, as I think, and I for the downfall of my race, as you think.'

The 1910 election resulted in a hung parliament; the Conservatives, led by Balfour, and their Liberal Unionist allies, won

Fairman and MEM c. 1911-12
Fairman was old and ill and the portrait highlights their estrangement

the most votes, but the Liberals, led by Asquith, won the largest number of seats. There was a second election in the December and the result was similar. The Liberals, supported by the Irish Nationalists, then formed a government that lasted until 1918 when, for the first time in their lives, MEM and her daughters were allowed to vote.

The Dulditch stories feature single episodes, which is what MEM believed a short story should do, but four novels from this period, *Olivia's Summer* (1902), *The Parish Nurse* (1905), *Rose at Honeypot* (1906) and *Astray in Arcady* (1909) give us more rounded portraits of life in villages like Dulditch. For these MEM had new publisher. This was Methuen, a new firm, founded in 1889. 'Mr Methuen writing from his private address makes request <u>for the 3rd time</u> for "one of my admirable books",' she told Tom happily. 'I wrote him a nice letter on this and now we are quite friends. He tells me he knows Norfolk well and his own people come from "that hospitable county". I have promised him the refusal of my next book but of course Hanneford will have to make terms. What will Fisher Unwin say?' Hanneford Bennett was MEM's agent and had taken over – not always very efficiently – many of the negotiations Tom Ordish used to undertake.

MEM did not handle the transition between publishers well; Fisher Unwin was not happy and wrote her 'forceful' letters, and Methuen threatened to take the firm to court. Meanwhile she flirted with yet more firms – John Long offered her £50 for the rights to *In Summer Shade* which she considered accepting, and Hurst and Blackett took *Fortune's Cap* in 1905 – Methuen disliked this story and had only offered £50 for it. The story was about a tweeny maid, an idea that had come from Margery, as MEM told Tom in some surprise. It was serialised in *Girls' Realm* and they paid £100 for it.

She was, however, still at loggerheads with various previous publishers about their practice of republishing old books as if they were new. She was dissatisfied with her agent, Mr Bennett, and trying to find a tactful way of transferring her custom to a new and more energetic agent, A.P. Watt, and all the while she was worrying about Methuen's new request for five years' worth of novels at a price she thought inadequate. MEM was always a difficult client to satisfy.

A long complicated explanation winged its way to Tom Ordish. 'I now have two literary agents and might have umpteen publishers – why all at once, I'm sure I don't know. Watt is an ... untamed sort of a creature quite different to little Hanneford who required a week at least in which to answer a letter. He (Watt) has set his mountain torrent of a mind on my writing a story for the Lady's Field. No use my saying I hadn't a story ready. How soon could I supply the 1st quarter? How soon the whole? When I gaspingly reply I can't do it under 6 months not having begun a suitable story he writes back by return: "Then when I get an offer for your story ready at the end of 6 months I go to Methuen." Quite useless for me to say I really think Methuen should have my next. He is absolutely without sentiment, is the torrential Watt. I wrote as courteously and kindly as I know how, to that bleating lamb, Hanneford and told him the sad news in as palatable a manner as possible. He has not even said Baa-a and it was days ago. He still has two of my old books which I think Methuen means to buy out and an unsigned story written in the Past to dispose of. These I have not taken from him but if he is "nasty" I shall. Fisher Unwin wanted the unsigned story <u>signed,</u> and he would have bought it with rejoicing (£150 out of my pocket). Long would have bought out the other old friends Parish of H and Lost Estate. This also I declined (£100 out of ma poche). So much does my pride cost me! I think that is all. I am sorry I have to behave badly to Methuen, but with the whirlwind Watt such repinings are as nought.'

In fact Methuen treated her quite well and undertook to republish most of her back catalogue. But in 1908, when *Heart Smiter* 'a slight little story' according to its author, written in just two months, was shorter than they had asked for, they only paid her £150 instead of the £220 they had promised for a full length novel. 'However, I had £130 [as well] for serial rights so it pays me,' concluded MEM. But by 1909 she was considering leaving Methuen – the problem was the perennial one of inadequate advertising – and, to her surprise, her agent agreed.

They sent a note of complaint to Methuen's manager and the firm apologised profusely, promising to do better with her next novel, but Mr Watt insisted on an interview with Mr Methuen himself. 'A.P. Watt is a real comfort to the grumblingly inclined,' wrote MEM. 'He never says "It's all right" when it isn't all right.'

Squabbles with her previous publishers continued. 'Hutchinson ask £50 for the Cedar Star and Out in Life's Rain or £25 for Cedar Star alone. Smith Elder complain they never had a penny back of the £50 expended and ask £10. So there I am. I am certainly not going to pay money out of my pocket for any of them ...' she grumbled. She did not have an exclusive contract with Methuen, however, for Hurst and Blackett republished *Moonlight* in a 7d. edition in 1911, paying her a paltry £25 for the privilege. To Tom's horror, she also allowed the *Daily Mail* to publish a 6d. edition of *The Sheep and the Goats* in 1912. It appeared on cheap paper, with a garish cover and the pages crookedly cut, but various well-known authors, Arthur Quiller Couch and Robert Louis Stevenson for example, published works in the same series. The *Daily Mail* paid 'hardly anything' but promised she would make money from royalties, and if sales were big enough they would re-publish some of her other works. Tom rightly described it as 'self-robbery'; the promised sales did not materialise and the *Mail* did not take any more of MEM's books.

However, for the most part things were at last beginning to go her way and newspapers were clamouring for her short stories. In December 1903 MEM was able to report that the *Daily Mail* had offered her twelve guineas for a 3,000 word story. She had offered them two to choose from and they had taken both, and Mr Watt was now forbidding her to accept less than four guineas per 1,000 words which meant she had had to turn down a commission from the *World* to write four 3,000 word stories for £20 'but I still have before me the horrible 80,000 word story for the horrible Lady's Field. A perfect nightmare it is!' she wrote cheerfully.

One of MEM's best books of this period, and the one of which she herself was most proud, is *Olivia's Summer* (1902). It is all about class - MEM was very aware of the shades and grades of social position which were at their most marked in country society and this novel examines the unnecessary misery they could cause. Olivia Greig, the vicar's daughter, is chilly and aloof but very beautiful. 'In her cool white dress and her flower-trimmed coarse straw hat, beneath which the bronze-coloured crinkly hair was neatly massed ... Her cheeks were a little too flushed for some tastes, perhaps ... [but] the chiselling of her clear-cut, delicate features was perfect.' MEM was very good at using a description of a woman to define her character. Olivia singles out one of the brighter village boys, Robert Sturt, for special attention in the form of music and reading lessons. He is only a few years younger than she is and falls hopelessly in love with his patroness. He does well, goes to Canada, makes his fortune and returns and persuades her to marry him. Her family and friends are scandalised, she is ostracised socially, but before the caste difference can destroy their marriage she is killed in a carriage accident. 'Olivia's summer having been vouchsafed to her, and being almost ended, it was better for her to depart before the winter came.' It is a perfect ending and the novel is by turns sad, funny and thought-provoking, a splendid tour de force, but again, it was poorly advertised, seldom reviewed and sold badly.

The Parish Nurse (1905) introduces a note of modernity into the countryside – though class and MEM's hatred of the clergy and their wives are never far from the scene. 'The vicar of the parish came in [to the parish meeting] with his miserable and unexpectant air, and held round a limply dangling hand for anyone to touch who liked.' The meeting agrees the parish should employ a nurse to look after the poor of the village and the vicar's wife snobbishly adds a rider to the advertisement; 'As the nurse will be required to be in daily association with the family of the clergyman of the parish it is desirable that she should be a lady by birth and education.' Nurse Geldart is duly appointed, giving MEM the opportunity to describe villagers suffering from various ailments – the senile old man who has to be put to bed each night wearing his wife's nightcap and who tries to take his own life by hitting himself over the head with a hammer, the woman with cancer of the ear who is denied morphine, the family of children with sores in their hair and on their skin, the lady with thrombosis in her leg. The nurse's insistence on cleanliness in the one case and complete bed rest in the other meet with resentment and opposition – there is much more to the plot but the message is clear: medical intervention made no significant difference to the villagers.

The sources of MEM's material for this book can readily be traced. Nurse Geldart was living in a boarding house when she saw the advertisement – Bertie's boarding house experiences, as recorded in her diary, are faithfully reproduced, even down to the Swedish man who was a fellow boarder. Margery had been a nurse and Rack was a doctor – they obviously contributed medical details. This time Methuen seem to have felt they had to address some of MEM's concerns, they advertised *Parish Nurse* widely and it sold better than any of her previous books.

For the most part MEM felt sympathy – if not empathy – for the poor. Throughout her life she kept notebooks in which she jotted down quotations, presumably because they appealed to her in some way or because they chimed with her own thoughts, and from time to time those quotations found their way, unattributed, into her texts. In one of the notebooks there is a long quotation from *Commonplace People* by George Eliot. 'Yet these commonplace people – many of them – bear a conscience, and have felt sublime promptings to do the painful right; they have their unspoken sorrows, their sacred joys …depend upon it you would gain unspeakably if you would learn with me to see some of the poetry and pathos, the tragedy and the comedy lying in the human soul that looks out through dull grey eyes and speaks in a voice of ordinary tone….' From Thomas Hardy she took 'The long suffering rank and file of the English Nation...' and from W.S. Henley, 'Oh the sad eyes of these poor might-have-beens ... '

But there were some families of commonplace people she simply could not abide. *Rose at Honeypot* (1906) tells of the experiences of a young lady who, unwisely, takes lodgings with the ghastly Jaggerd family at isolated Honeypot Cottage. Her fellow lodger is a game-keeper who protects her from the worst excesses of life with the Jaggerds, and they fall in love. It has been suggested that D.H. Lawrence got the idea for *Lady Chatterley's Lover* from *Rose at Honeypot*. This is rather far-fetched – the only similarity lies in the fact that a gentlewoman has a relationship with a gamekeeper – but there is evidence that Lawrence did read some of MEM's books and quite enjoyed them. Writing to Katherine Mansfield on February 9th, 1919, he included the throwaway comment 'and Mary Mann is quite good I think'. Given that Lawrence was often critical of other writers, this was something of an accolade.

Honeypot Cottage was a real place in Shropham and MEM was adamant that the Jaggerds of Honeypot were based on a real family. '[The public] live by having lies told to them. They have been surfeited by the stock peasant of fiction … Unquestionably the people I depict are actually true to life. I do not say that all our peasantry are like these savages who lived apart from the rest at Honeypot; for the purpose of my story I wanted Rose to get among a bad set. We have a man living in Shropham who killed at <u>least</u> seven of his children in the indicated method. The insurance people refused to insure his offspring again, since when they all enjoy fair health,' she told Tom. In *Rose at*

Honeypot Mrs Jaggerd fears for the life of her little girl. Her husband has had all her other children killed, by exposing them to cold, insisting she feed them on cornflour and water rather than milk and so on, so that he could claim on his life insurance policy. He is fond of their son, Alick, but has little use for baby Dinah.

Rose at Honeypot is also awash with instances of animal cruelty – a metaphor in MEM's work for depravity. Young Alick is a little monster who enjoys spearing live insects on pins to see them run round and round in desperate circles. He is only just prevented from putting the kitten in the cooking pot, he lobs stones at the gamekeeper's dog tethered in her kennel and, to his father's profound admiration, he once plucked a live robin. 'That was a master one, that was!' he cried proudly. 'He'd plucked'm as clane as a whustle, Alick had. I'm blamed ef he weren't a hoppin' round, a mask o' blood, when I come home; and Alick a'screechin' wi' laughin.''

Mrs Jaggerd is lazy and slatternly and the house is dirty and dilapidated and her cooking – in a frying pan full of blackened fat – leaves a good deal to be desired. Mrs Jaggerd has a fall, injures her leg and has to stay in bed; her husband gets a village girl, 'Aluss', in to help out, has a relationship with her and eventually they run away together. Rose and the gamekeeper mind the house, look after the children and Mrs Jaggerd – and set the tongues of Dulditch wagging. Rose's sailor husband arrives to claim her and the gamekeeper, defeated, marries Redelpha, the village schoolmistress, for whom he has no particular affection, because that will clear Rose's reputation.

Astray in Arcady is also set in Dulditch and takes the form of a series of letters from Charlotte Poole, who is staying there, to her ward and her son. The Manns let their property, Ivy Cottage (now called Ivy House) to short-term tenants in this way, and though the place is quite small, the guests were usually gentlefolk wishing to enjoy a long holiday in the country. Charlotte Poole is a successful London novelist who has come to the country in search of material. She is almost certainly a reflection of MEM herself, or of MEM as she would like to have been. Charlotte's sharp observations are in MEM's voice, her hatred of cruelty to birds and animals accords with MEM's own view, her love of little Nan, daughter of her ward, Hildred, who comes to stay with her, probably reflects MEM's feelings towards her own granddaughters.

Once again, class distinctions are at the core of the novel. The Hobbleboys at the Hall, an undistinguished, unintelligent couple, are treated with immense reverence by the other 'respectable' people in the village, the ghastly Major Barkaway, fat, idle Reverend Algernon Flatt and his odious, self-satisfied sister, Bertha. Charlotte Poole is both amused and piqued to find none of them have ever heard of her, or of the London friends whom she offers to invite to perform at the village fête, and they turn down her offer to provide items for the church 'because it might be seen as a slight to the Hobbleboys'. She tells Major Barkaway about the success of her play which is being performed on the London stage; he is totally disinterested and takes her to admire his pig. Bertha Flatt borrows one of Charlotte's novels and returns it, saying, 'I should not have thought a *nice woman* could have brought herself to write of such things,' commenting that it was poorly written and 'Mrs Hobbleboy has discovered two faults in the grammar.' 'And the earth does not open!' sighs Charlotte in disbelief at the young woman's rudeness. This may well echo Shropham's response to MEM's own work.

The person she likes most in Dulditch seems to be Mrs Chisholm, the hardworking, intelligent, capable wife of a tenant farmer, who is very conscious of her place. 'We heard the Hall called on you,' she tells Charlotte when first they meet, 'We don't call where the Hall calls … It wouldn't do.' 'And so,' comments Charlotte in MEM's voice, 'even in this lonely spot, with its mere sprinkling of civilized inhabitants, the stupid social law makes enemies of the few poor slaves who should be friends and free men!'

Nonetheless, in her relationship with the villagers, Charlotte Poole, like MEM, sees herself as a benefactor and comments with some bewilderment on how her gifts are received. She takes a basket of food to Mrs Moore, mother of good-for-nothing Clemmy, the under-gardener who steals Charlotte's eggs and who eventually, after she has dismissed him, goes to prison for theft. ' "You kin put it down," she graciously said, when I drew her attention to my basket. Ingratitude is the independence of souls. Judged by that standard, they are certainly not slaves in Dulditch.' To a modern reader the villagers' resentment of charitable gifts in lieu of a living wage is much more under-standable.

Charlotte is introduced to the villagers' cruelty when Syers, her gardener, shoots the woodpecker she has noticed in the tree in her garden. It continues as he empties nests and throws handfuls of live nestlings to the ground, she hears of village children who stoned a squirrel to death and of one who, like Alick Jaggerd, plucked a robin alive. It seems likely that some child in Shropham actually did this – it is hardly the sort of thing one would make up. Rather naively,

Charlotte attributes this cruelty to faults in the way the current generation of children is being brought up. She believes the parents and grandparents treat animals with respect, 'But, for the reason that they have learnt no better, the younger generation is of the opinion the animal world has been created for the purpose of providing targets to fling stones at, and victims for ingenious methods of torture.'

Charlotte/MEM is equally critical of the way children of her own class are treated. Her generation's children were left to their own devices 'as we treat the violets and primroses blooming round the roots of trees in the garden, tending them to the necessary extent, of course, conscious of their sweetness and beauty, letting them grow. In the present age, [children] are rare plants whose cultivation is a matter of never-ceasing care and speculation, whose daily history is the obtrusive topic, whose growth and training are considered of universal interest.' Little Nan is the only child of a widowed mother and is, undoubtedly, a spoilt brat, but it is equally clear that Charlotte pets and indulges the child as much as her mother does – and as MEM, very probably, spoilt her own granddaughters who were both wilful, naughty little girls. Nan is a thoroughly irritating presence in the book, however, knowing, demanding and often downright rude, though MEM probably intended her to come across as innocent and charmingly honest.

Meanwhile, both Charlotte and Hildred, her ward, are the object of unwanted attentions, Hildred from the Reverend Algernon, Charlotte from Major Barkaway. MEM shows quite a cruel streak in the way she makes Charlotte play with Major Barkaway, pretending that her fortune will be lost if she re-marries and leaving him to regret, and eventually retract, his proposal of marriage. She then ensures that he knows the story was a ploy she has used to test the sincerity of his offer. At the village garden fête MEM is recognised by Etta Milgay, an old friend from London who happens to be staying with her aunt, Lady Tatterbury, who is much further up the social scale than the Hobbleboys, and whom they are anxious to meet. All at once, after months of snubbing, Charlotte and Hildred become socially desirable. It is a deeply satisfying conclusion, with all the people who have annoyed Charlotte during her stay suitably embarrassed and humbled. No doubt MEM wished she could have done something similar to the people who irritated her in Shropham.

MEM was not really old at the dawn of the new century – she was only fifty-two in 1900 – but the world was changing fast. Maybe it was the 1800s becoming the 1900s; maybe it was the death of the Queen who had been on the throne since before MEM was born, or maybe it was becoming a grandmother; maybe it was the pace of change – whatever the reason, most of her early 20th century novels are nostalgic. The village stories harked back to the recent past, *Gran'ma's Jane* is set in the Norwich of MEM's childhood, *The Memories of Ronald Love* is a story of a brutal schooling in the 1850s.

The idea came to her from some correspondence she had with Frederick Hibgame. As we have seen, he wrote to MEM having read *Gran'ma's Jane* which is set in the Norwich of the 1860s and was hailed as 'a masterpiece' by the *Daily Mail*. He recalled having been taken to witness the hanging of Hubbard Lingley, the last man to be hanged in Norwich, in 1867. Lingley was accused of murdering his uncle, but three weeks after his death the real murderer came forward and confessed. *Gran'ma's Jane* begins with people assembling in the 'tea room' of her grandparents' home to watch a hanging on Castle Hill. Mr Hibgame had been a schoolboy at Mrs Priest's school in the 1850s, the same school MEM's brothers went to and where she herself went for a year to learn to read and write. Mr Hibgame clearly had a truly dreadful time.

MEM incorporated his stories into *Memories of Ronald Love*, barely troubling to change the teachers' names. Miss Elizabeth Paraman becomes Miss Eliza Paraman and the headmistress, Mrs Maria Priest, wife of Henry Raven Priest, the wine merchant, becomes Mrs Priestly, married to a wine merchant. MEM also invents, or describes, an affair between jovial Mr Priestly and Eliza Paraman, being carried on under his wife's nose, much to the amusement of the boys. This is not beyond the bounds of possibility in that the real Elizabeth Paraman was in her twenties when MEM knew her, and was some thirty years younger than Mr and Mrs Priest.

Unlike Fred Hibgame, who was the son of a respectable Norwich clergyman, Ronald is the illegitimate son of Dr Clough and pretty, flirtatious coquette, Nancie Love. The doctor discovers that she is two-timing him with Mr Tilly, the market gardener, and abandons her, but agrees to pay for Ronald's schooling. Nancie reluctantly marries Mr Tilly. Ronald sees very little of his mother thereafter; he has one holiday at home but Mr Tilly finds him a nuisance and the school deems his mother to be an unhealthy influence, so he is then doomed to spend all his subsequent holidays at school. Eventually, Nancie has a still-born baby and dies. Mr Priestly has a heart attack and Dr Clough is called in to attend him; Ronnie stows away in the doctor's carriage and is taken to his house where he meets the new Mrs

Clough, a kind woman called Eleanor, they take him in and all ends happily. However, most of the book is taken up with descriptions of the school.

In letters to Tom, MEM expresses her concern that Mr Hibgame is still, decades later, consumed with so much hatred and resentment about his schooldays. However, in 1910 she had a letter from J.D. Gooding who had been at school with Fred Hibgame and added his own memories of standing in the stocks and having his nose pinched when Miss Paraman administered a dose of senna. He described 'the torture chamber of Miss Paraman's bedroom. In her bedroom, in solitary confinement, I have spent many a miserable day.' Some of MEM's descriptions come, almost verbatim, from the letters. 'She was a woman uneducated and bigoted even beyond her class at that period,' runs one such description of Miss Paraman. 'She knew nothing, and could not have passed today an examination for the post of infant school-teacher. Little was there that she could teach but a religion of her own, and this she communicated with a cruelty and an ignorance by no means uncommon at that time, yet with a faith and fervour …at which the present age … can only wonder.'

Little Ronnie is beaten, in Miss Paraman's bedroom, with a busk from her corsets and with her hairbrush – the boys never knew which she would choose until the first blow struck. He is put in the 'stocks'; he stands on his book box with a dunce's cap on his head looking out over the rooftops to the hills beyond, believing the distant country he can see is America (again following a description in a letter from Fred Hibgame who also thought the distant hills were America); he is locked in a cupboard on the landing for an entire afternoon and evening and he is constantly hungry. Ronnie secretly buys 'hollow biscuits' from the nearby shop which are all he can afford. Like Fred Hibgame's brother, he runs away, is caught, brought back and punished. Ronald's final assessment of his school is Fred Hibgame's own. 'It is more than five and fifty years ago, but he is unforgiving still, and will go down to his grave execrating the memory of a woman who made little children suffer so.'

MEM also used Mrs Priestly's school in a short story, *The Coming of King Ackerman*, published in 1917. Ackerman King is a new boy at the school, his mother has died and his father is away at sea. He is unwilling to knuckle down under the regime, he laughs when he is put in the stocks, he dances a jig on his book box when he is forced to stand on it wearing a dunce's cap, and he complains about the food. Consequently he takes over from little Teddy Ball as the butt of Miss

Paraman's cruelty and on one occasion she spitefully reads him a story from the paper about a shipwreck, implying that it is the ship his father is on. When he asks whether it really is his father's ship that has gone down she tells him cruelly, ' … if it hadn't been the *Swallow* the paper is sure to have said so …' In *King Ackerman* the story ends quickly and happily; the little boy runs away, finds his house, meets his father who is home on leave and is rescued from the school for ever. *Ronald Love* gives a much more convincing picture of the long drawn-out misery suffered by a child who is unhappy at school for years on end.

Bertie in costume – there are numerous photos of her in village entertainments

The early 20th century also saw MEM flirting with writing plays. Mother and daughters were all keen theatre-goers. Bertie's diary records that they went to the theatre in Norwich about once a month, and much more frequently when they were staying in Yarmouth as they did for a few weeks most summers. It seems MEM had been taking her children to the theatre since they were small. In one of her letters she recounts how she found Bertie, dressed up and acting the part of Hamlet for Margery, 'such a smiling chubby Hamlet', two hours after bedtime. 'I suppose the good and wise people of the world would say I ought not to take Bertie to the theatre,' she sighed. 'She is obviously stage struck.'

MEM's attempts at writing plays were not a success and as early as 1907 Tom Ordish advised her to give it up. She admitted he was right. 'I must take your advice … I calculate I have lost £200 in giving up the time to them which would have produced me a novel … What set me on to the plays was the fact that <u>two</u> dramatists wrote for permission to dramatise the same short story. I thought if they – why not I?' In reality she had no intention of giving up her theatrical ambitions. By 1909 she was in regular contact with Richard Pryce, the playwright. Mr Pryce visited Shropham that December, and Bertie was disappointed to find that the man who wrote 'such charming letters' was small, slight, fair and nondescript. However, he was instrumental in getting at least two of MEM's plays staged.

Writing for the theatre is very different from writing a novel: a play is nearly all dialogue and that dialogue has to explain the action and the back story as well as introduce the characters. Mr Pryce's help was crucial and *Little Mrs Cummin* was the first play they collaborated on.

First Performance To-Night, Wednesday, December 1st, 1909

The Playhouse

LESSEE & MANAGER
Mr Cyril Maude

"LITTLE MRS. CUMMIN"

Preceded by "THE VISIT."

Playbill for Little Mrs. Cummin, 1909

This was based on the *Eglamore Portraits* in which young Mrs Eglamore's interfering mother re-organises her son-in-law's rather old-fashioned house and takes down (and damages) two valuable family portraits, replacing them with daubs 'after Landseer', by one of her cousins. The play is a much simplified version of the book and Mrs Cummin herself is a much softer character than the vicious mother in the novel, but it was relatively successful on stage. The celebrated actor-manager, Cyril Maude, was persuaded to put it on at the Playhouse in December, 1909. Lottie Venn was Mrs Cummin and Marie Lohr and Lennox Paule were Juliet and Horace Eglamore. Bertie went with her mother to see the plays and recorded that MEM was disappointed, but 'All the same, I predict that it will run. It is funny and makes you laugh the whole evening.' Even Laurence Gomme went to see it and wrote to congratulate MEM; he'd thought parts of it very good but disliked the 'tiresome mother'- which rather suggests he had missed the whole point of the story!

An evening at the theatre in the early 1900s might comprise a single play, several short one-act plays, or a combination of the two. The second of MEM's plays that made it on to the boards was a single act one, *The Visit*, based on what MEM believed was her best short story, *Freddie's Ship*. Cyril Maude used it as the curtain-raiser for *Little Mrs Cummin* with Henrietta Watson and Marie Lind in the lead roles. A couple new to the district reluctantly pay a courtesy call on the Vicarage and find they have arrived in the middle of a crisis. Word has reached the vicar that the ship on which his only son, a sailor, was serving, has sunk. The lady visitor is tasked with distracting the vicar's wife and preventing her from seeing the newspaper until he has been to the post office, some miles away, to telegraph for news. Meanwhile a telegram arrives which the visitor conceals. It actually contains the news that the son is safe; he never boarded his ship.

The original agreement had Cyril Maude himself playing one of the leading parts, but towards the end of January he pulled out, despite the fact that the show was still playing to packed houses. Bertie thought it was because he wanted to get back to his own theatre. Whatever the reason, and with just a week's notice, the play closed on February 12th. MEM was bitterly disappointed and in the end she made just £31 13s.4d. from her first theatrical experiment. She had hoped for at least £100.

In 1908 there is a letter from Richard Pryce about dramatising *Heart Smiter* in which he says, diplomatically, that he feels the piece 'wants something' but doesn't know what. MEM was determined that it would make a play and there was a good deal of correspondence about it with various publishers, all of whom turned it down. In the end, her agent placed it with Gaston Meyer who had a reputation for doing well with hard-to-place plays, and a Mrs Berringer was engaged to improve MEM's stage adaptation. MEM approved her changes and agreed they would share the profits equally; but there is no evidence that *Betty the Liar,* as it was renamed, was ever performed, except at a village entertainment in Rockland.

MEM did write a number of plays to be performed at village entertainments – the girls were very keen on amateur dramatics, or at least Bertie was because she always played the lead. Margery was towed along in her wake. MEM described one of these plays to Tom in April 1904. '[E]veryone in our crammed schoolroom was very polite saying it was too good for the occasion … But no-one breaks chairs or knocks the characters down, or makes a hellish noise in it and so we could not expect a success. Bertie was a widow and with the help of rouge she looked quite lovely, Marge, her maid, Dr Norris, a major, just returned from Africa ...' Reggie Norris, the local doctor, was a close friend. On the night of the second performance he asked the Manns' groom what he had thought of the play.

'I didn't like [it] at all.'

'Did you know', said the Dr impressively, 'that piece was written by your mistress and acted by your young Ladies?'

'That don't make no difference,' said the impartial critic, 'I didn't like it at all.'

MEM may have over-estimated her audience, but the failure to engage them may also have been because the play, like most of her others, was poorly written.

However, she was not alone in her belief that her stories could be adapted for the stage. In 1916 a reader asked for permission to dramatise 'your delightful story "A Family Party" that was published in Story Teller in 1908.' MEM wrote to Tom saying she had no intention of granting permission but might try to dramatise it herself. She did, and called it *Violet*.

She also wrote a number of other plays – *A Jacqueminot Rose*, a farce called *Something about Maria, How Marcus Plandane came back, Poisson d'Avril, Sister Helen* and *At a Boarding House*, most of which are based on short stories. Three other plays, *Rose, Mary* and *The Experiment* are based more-or-less unsuccessfully on novels (*Rose at Honeypot, In Summer Shade* and *The Patten Experiment*). She signed an agreement with Lewis Melville about *The Experiment* in 1909, but it was eventually co-authored with John Loughran in New York – possibly it was performed there. She also co-authored a three-act play, *Secret and Confidential*, with Hugh Norris. It takes place on board ship and centres round a bet as to whether any one of the women on board can persuade Commander Suckling to let her see the book of orders labelled 'Secret and Confidential' with which he has been entrusted. It is laboured and far too long to carry the fairly simplistic idea – though it has to be said that it is considerably better than the play Hugh Norris wrote on his own.

Amongst MEM's papers there is also a surviving typescript entitled *Mary Who Would*, grandly labelled 'For film production.' It is the story of a vicar's ward, Mary, a wilful young girl with whom, inexplicably, his curate falls in love. Mary goes away, makes an unsuitable marriage, spends a miserable time somewhere in Africa and eventually returns, a widow, to marry the curate. There are numerous locations which might have made the piece visually interesting, but the story is slight and the characters undeveloped.

We have no way of knowing whether any of these other offerings ever made it to stage or film set. However, it would seem that by 1912 MEM's theatrical ambitions were satisfied, or exhausted, for she did not even go to Liverpool in 1916 to see the re-run of *Little Mrs. Cummin.* It opened to rave reviews, but like its predecessor in London only ran for a few weeks. That and *The Visit* were published and she therefore continued to make small sums of money when they were performed by amateur companies – the fee for each performance was 21s. for *The Visit* and three guineas for *Little Mrs. Cummin.* But overall, MEM's play-writing was simply a time-consuming self-indulgence.

Chapter 7. Widowhood and war 1911-1919

MEM's hard-won success did not last long and the next decade was to be a difficult one. Rack was sent abroad in 1911 and she was distraught at losing him. 'Mother is in tears,' wrote Bertie, 'and the whole world is sad.' Bertie herself was still struggling to establish herself as an artist, and her relationship with Hugh Norris was becoming more intense. Dolly was still having health problems; the farm was still losing money, and Fairman was still drowning his sorrows in drink. Margery continued to look after the house, manage the servants and care for her animals and poultry and MEM went on turning out a book a year; maybe it was her way of staying sane in their increasingly difficult household.

Mary and Leslie Hewitt c. 1914

In October 1912 there was a crisis in Marlborough and MEM was summoned to help. 'Mary has been up to mischief at school,' Bertie wrote in her diary. 'She has done nothing terrible as far as I can make out, but she seems fated to create a continual disturbance.' Mary was fourteen and she may well have been naughty, but she seems to have been the pretext for MEM's visit, not the real reason. On the 15th Bertie wrote, 'Charlie is melancholy and going off his head ... is it our fault that all our menfolk turn to freaks – never in all our lives have we had a man we could turn to in any imergency [sic] never one we could rely on.' This is typical Bertie overstatement and very unfair – Rack was always willing to look after his mother and sisters, and for most of her life her father had taken care of his family responsibly. It seems unlikely that a schoolgirl's bad behaviour could affect her father so dramatically and Leslie's descendants interpret this episode very differently. Charles, they believe, thought Dolly was having an affair. There is a legend in the family that Charles took some sketches that Alfred Munnings had given Dolly and burnt them, then buried the ashes in the garden. We have no evidence to support this and we do not know whether the supposed affair was with Munnings or someone else, but family legends usually have some basis in fact. It is quite possible that Dolly did have a flirtation with someone, and that Charles, who idolised her, was mad with jealousy when he found out about it and burnt the drawings because she was fond of them and he wanted to punish her. Whatever it was, the situation was resolved and MEM was back in Shropham by early November.

She was still in touch with Tom Ordish, but as she had become more successful she had needed him less and their correspondence had dwindled from a letter a fortnight to half a dozen a year, so we have less detail about her day to day life. Nonetheless, many of her publishers' letters about royalties and fees were still addressed to him.

In 1911 she published *There was a Widow*, and in 1913, *Mrs Day's Daughters*. *There was a Widow* was the last book she published with Methuen, and once again MEM was sorry to see that they did not advertise it as one of their 'good' books, despite the fact that it was very well reviewed. Methuen had not made much money out of her previous work and were probably not sorry to see her go. 'Mr Methuen himself was a good friend,' she told Tom, 'and tried his best to push me into popular favour, but this new company, under the direction of … H.V. Lucas (who only makes anthologies and writes, when he does write, with a pen dipped in weak tea instead of ink) knows not Joseph.' (Exodus 1:8. It means 'has no knowledge of history'.) However, Mr Watt had organised an excellent three-book deal for her with Hodder and Stoughton, and *Mrs Day's Daughters* was to be the first of the three. The firm offered £250 for the first book, £260 for the second and £270 for the third. The other two books would be *When a Man Marries* and *The Victim*.

There was a Widow and *Mrs Day's Daughters* both deal with the difficulties women faced when their husbands died. Julia Delane is left penniless with three small children when her doctor husband dies. Her attempts to stay in her old home and act as book-keeper for her husband's successor lead to gossip and disgrace and she is forced to turn to her unwilling and unsympathetic relatives for support. Mrs Day's husband is taken to court for embezzlement and commits suicide rather than face prison. His friend, the self-made draper, George Boult, is charged with looking after the widow and her four spoilt children who are used to living in the lap of luxury. He provides for them by installing them in a grocer's shop which they are to run and manage. This is a tremendous come-down for the family; their social standing is ruined and it is all deeply embarrassing. In January

1913 such problems were to come much closer to home. Fairman died and MEM was left a widow.

Fairman's death certificate records the cause of death as, 'senile decay, nephritis, haemorrhage and heart failure', exacerbated, if not caused, by his heavy drinking. His lengthy and glowing obituary in a Norwich newspaper described him as a 'prominent agriculturist from a very old agricultural family...a fine specimen of an old style farmer who was keen to adopt ...any improvements...one of the most genial and hospitable of men, no one could be in his company without a sense of comfort and pleasant intercourse...'. It records the valuable role he had played in village life as a member of the local Board of Guardians, churchwarden and manager of the village school, and then goes on to describe his 'prominent novelist wife' and his children. 'Essentially a placid and amiable man he was universally respected...'

As Rack was away at sea it fell to MEM and her two unmarried daughters to decide what they were to do next. There was no way they could stay at Manor Farm. Fairman had been a tenant farmer and the lease on the property was due to expire; they were heavily in debt and Rack had made it quite clear he did not want to take over the farm. They could have moved into one of the two smaller properties in the village which they did own, Ivy Cottage or Mill Farm. Fairman left those properties to Rack, but MEM was to have the use of them for life. Some people thought that would have been a solution. Winifred Auld, Dolly's friend, wrote, 'I am so sorry you are leaving your house – it's a horrid nuisance. I suppose you won't go to Ivy Cottage? I am determined to go back to Shropham one day...'

But Mill Farm was tenanted and they needed the income from the rent, and Ivy Cottage was far too small for three women who had been used to Manor Farm with its six bedrooms, servants' quarters and big, light living rooms that, according to MEM's granddaughter, always smelled of lavender furniture polish and tobacco. MEM's position in Shropham was already diminished by her husband's death; moving into such humble accommodation would have been an added humiliation. There was only one option: sell up and move.

Letters from Bertie to Rack give some insight into the overwhelming task before them. MEM had lived in Shropham all her married life – over forty years – first at Church Farm, then at Manor Farm. Nothing had been thrown away. Fairman has already been described as a hoarder, and MEM was too, but now things had to go. First there was all the farm stock: Fairman's cherished red poll cattle, including his two prize pedigree bulls, Majestic Flaxmore and Magnus

143

Majestic, the horses, all thirty-three of them, including Bertie's beloved pony, Nancy, eleven pigs, 193 black faced ewes, 220 half-bred hoggets, twelve shearlings and six rams, hay, fodder and farm machinery, valued altogether at £4,349 16s. Then most of the furniture, ornaments and paintings had to be sold, along with all the stuffed animals. In the entrance hall alone there were stuffed birds, a stuffed otter, a bull's head and a horse's head, and on the landing were more stuffed birds, a case of 'freak lambs' and a dried wasp's nest! After that there was Fairman's considerable cellar – twenty-three bottles of wine, six of champagne, five of brandy, and no fewer than 277 bottles of various grades of port. MEM needed the money, but it is impossible that she would not have been aware of, and upset by, salacious gossip and people whispering behind their hands as the items were listed and put on view. The villagers had probably known for a long time of Fairman's drinking problem, but the size of his cellar provided confirmation of it. There were debts to be settled and servants' and farm hands' wages to be paid. The furniture and household items and personal belongings that they were keeping had to be packed; new accommodation had to be found – a daunting task at any age and MEM was sixty-five years old.

In addition to her personal troubles there was a much bigger threat looming on the horizon. War. MEM had been fretting about it for years and now it was beginning to look inevitable. She was frantic with worry, fearing that her precious Rack would be in deadly peril. In fact she was wrong. He was a surgeon, and hospitals were situated as far from the fighting as possible. Rack's biggest problem throughout most of the war would be boredom.

In a humorous story written in about 1911, MEM highlights the hysteria that was sweeping the country. The story is set in a small Norfolk village. It may have been Shropham; maybe something similar really did take place. *Bombs in Our Village* is a story of irrational panic. A villager walking home from the fields notices a strange object at the side of the road and immediately rushes round the village telling everyone to stay indoors as he is sure it is an unexploded bomb – even though, of course, he has never seen a bomb in his life. Everyone is terrified. Then the vicar's son comes along. Even though he recognises the object for what it is – an empty battery case – he cannot resist the opportunity to appear brave and fetches a bucket of water. To the consternation of all the villagers he approaches the 'bomb' dramatically, then picks it up and drops it in the water, walking away with it and telling everyone they are now safe. In the village there was undying admiration for the young man's bravery. MEM was showing just how gullible, uneducated and untravelled village folk were and the danger this might pose if there really was a war.

The last few months of 1913 in Shropham must have been hellish. Bertie's diaries describe how her mother was paralysed with inactivity, not knowing where to start. MEM herself wrote to Tom about how distressing she had found clearing out Fairman's den. 'It seems such a cruelty to tear down all the farm records he had kept for years, smoke dried, on his walls – my books, Rack's exams, Bertie's pictures – I began in floods of tears. But one hardens.' Eventually the girls sent their mother away and completed the packing themselves. But they were no happier about the move than she was. Bertie wrote in her diary about the new house. 'It is not a bad little house and the garden is nice in an old-fashioned, homely way,' before admitting, 'The thought of leaving here becomes more painful every day.'

Why they decided to move to Great Ormesby, a village about six miles north of Great Yarmouth, and not to Norwich itself where they had friends and would have been close to the theatre and art-world contacts for Bertie, we have no way of knowing. But they all liked the sea; they had had many happy holidays in Yarmouth, and perhaps houses were cheaper in a small place. There was a railway line between Ormesby and Norwich in those days so the cultural life MEM and Bertie so enjoyed was not inaccessible. What we do know is that they moved at the beginning of September 1913 and rented a house called The Elms. 'Orme' (as in Ormesby) means 'elm' and there are a great many houses there with names incorporating the word 'elm' so it is difficult to be sure which one was theirs. In almost her last diary entry Bertie recorded, 'Alice, Toby [their dogs], four cats, Poddles [the parrot] and a six foot lilium auratum arrived here this afternoon. The house is in a state of chaos – crammed with furniture – more in the coach house and more to come. Where it will all go I can't imagine.'

They were not particularly happy there and money was a problem. In a letter to Rack the December after they had moved, Bertie says, 'And remember, no Christmas presents this year – we haven't a penny...' Bertie was prone to exaggerate but they were certainly not wealthy.

Early in 1914 she wrote to the vicar of Shropham on MEM's behalf asking for news of various people in the village – MEM must have been finding it hard to settle away from the place and the people she had known for so many years. His reply was very full, and very sad, painting a vivid and depressing picture of how grim life was for elderly villagers in the days before the welfare state.

> 'Mrs Shaw is a sight. She, and her clothes, which are put on regardless of order, look filthy….Mrs Clarke and Martha are in despair. They washed her about a month ago and don't think she has washed since. No one cares to go near her as she says such horrid things about everyone, even poor Martha. She wanders the roads and they are worried about her setting fire to herself and her house. Mrs Elmer has little to live on and it is partly her own fault as she refused the 1/- or 1/6d a week to look after Ann Nobbs. She used to do some washing but did it so badly that she has lost that now. I am afraid farming is a bad lookout. Higher wages, higher rates and with the hay and corn looking poorly. You have your drawings but I am afraid Margery must want her fowls back very much…'

The letters and cards the family kept from this period not only give us an insight into what MEM and Margery and Bertie were doing, they also throw a spotlight on MEM's close relationship with Rack. We hear his version of the war, though he had to be very careful what he wrote; all his letters bear the censor's stamp on the envelope and, in a few, lines have been deleted. For the first time we get a clear idea of the sort of person he was. He was deeply concerned for his mother and wrote to her every week – sometimes every day – throughout the war, and offered both advice and financial help. He was obviously a highly intelligent man, and critical of those in power, both in government and in the navy, and he didn't mince his words. 'Eight consultants who are within the 'ring' are being paid £5,000 a year each for their services – they are the same useless antiquated old blaggards who have exploited us for years…' Almost all the films, programmes and documentaries that we are familiar with about the First World War concentrate on battles and the horrific conditions in the trenches. In Rack's letters we see another aspect of the war – the war behind the scenes – and it was equally ill-organised.

When the war broke out Rack was forty-one years old. He had never married, and when on leave from the navy he lived with MEM and his sisters in Great Ormesby. On August 14th 1914 in a letter to his mother he greets the declaration of war thus: 'It has fallen at last. Well now we must get it over with as soon as possible. Is the financial panic affecting you in any way? Let me know.' Another letter a few days later says that he has put £200 into bonds with a good rate of interest and advises his mother to invest £500 in the same way.

The Manns were also getting news from the other side of the Channel. They had friends in Belgium, the Andreas family, the children of MEM's mother's friend who had spent so many weeks with them in Shropham. Their letters are addressed to 'Dearest Mrs Mann' and are written in excellent English and the writer asks for news of them all and of their pets – Poddles the parrot seems to have been a great favourite. The letters come from different places; the Andreases kept having to move to escape the bombing and the invaders. 'What terrible times we are living in!' runs one of the early letters. 'Who would have thought that a so-called civilized country could have behaved in this outrageous way.'

MEM was obviously very scared that the East Coast would be invaded. Rack reassures her that this will not happen because the Royal Navy and Naval Volunteers were guarding the coast, but suggests that if she really finds it impossible to live there then she should put the furniture into store and move up to Ardrossan in Scotland where he was stationed and he would find her rooms. She did go up to Scotland to visit him, travelling First Class, for which he insisted on paying. They went to a social event together, a 'ladies night' on board his ship, but she did not leave Great Ormesby. In a letter to Tom Ordish at this period she tells him that Rack has advised her to dig a hole in the garden and bury the household silver to keep it safe from the invaders – one suspects that Rack, like Bertie, sometimes got irritated by her incessant worrying and that this advice was not wholly serious. In another letter Rack scolded her mildly: 'I wish you would not call every ship of war a battleship. Bertie knows the different classes and would explain them to you …We are getting quite a big base established now, 3 ships, 3 submarines and a detachment of terriers. My sick bay (on his ship) is only about 1 foot wider than our bathroom at home and the lighting is vastly inferior…I don't know how we would cope if we got a lot of wounded…'

In fact MEM had good reason to be nervous. Great Yarmouth, just down the coast, was the first town in the UK to be attacked by the Germans. A flotilla of seven German cruisers and their attendant warships shelled the town on November 3rd 1914. The shells landed harmlessly on the beach and no damage was done, but it was the first attack on the British mainland in 250 years and caused a good deal of panic. As a result, a special train with two twelve-pound naval guns was commissioned to patrol the coast from Yarmouth to Mundesley. It never fired a shot, despite the fact that Great Yarmouth was shelled twice more. Predictably, the train was never where it was needed when it was needed. A second unsuccessful bombardment of Yarmouth took place on April 25th 1915 and there was a third attack on January 14th 1918, by which time the Manns had moved to Sheringham. This time over fifty shells were fired and some reached the town, resulting in some damage to property and four deaths.

Great Yarmouth was also the first place in Britain to be attacked from the air. On June 18th 1915 two zeppelins crossed the Norfolk coast at Bacton; one headed south towards Great Ormesby and Yarmouth; MEM saw it overhead. It reached Yarmouth and dropped its bombs, killing two people and injuring three more and another of its bombs actually fell 'in a field just five minutes walk' from MEM's house. The other zeppelin headed west towards the Humber estuary and dropped two bombs on Sheringham because the captain thought he had reached Hull; the weather conditions were very bad and visibility was poor. One landed on wasteland and didn't explode, the other fell through the roof of a cottage in Whitehall Yard and landed in a bucket in the kitchen! One of the men in the house rushed outside with it and put it under a tap. In 1916 a Royal Flying Corps base was established at West Denes and foiled two more zeppelin attacks on Yarmouth – one on 27th November 1916 and one on 5th August 1918. The Norfolk coast was not quite as safe as Rack wanted his mother to believe.

When war was first declared young men rushed to join up. Long queues of excited youths and slightly older men formed outside recruiting offices up and down the country – anxious for adventure, for honour and to accept the 'King's Shilling'. In September 1914 Rack wrote, ' ... it is splendid how everyone comes rolling up. In spite of all our crude sentimentality and our cursed politicians we are still a great nation', adding inconsequentially, 'I saw my first 10/- note yesterday – what a shoddy looking thing it is...'

Neither Staff Surgeon Rackham Mann, nor the volunteers who so impressed him, could have foreseen the slaughter that was to follow, and the general feeling in the country that September was that it would 'all be over by Christmas.' But the men's idealism would soon be shattered. Initially, conscription was unnecessary, but as the war progressed the government found that fewer and fewer men were willing to enlist, so, in order to replace the casualties, conscription was introduced in January 1916 for men between the ages of eighteen and forty-one, unless they were widowers with young children or ministers of religion. By the end of June that year the losses were so great that the upper age was raised to fifty-one. Conscientious objectors were treated as criminals by some women who handed out white feathers, symbols of cowardice, in the streets. Altogether over sixty-five million men from thirty countries fought in that terrible war, and nearly ten million of them died. With the exodus of young men, young women took jobs that had previously been denied them, becoming the drivers of buses, trains and ambulances and working in munitions factories.

As the war dragged on, MEM and her daughters would have read the daily reports in the newspapers and witnessed at first hand the grief in their village as news came through of husbands, sons, brothers and nephews who would never be coming home. The arrival of the telegraph boy knocking on the door with a telegram in his hand was a continuous nightmare for women everywhere. MEM, Bertie and Margery would have known many of the bereaved and remembered some of the young men they mourned. The war memorial on Great Ormesby village green lists thirty-four dead, and of these, only three are buried in Great Ormesby churchyard. Robert Derry and Frank Whitby came home with severe wounds from which they died. William Lawrence Mickleburgh was in the Royal Navy Volunteers that Rack had told his mother about; they sailed all kinds of small ships up and down the east coast, on the lookout for mines and German ships. William was on the trawler, *Quintia*, and was killed on November 26th 1918 – two weeks after the ceasefire had been declared. All the rest of Great Ormesby's dead were buried abroad, in graveyards in France, Belgium, Egypt and Iraq; others have no known grave – they are just a name or service number in the official records. Watty and Jane Nickerson, John and Martha Beck, George and Lydia Page, George and Mary Sizer and George and Marion Thurston all lost two sons. So did Alfred Crowe. Already a widower, the war was to leave him without either of his boys. George Crowe was twenty and buried in Egypt, his brother, Percy, was twenty-two. He 'Died of his wounds' (MEM used the phrase as the title of a short story) and was buried in France.

In Marlborough they were 'horribly saddened by the deaths of all their boys in this nightmare of a war' MEM wrote in June 1915. '72 were already killed when I was there, and there have been many since. Some of these were friends of my grandchildren and pals in their domestic circle. The last day I was there Charles came in with tears on his face to announce the death of one dear boy of whom they were all specially fond ...' By 1916 she was writing to Tom, more presciently than she knew, 'No child of the present generation will be bothered to learn history before the Great War. The things which were outstanding Thermopylae, Crécy, Waterloo etc. have all been surpassed. Nothing seems to be of importance beside what we have seen.'

Towards the end of the war MEM had a letter from her brother Frank in London. His son, Geoffrey, was a serving soldier and had been wounded in the foot. 'I only wish the people responsible for this blasted war had to take his place,' wrote Frank, adding that his youngest son, Philip, was 'going from one recruiting office to another.' Philip was just seventeen, so not really old enough to enlist. Geoffrey recovered from his wound and re-joined his unit. Early in 1919 he was awarded the George Cross for an incident that had occurred on the 27th of October 1918. He was awoken that night by the sound of an explosion and rushed out of the barracks, still clad in his pyjamas, and drove away a truck loaded with ammunition, part of which had already caught fire. He then helped put out the flames. Had the lorry and its contents exploded, everyone in the barracks would have been killed.

None of the horrors of the Western front, or the tragedies MEM was seeing in Great Ormesby, affected Rack directly for the first year of the war. He was marooned in Scotland and struggling with inadequate facilities on board his ship – and boredom. 'October 1914. Nothing to tell you. Nothing ever happens in this god-forsaken hole. I sleep as much as I can and I walk about 4 miles every day for my health...occasionally a young local woman comes with me, through pity, I know she looks on it as her contribution to the war effort! I can't write what I mean but you can probably guess.' Rack was a handsome man and clearly he was no saint! He tells his mother about the huge supply of knitted goods, thermos flasks and chocolates that they were being sent, adding, 'I hear Antwerp has fallen – I fear the Belgians have always been poor fighters....'

As well as the war, MEM had another worry constantly on her mind – Dolly. In the autumn of 1914 Dolly was in Bournemouth to recuperate from a spell in hospital, and was accompanied by her two teenage girls, Mary and Leslie, and her mother-in-law, Mrs Hewitt, whom she disliked intensely. She wrote to Bertie. 'I am enduring arguments with Mrs H. and wish I could cultivate your indifference. There is no sign of decay and she is more alive than anyone I know. I know that only you would understand what I feel with her.... The ugliness of age which makes me feel physically sick; at the same time the intense youth of the children. They live in perpetual rag-time [the

150

syncopated dance rhythms called 'rag-time' were at their peak between 1897 and 1917 when they started to be overtaken by jazz] I wish I could be more amusing when I write to you but you remember in our ancient literary pursuits you always did the comedies.....'

At this point MEM was proposing to pay for her to have medical treatment, and wrote to Rack about it. He was obviously completely fed up with his sister and what he assumed were her imaginary ailments. 'The only thing I can suggest about Dolly' he wrote, ' is that you take away her sulphonal, take away her stays, send her for a 5 mile walk daily and refuse to discuss health and sleeplessness. A specialist would say "you must send her to my home and have a course of electro treatment" and charge like the devil, and have her in his clutches forever and a day...What is there about the war to depress you. It is going well I think ...Tell Dolly to buck up and not to imagine things.' Sulphonal was a hypnotic drug, a combination of mercaptan and acetone. It was used to treat insomnia, but it was slow acting and could be addictive. Dolly was becoming dependent on it.

Rack's irritation with Dolly was probably compounded by the boredom he felt in Ardrossan. He was not the only person affected. More and more soldiers and sailors going ashore were becoming drunk; some fell into the sea, some tried to swim in puddles, some died. 'There have been 5 deaths in one month' Rack told his mother. But that was about to change. In March 1915 Rack left Ardrossan and sailed to the Dardanelles, and he was worried – though he wasn't able to tell MEM why or where he was going. All he wrote was that he had heard that the French only had 8,000 men in the field and that Paris had only been saved by 'the marvellous fighting of the British Army.'

The Dardanelle straits, a very narrow channel between Europe and Asiatic Turkey, were a vital supply route, essential for getting supplies to the beleaguered Russian army. The maximum width is about six kilometres; in the area known as 'the narrows' a distance of no more than 1,600 metres of water separates the two shores and the straits are overlooked by steep and heavily fortified cliffs – the Gallipoli Peninsula to the northwest and the coast of Asia Minor to the south. The wildly varying currents in the straits made navigation difficult. The naval attacks upon the Dardanelles on the 19th and 26th of February 1915 had, nevertheless, succeeded in achieving the first element of naval Commander-in-Chief Sir Sackville Carden's three-point plan for seizing control of the waterway and thus gaining access to Constantinople and a supply route to Britain's ally in the east. But the second stage of his plan had not worked – hence Rack's rapid dispatch to the region. The guns on either side of the narrows had not been neutralised and they had renewed their attack on the fleet of sixteen allied battleships and other smaller vessels which stretched in a line for almost 10km along the narrow strip of water. The whole advance proved a heavy failure, for as well as the bombardment there was the presence of an unsuspected, drifting, minefield that had been laid on the 8th of March, just days after the first British attacks. Five allied warships were sunk or disabled by mines and the loss of life was huge. On the 23rd of March, Winston Churchill reluctantly reported to the War Cabinet that the naval attack upon the Dardanelles had failed. The disaster would damage his political career for the duration of the war.

As a surgeon, Rack was not involved in fighting, but for the first time in the war he was under huge pressure, and his sick bay was, as he had foreseen, totally inadequate. But at the time, he was banned by the censor from telling MEM any of this. She was obviously still writing to him about her fears of invasion and things she read in newspapers. He tries to reassure her '...<u>never</u> believe any German statement'. He goes on to elaborate on the way the Germans were using propaganda to undermine the Allies' state of mind, and tells her sharply that the reason she cannot get a servant (another problem which features regularly in her letters) is because 'they are all working in the dynamite factories...' Later she did find a servant – Bessie – who turned out to be totally unsatisfactory and MEM dismissed her. Rack wrote again saying she must offer higher wages to get someone suitable – he would pay the difference.

MEM was constantly worried about money and it is hard to be sure whether she was genuinely hard up or just very careful. She still had some income from her writing – around £150 in 1915, at least £200 in 1916, the same in 1917, and £100 in 1918 from her books alone. She could still command twelve guineas apiece for her short stories, though we do not know how many of those she published during the war. But she was slowing down. Her last book was *Pedlar's Pack*, the collection of stories she published with Mills and Boon in 1918, and in one of her later letters to Tom she told him she was desperately trying to save something for 'those who come after.'

She had a regular income from the rents on the properties in Shropham, about £135 a year after the agents had taken their fees. She had also invested some money. In September 1918 Miller, Stevens and Jones wrote that War Bonds she held to the value of £1,048 8s.6d. would raise £52 8s. 4d. that year. Another deposit she had made raised £31 4s. 0d. From a different bank she received £21 15s. 4d. But she was not wealthy. She was paying the rent on the house they lived in. She paid the servant. She bought the food, she clothed herself and her daughters. While she was at home, Margery contributed nothing financially; Bertie had some income from her illustrative work though this does not seem to have amounted to a great deal and was spasmodic. Rack helped his mother to make an Income Tax Repayment Claim, from which she eventually received the substantial, one-off sum of £406 which, with a contribution from Rack, probably went on the house they eventually bought in Sheringham.

In the boxes of MEM's papers in Norwich Record Office there are many stories written about the war, though none of them are precisely dated. Some are typed, some are handwritten. Some are labelled 'Not for Publication' – at the time they were written they would have been considered unpatriotic – but MEM's great-great-grandchildren, her closest surviving relatives, have given permission to reproduce the one below. They can all be read in full in the Record Office. We suspect that most of the stories are based on true events, recounted to her by Rack or by friends. They all make very sad reading and present the war from a very human angle. The first one shows the terribly difficult moral choices that could face young men elevated to officer status beyond their years. *Keep the Home Fires Burning* was the title of a popular wartime song. This story is quoted in full.

Keep the Home Fires Burning

'We were going through P... on our way to ..... (Colonel N. told me the story. But it does not concern the tale where they were going or on what military duty bent.) The village presented the appearance with which we were too familiar – a ghastly, heart-breaking panorama of ruined homes, of pleasant fields ploughed up by devastating shells, of blooming trees blasted with the deadly hail of guns.

In the midst of this hideous zone of destruction one house – a small farm-house, with smaller buildings clustered about it, stood intact, having, in some wondrous way escaped the fate of the rest. We slowed down the motor at the sight of it. It looked as if it might even be inhabited, if so we could ask to be directed on our way. Peters, who spoke a little Flemish, got down. Hearing the motor a woman with an infant in her arms came to the door of the farmhouse. A young woman in her picturesque peasant's dress, fresh and neat, black-haired and smiling. An orchard of blossoming trees framed the background to the little place, and she made a picture, as she stood there, framed in the doorway, the sunny garden where flowers grew amongst the cabbages at her feet.

To the left of the house were a couple of fields which shells and shrapnel had also practically spared; in the corner of one of these a man was digging, and as he dug he sang. A note or two of a tuneful, youthful voice reached us as we sat in the car. Peters, going towards the house, stopped by the hedge to listen. Then he came back with a puzzled look in his eyes.

'That fellow is singing in English,' he said, 'Listen. Do you hear? 'Keep the Home Fires Burning.'

The rest of us got out of the car and went to look. He was so busy digging, so loudly singing, he neither saw nor heard us – a robust looking young fellow, almost a boy, the sleeves of his khaki coloured shirt rolled to the elbows, his earth-stained, shabby khaki trousers pushed into the top of long boots, many sizes too big for him.

'Well, it's just a pity we happened to be on that particular road on that particular spring morning. I think if any one of us had been alone we would have just pressed on, said nothing, and conveniently forgotten the incident. As it was we couldn't – there were half a dozen of us – we had orders: locate enemy, search for deserters.

Oh yes, he was that. He had crawled away, terrified in his first battle – a Yorkshire boy. The woman had hidden him, loved him, married him. For nigh on a year now he had planted her cabbages and tilled her fields.

He cried – like the boy he was. So did she! It wasn't a pleasant business. Very far from it, take my word. War is war we know – but – ...'

'What became of him?'

'Court marshalled, and yes, shot of course. Peters who is a sentimentalist put a cross above him with the inscription, 'Died in Action'. Perpetuating a lie, as you say, but it seemed to be a relief to Peters.'

Died of his Wounds is a poignant story of a young woman sticking to what she has been taught is 'proper' behaviour, and dealing with a dilemma which many, many young women must have faced.

Years after the event she recounts her enduring guilt and sorrow to a slightly older man whom she has befriended in a lodging house in London where they are both staying. She explains how a young soldier, on the last evening of his leave before he went back to the front, took her out for a meal – a rare treat for her. After the meal he tried to kiss her and wanted to take her up to his room – but she refused. As she walked away she was aware of him watching her leave. He had given her a lovely evening with good food – but she gave him nothing in return. She later heard that he had died of his wounds. MEM meant the title to have a double meaning: the wounds that killed the young soldier and the wound of the girl's refusal of him on his last night in England.

In *An Open Air Service* MEM yet again shows her contempt for the clergy. She was personally devout and a church-goer, but she rails against the content of the services being given for fallen soldiers and their families. To her, they were without feeling, simply emphasised the power of the church and were no help at all to the grieving families. She felt they should contain more poetry and humanity, and she quotes from a book called *Rough Rhymes of a Padre* in which the Padre tells the story of a soldier wounded on the battle field. The soldier is sure he will die and indeed dreams that he is dead, but then cannot understand what he finds. He is sure he is 'on the other side' but there is no great judgement court, no throne, no one official at all, just someone before him who has known love and suffering for others. And that is what they should be concentrating on in services for the dead, MEM says – love, comfort, and understanding – not power, authority and hellfire.

Bertie's lover, Hugh Norris, was a naval surgeon like Rack, and for a time was posted to North Africa. But he had literary pretensions; he had already written two books, *Rice Paper* and *China Trade*. He wrote a play called *Playing the Game*, which he sent to MEM – he often wrote to her as well as to Bertie. It is set somewhere off the coast of Africa. The First World War gave rise to a crucial change in the relationship between Europe and Africa. Over two million people in Africa made huge sacrifices for the European Allies and 165,000 men lost their lives. Not since the American War of Independence, when 14,000 slaves and freemen fought as black loyalists alongside the British, had such a huge number of people of African descent been involved in fighting for Europeans. Very few were combatants, most of them were used as porters. They were recruited to carry heavy weapons and supplies, were badly paid and given food which was either of poor quality or entirely foreign to them. While travelling through unfamiliar territories they often fell sick and were affected by different types of malaria. Hugh's play reflects all this. In most ways it is a totally forgettable piece, badly written and with no discernible plot, but the appallingly racist language of both officers and men provides an unpleasant insight into the time and its attitudes.

It begins 'Scene. A mud fort, thatched huts, a mud parapet at the back – barren hills. A surgeon is lying asleep on a chair in a white tunic which is blood-stained. He has been shot and the bullet is lodged in his body. His helmet is on the floor, his pistol hangs on the back of his chair. Nearby stands a Somali soldier with a rifle and bandolier – an ammunition belt. Enter a man – his right hand has been amputated and his arm is wrapped in a bloody rag.'

The play goes on to describe, in lurid detail, the injuries of both men and the fact that there is no one who can really help. The Somalis were being treated disgustingly, so many of them were fleeing from the army into which they had been conscripted by the colonial powers. The only person available to remove the bullet from the surgeon was the chaplain, who was totally untrained, so the surgeon instructs him in what he has to do. He is to use a ceramic tipped probe to locate the bullet – then withdraw the probe. If it has a black mark on it, that means it has made contact with the bullet, which he can then withdraw using a small pair of forceps. However, the chaplain never performs the operation because at that point a nursing sister comes in. She is very pretty and all the men want to marry her. She reaches for the surgeon's gun and is about to shoot herself as she thinks that the end is upon them, when her fiancé arrives out of the blue and in the nick of time to rescue them all!

If this piece is typical of Hugh Norris's writing it is difficult to understand why MEM ever collaborated with him. We can only presume she did it for Bertie's sake, for by the time war came Hugh and Bertie's affair was well established. By 1916 it would seem that Bertie was in Southsea, for MEM kept a letter from Hugh in which he told her that Bertie was well, had been working hard in the garden and was losing weight as a result. He was on board his ship, but the implication is that by this point he and Nina had separated and Bertie was staying in his house. Rack remained friends with them all and was able to tell his parents that when the war was over Hugh was planning to divorce Nina and marry Bertie. Nina knew, and he had been in correspondence with her about what her finances would then be; they had stayed in touch though any relationship between them seems to have fizzled out.

It was an extraordinary situation. Divorce at that date was rare – there were just 1,100 divorces, nationwide, in 1918 – and for the women concerned it was still shameful. Middle class men wishing to divorce their wives and marry their mistresses usually employed the services of some lower class woman who, for money, would act as the guilty party and be found in the man's hotel room by a chambermaid. For a woman like Bertie Mann to be cited in a divorce case was all but unthinkable. It seems that this is what they were planning, but it was not to be. In May, 1916, Hugh was sent with the fleet to the North Sea on the battleship H.M.S. *Indefatigable* to take part in what was to be the biggest naval battle of the war. The Battle of Jutland started on May 31st 1916 and Hugh's ship was hit after just twenty-five minutes. The *Indefatigable*'s magazine exploded and the ship sank with the loss of 1,017 lives; only two men survived and Hugh Norris wasn't one of them.

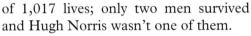

Self-portrait of Bertie as a mermaid, possibly prompted by Hugh's death at sea

It was the great tragedy of Bertie's life and friends and family treated her as if she were in fact a bereaved widow, or at least fiancée. Dolly wrote to say, 'My dear Bertie, I am simply heartbroken for you and can do nothing but cry and cry....' She goes on to say that she had a premonition of his death just before it happened. Sixteen year old Leslie wrote poems for 'Auntie Bertie' referring to her loss, their friend, Winnie Auld, sent a letter of sympathy adding, 'How glad you must be that you went up to London to see Hugh Norris such a short time ago. How little anyone needs to think of the future just now.' Her cousin Simon sent condolences from the family in London. Bertie's affair with Norris seems to have been common knowledge – and totally accepted, which does not accord with what we think we know about Edwardian middle class behaviour. MEM penned several stories on the theme and Bertie herself wrote melancholy poems of which this is a typical example:

157

Lovers

They whisper in the firelight
Words of love I do not hear,
For my whole soul is listening
To the dead voice in my ear.
Their cheeks are red with kissing
Their life as rich as wine
My face is pale as sea foam
For a drowned mouth kisses mine.

The sea's a bed
Where sleep the dead
As they ne'er slept before.
It rolls and swings
And idly flings
The crested waves to shore.
The dead it keeps
In misty deeps
To leave them never more.

Hugh's will left everything he owned to Nina, but Bertie had already received his wartime diary. He had started to write a diary at the beginning of the war and in August 1915 he sent it to Bertie. It is a series of loose pages of brittle, yellowing paper, rolled into a tube, addressed to The Elms, Great Ormesby, and it bears the censor's stamp. Presumably it got through because the events Hugh was recording were in the past by the time it reached the censor. Someone typed it up for Bertie, and no doubt it was a treasured possession. For the rest of her life she clung to memories of Hugh, cutting out the centre pages of her first diary so she could paste his letters into the space. One of them is in her handwriting and is still sealed in its envelope – it is probably a letter she was planning to post when the news of his death came through.

Nina was still close enough to Rack to write to him about her finances. In a letter to MEM on the 24th July 1916, three months after Hugh's death, Rack said that he had told Nina she would have, 'an army pension of £200 a year for herself and £40 a year for Lavender, there will also be a one-off payment of £400 from the navy and £200 from Hugh's life insurance.' He assured his mother that Nina bore her no ill will, but by then any friendship Nina had had with the Manns was a thing of the past. In November 1917, just a year and a few months after Hugh's death, she remarried and would live on to the ripe old age of ninety-three. Lavender was killed in a freak accident at Brooklands race track in 1926. The race was over and she was being driven round the track at 100 m.p.h. by one of the competitors, Cyril Bone, when the car spun out of control and they were both killed outright. MEM was still alive in 1926 and she and Bertie must have known of the accident – it was front page news at the time, an unwelcome reminder for them both of what might have been.

As usual, MEM put her children's experiences to literary use. *The Man of the House* is poignant and probably descriptive of the Manns in the months after Hugh's death; it is another of the stories 'Not for Publication'. It is written in the voice of a dog who is the 'man of the house'. He lives with three ladies, but only one of them is his mistress. She laughs and plays with him, feeds him biscuits, and whips him, but he doesn't mind because he loves her. 'One of my ladies is old and does not care to go out, and sits alone when my young ladies have gone to help at the local canteens and hospital. She thinks sad thoughts of all the people she has loved and will never see again.'

At the end of the story the dog says, 'It is only when she plays with me that my mistress laughs. Often she takes me in her arms, and whispers in my ear that she has no one but me now, and if I give her a sly lick to her face I find it salty to my tongue. She wears a long black veil on her hat now when she takes me for walks, and no one we meet ever stops to ask her for the soldier man who went away.'

The reference to helping at a local canteen and the hospital is the only indication we have of what Bertie might have done during the war. At the beginning of the war, Margery, who had worked as a nurse

Margery (seated second from right) and her nursing companions at Great Yarmouth in 1915

in 1900-1 but had never completed her training, went off to work in a hospital in Great Yarmouth caring for wounded Belgians. How long she stayed there we do not know, but a post card that she sent to MEM shows her in her nurse's uniform.

MEM also began to incorporate the theme of divorce into her stories. She had already explored the idea before Hugh's death and before there was any talk of his divorcing Nina. In *The Wedding Day*, a story in the collection *Bound Together* which was published in 1910, MEM has Adriana's mother reject the idea of leaving the husband with whom she is no longer on speaking terms. 'I would never seek a public separation. The disgrace of your father's conduct would then fall on your innocent head.' Within a decade, however, divorce was becoming much more common, though MEM never wholly approved. Another short story, *A Boy and Girl Marriage* published in *Pedlar's Pack* in 1918, sees rebellious Ida make a foolish marriage to the impoverished and unsuitable Maxwell Brunson. Her family seek to extricate her from him by employing private detectives to spy on him to find grounds for a divorce. He enlists in the army, and seeing him go off to war makes Ida change her mind; she defies her family and remains his wife. He is killed a few weeks later.

In 1917, when divorce had come very close to her own family, MEM published *The Victim*. It could more accurately have been called the victim<u>s</u> because the novel deals with the widespread fallout from an affair. The novel opens with Elaine Quaile writing to ask her husband, Richard, for a divorce. He refuses. She has left him some time previously and is living, very happily, with her lover, Lieutenant Eustace Barr, in a rented cottage in a small seaside town which every summer attracts crowds of visitors. They have little money and are dependent on Eustace's allowance of £200 a year from his clergyman father, an allowance which will be stopped if he is discovered 'living in sin.' Needless to say, two of his father's neighbours rent a holiday cottage nearby and news of Eustace's affair does get back to his father. He is summoned home and found a job in the colonies; Elaine is given £100 to buy her silence. The affair damages Elaine, her husband, the child she has with Eustace, her sister-in-law and her former lover. No-one emerges unscathed. MEM acknowledges that morals have changed but her message is clear – adultery doesn't pay. One wonders what Bertie thought of *The Victim*.

Towards the end of 1916 MEM decided they should move house. She had never liked the place in Great Ormesby, she says so in several letters but never explains why. Perhaps she also thought that a change of scene would be good for Bertie. Rack advised her to find somewhere nice and be prepared to pay for it. 'I have told you a 1,000 times you must give more rent. I want a comfortable place to stay when I come home on leave.'

The place they chose was in Sheringham – a bit further up the coast – and again we don't know why, except that in the early 1900s it was quite fashionable and popular with a 'good class' of tourist. They found a property in Cromer Road called Springfields. MEM wrote to Rack about the house. He replied, having obviously made good his promise of financial help. 'So glad the cheque arrived and that you have got a house at last... but what a terrible name ...Winnie tells me that poor young Ronald Becket has been killed. They went into battle with 1,000 men and emerged with just 40 and the colonel. I went to see them last year in Troon, and one of the soldiers there said that he supposed 50% of all of them would be dead by this time next year. He wasn't far wrong...' Rack was still in the Mediterranean and not enjoying it much. 'The food here is beastly and we have now even run out of cheese..' He goes on to say how awful and feeble he found the Greeks, how unattractive were the Greek women with their 'sharp red noses' and that they had deserved 'everything they got ... but nothing of it will be reported in the papers'.

MEM seems to have been happier in Sheringham, but she still found things to worry about. She may have become resigned to the threat of invasion, but she now became obsessed with the idea of German spies. She was convinced that she had seen a spy on the Sheringham cliffs and wrote to Rack about it. He was sufficiently worried to contact the local police, who on investigation found that it was just a local man. MEM was charged with wasting police time and fined £5. Rack paid. She did, however, have the grace to turn the incident into a story *The Abode of Peace*. Miss Lark, a spinster school teacher is taking her holiday in a small seaside town when war is declared. She is very patriotic and finds the idea of a war exciting. She makes friends with a charming man who is staying nearby and tries to protect him when the police come looking for him because she believes the cock-and-bull story he has told her. He turns out to be a German spy! *Charming Hospitality* continues the theme. Two particularly ugly, taciturn, elderly Belgian refugee women are offered a home in a seaside resort – and turn out to be German spies.

In December 1916 there was a general election – and Rack wrote, 'I think the new government will be a distinct improvement on the old one – but that isn't saying much. At any rate that woman Asquith's influence is gone...' The election was won by David Lloyd George, a Liberal, a Radical and the founder of the welfare state, not an appointment to find immediate favour with the Mann family. 'How are you for money in these hard times,' Rack went on. 'Shall I send you a cheque?' Money was rapidly losing its value as the war progressed (see the table at the beginning of this book), MEM's income from property and investments was dwindling rapidly and she was publishing less and less. 'I will have some tales to tell you when I get back. I think the war will end this year...' Rack was wrong of course. The war dragged on until 1918.

His letters from 1917 are all censored and bland, and much of what he wrote now seems obvious and rather trite. For example: 'I hear the Revolution in Russia was awful and that thousands of people were massacred....' Rack was obviously still somewhere in the Mediterranean, though not allowed to say where, and talks instead of bathing, the irregularity of getting letters and what he sees as the totally irresponsible reporting in some of the daily papers. 'July 25th. ... all the papers we have had in this mail are full of whoops and howls about air raids. The filthy Daily Mail is particularly disgusting on the subject. Can't these journalistic swine see that they are playing the Hun's game? In this horrible war people must expect to have a few bombs dropped on them – the Huns want to weaken our air force at the front and the papers are doing their best to help them...'

When there were no casualties to treat, life on board was boring and the men did what they could to cheer themselves up. Boxing matches were arranged and a ball – preceded by dancing lessons which they all had to attend. He sent MEM a long description of the event. 'All the men on board attended it – many dressed as women, and those had spent weeks making their dresses. A few looked quite fetching! There is nothing to see. Tennis and boxing bores me and I have read more trash recently than I ever did before in my life... No news. It is too hot....' He describes to her a group of Scottish women they had met – all nurses on board one of the other ships who had their hair cropped like men. It was thought at first that they were trying to be men; it turned out that the ship was running alive with head lice and they had cut their hair in order to try and eliminate them. In another later letter he wrote, optimistically, 'If everything goes well I ought to be home by the end of October or the beginning of November...'

In 1918 rationing was introduced for the first time. Food was in short supply due to the German blockades and inadequate food production in England. Rack wrote, 'I am afraid you don't get much to eat – I hope you buy all you are allowed to have and eat it. I can let you have any money you want. You mustn't mind the expense...'

His concern was not unfounded, as MEM showed in a story she wrote at the time – another of the 'Not for Publication' ones. *Shopping in our Town 1918* is a short story about a respectable lady living on her own means. Food became more and more expensive and incomes from investments were reduced as interest rates fell. Coupons were issued for eggs and meat. A lady – obviously MEM herself – goes into her local store and becomes desperate when she realises that she cannot afford both eggs *and* bacon. There are other women in the store and the shopkeeper leaves her to serve them. She watches – they are bringing back bottles to have them refilled with beer and whisky. They buy more drink and food as well. When they have left the lady asks the shopkeeper how they can afford it. He tells her that many people have more money now than they have ever had, their husbands are working or in the armed services and they get benefits from the government. The old lady sighs heavily, saying how difficult things are her now. 'Fact is, in the present day, we're all out robbing or being robbed,' says the shopkeeper. 'Got to make the best of it.' No doubt it genuinely was difficult for MEM: she had no idea how long she would live and whatever money she had must be made to last.

Times had changed, things would never be the same again, and for people of MEM's generation in particular, this was very hard to bear.

Chapter 8. A life's work

By any standards, MEM could write. Her plots – like those in many novels before and since – are often contrived and rely on improbable coincidences, but she always has control of her material, the twist, the turn, the sting in the tale always comes at just the right moment. The beginnings of her novels capture the imagination, her endings are satisfying if often tragic. Her characters are usually believable – after all, many of them were based on real people. For the most part their conversations are convincing; they speak simply, there is a creditable lack of moralising and her rendering of the Norfolk dialect has been praised by many who know it far better than the present authors. At its best, her descriptive writing is lyrical. She may often have been bored by Shropham, but her depictions of the sights and sounds and scents of the countryside are beautifully evocative. She loved gardens, knew her flowers and described them lovingly. She is also exceptionally good at descriptions of dress. The best of her novels – *The Patten Experiment*, say, or *Olivia's Summer* – have a message of some importance to convey. Plot, structure, characterisation, dialogue, description and message are all qualities we look for in a novel and MEM did most of them well, most of the time, as these two quotations from reviews in the *Academy* recognise: 'Her sense of form, the rise and fall of her sentences and her immaculate grammar remove her leagues from the slipshod and amateurish majority of writing women.' 'I have enjoyed her book and it has taught me something. And is not this distinguished praise?' So why is she so little remembered? Why is she not considered one of the 'great', or at least one of the 'good' Victorian novelists?

In part, it is because she wrote too much. An article in the *Daily Mail* on June 28th, 1922, discusses the work of J.E. Buckrose, another overly prolific (and forgotten) writer. The author compared them: 'It was that [same] trouble which prevented Mary Mann from adding to the permanent stock of English novels. She turned out book after book at six monthly intervals and ruined her delicate talent ... Once the present author reproached Mrs Mann for doing so. She replied that the writing of novels was poorly paid ... "Few reviewers," she said, "distinguish between good and trumpery novels; the public reads anything; it is hard for the novelist to live." '

The public certainly had a great many novels to choose from. John Sutherland (*The Longman's Companion to Victorian Fiction*, 1988) estimates that there were around 7,000 novelists at work in England in the Victorian period, just 238 of whom (including MEM) made it into the 1999 edition of *The Cambridge Bibliography of English Literature 1800-1900*.

We do not have anything like a complete picture of MEM's earnings. While she carefully hoarded letters written by her little brothers to their parents, mourning cards for long-dead family friends and invitations issued to her by neighbours when she was a young bride, her business records are sketchy. She touted her novels from publisher to publisher and switched allegiance whenever she was offered a better deal. Some publishers – H. Henry and Co are the prime example – seem to have taken advantage of her naivety; others, notably Methuen, seem to have treated her remarkably well while not making much of a profit for themselves. None of her novels made more than £300; many made considerably less than half that sum. MEM's early short stories for magazines seldom brought in more than a few pounds apiece – in 1900 she was delighted to get six guineas for *Lest I Forget*, the most she had ever had, though after Mr Watt became her agent he did negotiate a minimum rate of four guineas per 1,000 words. It is doubtful whether, all together, her plays made as much as a hundred pounds. In the whole of her thirty-year career it is unlikely that MEM's total earnings exceeded £10,000 (something like £250,000 in modern money). Had she been solely dependent on her writing, she would, indeed, have found it hard to live.

Her working methods seem to have been as chaotic as her financial record-keeping. She stored numerous drafts of her unpublished and published works, but we only find hints about the way she worked in the morass of papers she left behind. There are exercise books filled with scribbled, barely legible notes for stories, sheets with lists of characters and their attributes ('A man, young, rich, motorist, property, game, presents, poacher' or 'Athletic girl, heaps of vitality, little sentiment' or 'Chauffeur, animal person, falls in love with Sam's girl'). In other notebooks she made long lists, of possible names for her characters, and there is even a printed sheet from the Registrar General listing common given names for men and women that she could consult if imagination failed her. She kept notes of words not to use: 'don't use vicinity for neighbourhood, endorse for approve, mutual for common' and so on – but where those strictures came from is not clear.

Nonetheless, she left behind a body of work of considerable, if variable, quality. For the most part she wrote about what she knew so

165

most of her novels are set in villages or small country towns. Her characters are farmers, landowners, clergymen, tradesmen and labourers, people with whom she lived cheek by jowl for all her years in Shropham. Snobbery and the infinite gradations of social status recur in novel after novel. 'Because our father kept a linen draper's shop in the place there are people who won't be friends with us,' Clara Fisher tells her unworldly clergyman brother in *The Sheep and the Goats*. '[A]nd,' she went on, 'there are others who expect to be – father's and mother's friends, not refined people at all, some not even educated. To know them would give you no pleasure. To ask them to your house would offend the other people – the people with whom you are now equal who should be your friends.' MEM's father was a draper; she had seen her family move up the social scale from Pottergate Street to Town Close House, and by the time this was written, in 1907, she had seen most of her brothers move down the scale again, from running their own business to taking relatively menial paid employment. Her father was cultured and educated, but no doubt some of his business colleagues were not particularly refined.

Social position was immensely important in her novels. The hospitable Miss Potters in *Mating of a Dove* were socially unacceptable because 'their names did not appear in the Clergy list, and [they] were not of a county family.' In the short story *A Boy and Girl Marriage* Ida's family disapprove of her husband because 'You know he has chosen to make friends with people below him in station – people you can't possibly associate with.' In *The Eglamore Portraits*, Juliet despises Clarence Eglamore's relative, good-natured, sensible Suzy, because she is not quite a lady. Angela Mayes in *Moonlight*, the 'home-petted' daughter of a bankrupt farmer, goes to work in Onesimus Parker's department store and feels herself to be a cut above the other young people she works with. When prompted by his wife, her Uncle Fred eventually agreed, 'A man couldn't allow his own flesh and blood to wait behind the counter of a country shop, and a country shop in his own county,' he told his friends. She is rescued by him and her Aunt Stella and lives with them in comfort and respectability before marrying the local vet, her social inferior.

In *A Winter's Tale*, the servant, Penelope Bye, is murdered by the 'gentleman' with whom she has the temerity to have an affair. Mercy Morrison's mother in *Out in Life's Rain* was a 'serving maid removed from her proper sphere'. In *Fortune's Cap*, Tilly, the tweeny maid, is the only person willing to put up with difficult, disabled Mrs Carrow and becomes her companion. The other servants are shocked: ' "I never see sech a sight! For a lady like her to demean herself with a tweeny maid", the servants said, who are always great sticklers for the maintenance of caste, and never like to see a member of their own profession put out of her place. "The old woman's dotty, sure as eggs." '

In the Dulditch story, *The Setting Sun*, the farmer and the old shepherd reminisce companionably about the fifty years they have been master and man. The shepherd is retiring and, for the first time in their acquaintance, the master shakes him by the hand. Similarly, in *Lost Estate* Bob, the coachman, is permitted to shake young Peter Merry's hand – but only because it is Peter's birthday.

To demonstrate the gulf between family and servant in *Rattle's Wife*, Millicent tells Dot, her improbably-named husband, that her mother calls all her maids 'Parker' because that was the name of the first one. One had been very good looking and had been caught trying on Millicent's clothes – and what was worse was that she looked better in them than Millicent did. Dot's brother, Rattles, has just married Nora, who is extremely beautiful and Dot and Millicent are on their way to meet her when this conversation takes place. When they arrive Millicent is horrified to find that Nora was 'my mother's parlour-maid. The Parker that tried on my blue hat!'

In *Mating of a Dove* Dr Lammb [sic] is uncomfortable to see how friendly Amy is with the Grands. 'It was something of a shock to him to see the delicate lady with her unmistakeable air of race and breeding, kissing this carpenter's mother as naturally as if she had been her own.' MEM remembered when 'the idea of social equality at that time was a craze which one thought of with a shudder. Bliss Saddlebow, unconscious of any want of charity, considered herself, a rich and prosperous merchant's daughter, as removed from a girl out of a glove shop as if they had been different races.' (*Mattie, a Portrait*). This may well have been how MEM saw herself in relation to her brother's wife.

Women's status was bound up with their husband's position – something of which MEM would have been painfully aware. This forms the theme of *There was a Widow*; when Julia Delane, the doctor's wife, is widowed she loses her status as well as her income and has to rely on the grudging charity of her relations. In *Mrs Days' Daughters* it is anathema and social suicide for Mrs Day and her daughters to have to run a grocer's shop when her husband dies and leaves them penniless. 'I do not really think I could keep a shop' she said, 'above all, a grocery shop. I could not undertake it, Mr Boult; and I am sure the girls would not like it at all; nor my son.' But Mr Boult, friend and adviser to the late, disgraced William Day, and charged with looking after Mrs Day and her children, was adamant. Not only did she have to take the grocery shop, she and the girls were expected to make and sell their own Christmas mincemeat and take in and look after a lodger. When the girls are given tickets to go to the Assembly Rooms their reduced social status is made painfully clear to them. 'By a good many present, the sisters were recognised, and here and there a smile was turned on them, and here and there a cool, discreet little bow was made. And more often the people who knew them, having involuntarily looked, looked away again; for them the girls' presence there, in a fashionable company and the most expensive seats, was an offence.'

Bessie and Deleah Day, and girls like Helen Smythe, Amy Dove, Olivia Grieg and Rose Abra ignored the social rules at their peril *(Mrs Day's Daughters, Parish of Hilby, Mating of a Dove, Olivia's Summer, Rose at Honeypot)*. Class runs like a poisoned river through almost all MEM's work. Even the villagers of Dulditch could be exposed, almost as anthropological specimens, to the fascinated gaze of her readers because they and her public were so far apart on the social spectrum.

There were some groups for whom she had especial contempt. In previous chapters we have noted her distaste for socialism and her hatred of people who abused animals, but MEM's real venom was reserved for the wives of clergymen. Mrs Bramleigh Jones in *Among the Syringas* is lampooned as 'That zealous disciple of her husband's creed "Love your neighbour if his position is higher than your own".' Mrs Martell in *Mrs Peter Howard* is officious, unkind and insensitive, browbeating her down-trodden daughter, Adeline. Monica Bell (*Mating of a Dove*) soon learns to be contemptuous of her husband's parishioners. 'And give them soup and money,' she exclaims when it is suggested she should do more in the parish, 'and shake their disgusting-feeling hands, and beg them, as a favour, to come and hear us pray for them!' From sanctimonious, tract-writing Anna Pearson in *The Parish of Hilby*, to Mrs Dodman in *The Patten Experiment*, MEM made it clear that she despised clergy wives. Mrs Dodman 'knows nothing of wit, of beauty, of genius, of the nobility of men's minds ...nothing of her own times; the advent of science is but a name to her, the region of letters is almost totally unexplored ... But with her own and her husband's narrow interpretation of the Christian doctrine she is acquainted, and performs the duties she conceives to be hers rigorously in her limited sphere, being accounted among her "set" a splendid clergyman's wife, and a good woman.'

The women's husbands fare little better. Mr Freeman in *Parish of Hilby* was contemptuous of all parsons. 'Here's this lazy beggar, here; pretty nigh three hundred pounds a-year o' the country's money goes into his pocket – for what? For standin' up twice on a Sunday and makin' a fool of himself in public, and for twaddlin' round the rest o' the week from one house to another, settin' folk by th' ears!'

Weak, ineffectual clergymen are stock characters in MEM's work – men like Cecil Garnett in *In Summer Shade*, Reverend Clay in *Parish Nurse*, Reverend Grieg in *Olivia's Summer*, the children's neglectful father in *Cedar Star*, lazy, selfish Reverend Melancthon in *Among the Syringas,* or the hen-pecked Reverend Pearson in *The Parish of Hilby*. By 1891 the Vicar of Shropham was George William Watson, a married man in his late thirties who clearly had a crush on MEM. Some rather silly and inappropriate letters from him survive, pleading for them to be friends and for her not to turn her back on him – all of which very probably reinforced her poor view of the clergy. 'In a little place like this' she told Tom, writing about one of Mr Watt's predecessors, 'you can't dissociate the priest from the person, his precepts from his practice ...'

Perhaps most damning of all is her portrait of lazy, complacent Cyprian Every in the story *An Undelivered Message*. 'It was really wonderful, and a thing to be devoutly thankful for, how often he could preach the same sermon, even his wife not recognising that it had done duty before.' He made no attempt to convert people because 'It was considered more dignified in the Church of England to do nothing.' One day a stranger comes to his church. The service is, as usual, lacklustre, the sermon is another repeat performance. The man turns out to be a wealthy local ironmonger and Cyprian's wife insists that her husband go to see him the next day to ask for a donation for the church. He arrives just as the man's body is being removed; the ironmonger has shot himself. People say that it was a good thing that he went to church so soon before killing himself and Reverend Every agrees, but 'deep down in the clergyman's heart, though he breathed not a word of it to mortal ear, there must have lurked a suspicion that the whole service had been as cold as the night from which [the ironmonger] had come, as dreary as the grave to which he went ... once at least in his ministry of thirty years it had been given him to justify his calling as the servant of God, to whom had been committed a message to deliver. And he had failed to deliver it.'

Small wonder then, that MEM was unpopular with most of the local clergy. In fact, she was more than unpopular. In October/November 1904, 'Old Dr B' threatened to bring a case against her. On October 31st Bertie drove her mother to Attleborough to see her solicitor and recorded in her diary that 'It seems the slander case is to proceed.' The following day 'Dr B' and a Mr Clarke came to see MEM. 'I suppose,' wrote Bertie, 'he was afraid to face mother alone.' Bertie knew little about legal matters; after her father's death she wrote about Mr Salter having come to value their possessions 'for probit [sic], whatever that may be', so it is quite possible that the case was for libel (written defamation) not slander, which is verbal. Either way, it does not seem to have gone ahead. Bertie and her father made sure Mr Clarke was unable to support the aggrieved Dr B and MEM seems to have managed to talk her way out of trouble. We cannot be sure who 'Dr B' was, but it seems quite likely that he was the Reverend Frederick William Bussell D.D., of Mundford. There were a number of local clergymen whose surnames began with a 'B' - but he is the only one with a doctorate.

Much to her surprise, in 1900 a Mr Bickley wrote an article in the *Church Gazette* called *Parsons in Fiction; Mary E. Mann.* It seems to have been complimentary and she was delighted both with his support and with the publicity.

MEM had problems because her characters were too easily identifiable. The blind shopkeeper, for example – Mrs Batty in *Lost Estate* – was surely based on someone MEM knew. In summer, the old woman's right arm was constantly swollen with wasp stings from the wasps that got into the sack of sugar; she sold clo' balls (clove balls – probably like aniseed balls) and home-made toffee, she had a sixth sense that told her when someone was trying to steal from her, and she had no difficulty in distinguishing a sixpence from a metal button by touch alone. It was an affectionate portrait and years later 'Mrs Batty's' grandson ran the local garage and was proud to claim she had been MEM's inspiration. It is unlikely that many villagers in Shropham would have been quite so willing to be associated with MEM.

One of her short stories, *The Eerie*, published in 1910, is a rather unkind portrait of Kate Nichols, her friend since childhood. Kate was something of an eccentric, an artist, an etcher, president of the Norfolk branch of the RSPCA and the founder of the Woodpecker Art Club. She appears in the story as wealthy Judy Harrison, 'beauty lover', holder of soirées, with an eclectic mix of friends which includes tramps and titled gentlemen with their own private observatories. The police regularly warn her to be careful of the people she mixes with; she frequently invokes them to prosecute tradesmen over-working their horses or men abusing their dogs. She has gipsy looks and frequently wears black but always with a splash of bright colour – scarlet or orange – to enliven her dress. Those last details could have come straight from Kate Nichols' obituary. MEM peppers Judy's speech with words in italics for emphasis; Kate Nichols' surviving letters are full of emphatic under-linings. Judy's protégés in the story are Cavazza the mystic and her housemaid, Kitty, who hears voices and was 'called' to work for Judy. Cavazza is handsome and charming but there is nothing remotely mystical about him – his prophecies rely on observation and common sense. Kate Nichols was entangled with Alasdair the Palmist, according to Bertie's diaries. He was handsome, charismatic and a good showman, but MEM and Bertie were sure he was a charlatan. Kitty and her husband have plans to rob Judy of her jewels. The plot is foiled and Judy is fatalistic – 'It was not the first time by a great many she had trusted and been deceived. It was nearly certain not to be the last.' Kate Nichols was not a wealthy woman but she was comfortably off, and though we have no reason to suppose she was robbed she certainly gave her money away very freely to people she believed were in need. On her death she left just £89 15s. 10d. One wonders whether MEM's friendship with Kate survived the publication of *The Eerie*.

However, she was equally happy to be uncomplimentary about her own family. We have already noted how she used her bossy, managing mother and dreamy, unambitious father in a number of novels. In the story *The Old Birds*, in *Through the Window*, she puts her own marriage in the spotlight. An elderly couple whose children have long since flown the nest no longer have anything to say to each other and the husband has grown taciturn and bad tempered. The wife decides to take an extended holiday visiting her children and secretly doubts whether she'll ever return. She writes home frequently but all she gets for answer is a brief note from the cook, dictated by her husband, that tells her all is well. Nonetheless, she misses him, and when one of cook's letters contains the intelligence that 'master has a cold' she happily goes back to 'her owner, her master, the father of her children.'

Charming, feckless, selfish younger brothers, of whom MEM had several, also feature in novel after novel – Philip Harleigh in *Mrs Peter Howard*, Alfred, the drug-addicted medical student in *Susannah*, Herbie Rolfe in *There once was a Prince* and Andy Bain in *Among the Syringas*, to name but a few. MEM also used what she could learn from

**Frank Rackham, with one of his grandchildren,
the only one of MEM's brothers to survive her.
He was always known as 'Old Chap'. He died in 1931.**

her family about jobs. MEM's granddaughter believed that one of their relatives had a market garden for a time at Thorpe, like uncouth Mr Tilly, the market gardener in *Memories of Ronald Love*. MEM's sister-in-law, Fanny, had been a shop-girl in a department store and she may well have talked to MEM about how hard the job was on the feet, how to fold fabric – 'lay the roll at the edge of the counter, and ... get the material level before folding' – how to flatter customers and how to look busy at all times. MEM put Fanny's reminiscences to good use in *Moonlight*.

She also used her own children as models. Bertie, strong-minded, resourceful, unconventional and intelligent, appears in different guises in novel after novel – as naughty, honest Betty in *Cedar Star*, plucky Rosamund in *The Patten Experiment*, as the eponymous heroine in *Susannah* or as Daphne Snare in *Heart Smiter*. Margery appears seldom, once as innocent, child-like, independent Amy Dove in *The Mating of a Dove*, and again as Nora Chisholm in *Astray in Arcady*, pretty, sensible, a rearer of turkeys and chickens, with no hope of marrying because she never meets men of her own age. 'It is a pity, one feels, as one watches the girl going sensibly through her useful days; as one listens to her and looks at her strong figure and healthy face.'

The pretty, spoilt, child-wife, heavily reliant on her mother, who appears in story after story, was probably based on Dolly, and to some extent on the young woman MEM believed herself to have been. Millie Howard, Monica Dove, Juliet Eglamore and Lally Garnett were all of this type. An unpublished story, *The Coddles Adventure,* was probably intended to amuse her own children rather than for public consumption. Two motherless little girls, Margy and Molly, decide to run away for the day. Their big sister, Linda, knows of their plan and lets them take Nip the dog with them. The children roam the countryside, playing in the woods, paddling in the stream and picking flowers. Nip chases and kills a turkey and some chicks. Eventually the children tire and go home – to be met by their distraught father who is so angry and relieved to see them that he whips them both with his riding crop. It is an innocent little story, the children's names echo those of the Mann children – and the family had a dog called 'Nip'.

Hugh Norris and his wife, Nina, appears as Edward Harringay and his weak, pretty, clingy wife, Violet, in *Cedar Star.* Nina was deaf – so was Violet. Like Hugh and Bertie, Edward and Betty have a relationship; there is then a boating accident in which Violet drowns. Just before their wedding Edward confesses to Betty that he did not save Violet when he could have done, but pushed her away, knowing she could not swim. Betty is horrified and rejects him – he flees to Africa and dies of fever – she receives the news of his death just as she is about to relent. This is a story of what-might-have-been, as was Hugh's and Bertie's, and has a similarly tragic outcome. In the same book there is an unpleasant episode when Betty is so irritated by a pathetic little stepbrother that she forces him to pick up a black beetle. One wonders if MEM was remembering a letter sent to her by five-year old Rack while he was still in the schoolroom at Manor Farm having lessons with his sister. The governess got him to write a little letter to his parents who were away from home on a short holiday. The thing that he was most anxious to tell them was that 'Berty picked up a beatle'! She was three.

Margery and Rack's medical experiences are put to good use in novel after novel. 'In my second year at St Michael's Hospital,' says Marion Mott in *When a Man Marries,* 'the conditions became more bearable, the worst of the drudgery was over – the cleaning of brasses and rubbing of floor, and endless emptying of basins. At the end of the third year I was finding existence within the hospital walls full of interest …' Poor Margery never really reached her second year as a nurse, but no doubt she had observed how things improved for those who did.

Not only MEM's characters, but also their names, were often only thinly disguised. In the unpublished *Good for Nothing* one of the young men is called Fairjoy Fielding – obviously an adaptation of Fairman. Nina Norris's maiden name was Dyson, and a Nellie Dyson appears in 'Heart Smiter'. Little Philip in *When Arnold Comes Home* has the surname Margetson and a Mr Margetson was on the Board of Guardians of Wayland Workhouse. As we have seen, in *Memories of Ronald Love* the names are virtually unchanged. In the village stories Shropham names are easily recognisable – Nobbs becomes Hobbs, Brame becomes Brome, Mrs Eke the farmer's mother becomes Mrs Eke the shopkeeper, the Gal La'rences may not have belonged to that family but there were certainly Lawrences in Shropham – and so on. When MEM came across a name she liked, she used it – her granddaughter's husband, Guy Vallance, lends his name to Major Vallance in the short story *After All*, for example, and her husband's horse, Depper, gave his name to the miserable husband in *Women o' Dulditch*. Her niece Phyllis was known as 'Pig' to her family; a little girl called 'Pig' whose real name is Phyllis appears in *Among the Syringas*. There are endless other examples. MEM also used real places. Kirk Hall, the house of horrors in *Confessions of a Coward and a Coquette* was the name of Fairman's brother's farm. There was a Honeypot Cottage in Shropham, over by Honeypot Wood. The Maid's Head Inn in *Moonlight* is based on the real 'Maid's Head' on Tombland in Norwich. *The Sheep and the Goats* was apparently set in Marlborough where Dolly lived.

MEM's own marriage was not particularly happy and many of her novels present quite a jaundiced view of the institution. There are weak husbands overshadowed by domineering wives like Mrs Cummin and Anna Pearson (*Eglamore Portraits* and *Parish of Hilby*), and bullies like William Day and Mr Bloore (*Mrs Day's Daughters* and *Avenging Children*). Young brides like Miriam Elgard, Millie Howard and Monica Bell (*One Another's Burdens, Mrs Peter Howard* and *Mating of a Dove)* are quickly disillusioned, and sensible girls like Polly Freeman, Bessie Day and Georgy Waller marry men who can look after them rather than men they love. (*Parish of Hilby, Mrs Day's Daughters* and *Lost Estate*). Happy marriages are few and far between in her canon. Bertie seems to have absorbed her mother's views; in one of her diary entries in about 1910 she writes 'Nine out of ten women have to marry the man they can get, not the one they want.' This piece of cynicism seems to have been prompted by her friend Madge becoming engaged to Dick Harvey after having had a relationship with his (married) uncle. Bertie was a snob and thought Dick a yokel. 'How can pretty well-bred Madge contemplate it?' she wrote. 'The uncle is rough too, but big and handsome ...' In one of her many notebooks MEM recorded various quotations which presumably reinforced her view of marriage: 'There are no persons so far apart as those that are married and estranged' (Anon) and 'When you are married there is nothing left to you, not even suicide, but to be good.' (R.L.Stevenson)

In fact, suicide is another theme that recurs remarkably often in MEM's work. In a letter to MEM from her friend, Mary Lee, when she was still a girl there is a – probably jokey – question. 'Has Georgy committed suicide yet?' Georgy was one of MEM's younger brothers, who actually died in his own bed, of pneumonia, at the age of forty-eight. Presumably as an angst-ridden teenager he often threatened to kill himself when things went wrong. But suicide was something with which the whole family seem to have had an unhealthy fascination, as witnessed by the fact that two of MEM's daughters and one of her granddaughters killed themselves, and a second granddaughter made at least one unsuccessful suicide attempt. What is chilling is the way the family regarded it. Writing to Bertie after the death of MEM's granddaughter, Mary, in 1937, Simon, Frank's eldest son, wrote of her 'final magnificent gesture', her 'courage and dignity' and suggested that 'the manner of her death is a justification of her whole life' – a strange comment on the death of an unhappy and rather unstable young woman. Suicide seems to have been perceived as a perfectly acceptable solution to problems in the Mann family.

We know it was relatively common in village society. Men – and women – who could no longer face the on-going battles of daily life, who could no longer work or who feared the workhouse, for whom one more tragedy was the straw that broke the camel's back, might seek death as a welcome release. 'Making a hand of yourself, as it was called in the village, was a sin and a crime and suicides were not always afforded a proper burial, so doctors often fudged the issue. Deaths were frequently recorded as accidents when they were no such thing – even Dolly's overdose was listed on her death certificate as 'accidental' to enable Charles Hewitt to give his wife a proper funeral. In the story, *White Chintzes* a man's wife is found dead. The doctor comes to examine her body. 'I can give you the certificate all right,' he tells the husband, 'but look here,' and he invites him to smell the empty glass lying by her bed.

Drowning was a popular method of killing yourself in water-logged Norfolk, and MEM was in no doubt about how unpleasant a death it would be. Mrs Day's disgraced husband committed suicide by poisoning himself with a capsule hidden in his watch. She considers drowning herself. She had no illusions about the enfolding in the 'cool and comforting arms of death.' She knew quite well the horror of it, the choke, with the rank, foul-tasting river in her mouth, its weeds and offal winding her limbs. But that would pass, and she would be out of it. Far rather be dead at the bottom of the river than married to her benefactor, Mr George Boult.'

Hanging was also common. This was not always easy and MEM records cases where men went to extraordinary lengths to find a way of doing it. The ghastly Maher Crouch in *Lost Housen* makes numerous attempts to find a solid enough part of his flimsy walls to hold a nail which would support his noose. Angela Mayes' father, in *Moonlight*, tries to hang himself from a beam in his barn but it is rotten and gives way. Undeterred, he hangs his rope from the top of a ladder, but he is a tall man, his feet would have touched the ground, so he put himself in a kneeling position. The fortitude it must have taken to allow yourself to dangle in that position until you finally suffocated beggars belief – but MEM may well have heard of such a case for in *Astray in Arcady* the Chisholms' old shepherd is driven to the same straits to hang himself from the low beam in his shed.

One of MEM's short stories, *To London Bridge* is entirely about suicide. A young man, worrying about his gambling debts, meets a beautiful young woman on a train. They discover they are both contemplating suicide and are both carrying revolvers. They make a pact to throw the guns out of the window before the train reaches London Bridge. She turns out to be a jewel thief and is arrested on arrival at the station; he goes off to explain himself to his family. MEM seems to suggest they might both have been better off if they had killed themselves.

Her characters take their own lives in various ways – hanging, shooting, drowning or cutting their throats with the lethally sharp razors with which they shaved. It happened. In 1887 MEM wrote to Tom, 'A great friend of ours, by name Tom Jarrod was coming to stay with my mother this Easter and coming on to us. Instead he cut his throat. Why we can only guess at. He was young (28) very handsome, very rich, the petted and idolised son of an old man who only seemed to live for him … I cannot bear to think of it,' she added, ' and yet can think of nothing else.' Rack may have encouraged her obsession. At Manor Farm in the 1890s a young man was staying with the family. He was depressed, and as a precaution against him killing himself, so MEM told Tom, Rack removed his razor. In a letter home from the Gloucester Royal Infirmary where he was working for a time in November 1896, Rack also writes quite casually of a young man who had attempted to commit suicide by taking an overdose, 'It was the usual love affair' but the stomach pump had a 'calming effect'.

Even when she did not have them kill themselves, MEM often disposed of her excess characters in a rather cavalier fashion. In September 1913 *The Athenaeum* reviewed *Mrs Day's Daughters* which they saw as dreary and unromantic. The reviewer also commented that he could 'see no necessity, artistic or other, for the death of little Frank', the youngest Day child, who was killed in a carriage accident. The *Sheffield Telegraph* in April 1901 recommended *Among the Syringas* but thought 'there [was] a little too much infanticide'! This was certainly true of *Lost Estate*. Georgy Waller and her four sisters come to stay with Reverend Budsworth as his wards. Only Georgy is given a name and a personality, the others are just 'the little Wallers' and they are killed off, unmourned, in an epidemic when they are surplus to requirements!

Rack's medical career also introduced MEM to the seamier side of life in other ways. In *Susannah*, Sukey's brother, Alfred, is a medical student and an opium addict. Opium, in various forms, was the key sedative drug in 19th century hospitals and drug addiction amongst medical students was not uncommon. Rack's fellow student, Frank Marsden, became addicted to opium but managed to kick the habit. Through Rack he then met and fell head over heels in love with Bertie who was in London at the same time as her brother. Bertie was a flirt and a tease, it is clear from her diaries that she was well aware of her own attractiveness and the power she could exercise over young men. With Frank, the attraction, all too literally, proved fatal. Bertie was playing games and when she told Frank – repeatedly and none too kindly – not to be so silly as to think she would marry him, he was devastated. He turned to opium again, there was a particularly frightening episode in 1896 when he turned up at her lodgings, high as a kite, and made a scene, and he wrote her pathetic letter after pathetic letter. She sent copies of the letters and her account of the incidents home to her mother for advice. 'Don't you think them very feeble and sickening?' she asked, adding unsympathetically that what she really wanted to reply was 'Dear Frank, Don't be such a silly fool.' It is not always easy to like Bertie. The details in *Susannah* – like Sukey searching for track marks on her brother's arms and legs when she bathed him during his last illness – very probably came from Rack. The short story, *Sister Helen,* and the play of the same name, also centre around opium addiction – 'it is killing all moral sense in me as well as in the miserable wretch I am tied to,' exclaims Nurse Edna miserably as she tries to blackmail Sir Peter Bennett, the surgeon who has murdered his first wife, into giving her yet more money. Sometimes MEM did not apply her new-found knowledge very appropriately. Angela Mayes in *Moonlight* 'craved for stories as the poor wretch with the morphia habit craves for the drug which brings him oblivion.' Reading certainly enabled Angela to forget her surroundings for a while, but it is a rather crass comparison.

The world MEM lived in was changing fast and she tried to keep her novels up to date. By the 1880s it was quite acceptable for respectable young women to ride bicycles. The Boyan girls in *Patten Experiment* had bicycles; young Mrs Peter Howard angers her husband by cycling to the woods for a picnic with Captain Gressley; MEM's own daughters, Bertie and Margery, cycled. Bertie wrote in her diary of one stormy night when she and Margery had been to Norwich by train, leaving their bicycles at the station. Trying to cycle the three miles home in the dark and the driving rain both bikes developed punctures, the girls had to push them home and arrived soaked and mud-bespattered. MEM saw this as healthy: in *Moonlight* she describes two girls with 'rain-soaked hair and rain-washed faces, their ungloved hands thrust in the pockets of their jackets, and [they] had taken nothing but good thereby to health, spirits and complexion.' Tom Ordish was also a keen cyclist though he took it up quite late in life; he writes to MEM about his efforts to learn to ride. He took cycling holidays and on several occasions she suggests, quite seriously, that he and Lily ride up from London to see her – a distance of around 100 miles.

MEM was probably too old to learn to ride a bicycle herself, but she certainly travelled by car. As early as 1908 the Salters from Attleborough took her for a drive as a birthday treat. Cars were almost unknown in villages like Shropham at that date and the passage in *Parish Nurse* where the villagers talk about the car that the nurse arrived in may well have been MEM recording Shropham villagers' comments verbatim. 'Fust time as I seen yew a-flyin past without nothing, as yer may say, to keep yer a-goin ...' 'Tis as good as a merracle, ain't it?' Motor vehicles would remain an unusual sight in country villages for many years and horse-drawn vehicles co-existed with them for a generation. In 1911, the Hemsworths at Shropham Hall had a car and chauffeur – but the family at Shropham Villa still had a carriage and coachman.

Women smoking cigarettes was something else MEM had to get used to, and like cars, she used the practice as a symbol of modernity in her novels. Old fashioned Mrs Derrington Bell, Monica's mother-in-law in *Mating of a Dove,* is described thus: 'She was only sixty ... Many women at her age smoked their cigarettes after dinner, wore sailor hats, bicycled, and pretended to like it.' MEM could not bring herself to believe that these modern habits were enjoyable though, nor could she sympathise with hard, self-controlled, judgemental Mrs Bell, a vicar's widow. In *Moonlight*, worldly-wise Stella Mayes tries to encourage Henry Scard to smoke and relax by lighting up a cigarette of her own, though when he still refuses to smoke she throws it away, admitting that smoking doesn't really give her any pleasure. Even Mrs Carrow's Siamese cat in *Fortune's Cap* was given the inexplicable – but modern – name of 'Cigarette'.

Society was changing. *Grandpapa's Granddaughter*, originally serialised as *The Interfering Pauline,* but published in book form in 1915, was all about the contrast between the old and the new. Old Mr Coutt is house-bound and senile and has completely lost interest in his estate. This has been ruined by his extravagant lifestyle and his two spendthrift sons, the farms are going to rack and ruin, the cottages are dilapidated and his agent is just about holding things together by selling off parcels of land piecemeal to their nouveau riche neighbours, the Calemhursts. Both the Coutt sons are dead. Each had a daughter, and those daughters come to live with their grandfather. Vivia is a modern young thing who dances and goes otter-hunting with the footman and spends her evenings tête-a-tête with her grandfather's agent, Roger Stilman. Pauline is old fashioned and shocked by her young cousin's ways. 'She was living in a socialistic age. Heaven alone knew to what pulling down of strongholds, to what levelling processes it was tending.' Pauline tries to take charge and is gradually made aware of their financial situation. The agent is a member of a new social class, intelligent and educated, but Pauline's father has taught her to despise such men – 'laughing indulgently [he] had pointed out to her that a good deal more than an education at a country grammar school and a few years in an office of a provincial town went to the creating of even the outward semblance of a gentleman.' But Pauline's father was wrong. By a series of improbable co-incidences Roger inherits the Calemhurst estate and the novel ends with Pauline set to marry him. Vivia, meanwhile, has happily married Harry Grey, one of the tenants, completely oblivious of the social impropriety involved, and old Mr Coutt has died. A microcosm of the social order has been turned on its head. However, MEM clearly sympathises much more with traditionalist Pauline than with hoydenish Vivia.

As well as changes in manners, MEM's generation saw many technological changes, one of which was the march of telegraph poles across the landscape. To MEM they were almost mystical. Little Lolly Rolfe, having run away from her brutal stepfather in *There Once was a Prince* passed tall telegraph poles 'murmuring strange, inarticulate secrets to Lolly, listening with her ear against them, for the story of the mysterious messages flying along the wires overhead.'

But however hard she tried to embrace modernity, MEM was nostalgic for the past. She wrote of the apparently easy relationship between master and hand 'before the days of the agricultural depression which put an end to such innocent festivities in thousands of homes.' She disliked modern fashions in dress with their 'high collars [and] stiff neck-bands hiding a girl's chief beauty, her round white throat,' and yearned for the days when women didn't have to pretend to be young. Mrs Day was a 'pretty woman of medium height, middle-aged, as women allowed themselves to be, frankly, fifty years ago.' MEM hankered after 'the unenlightened days when customers could depend on the civility of shopkeepers' and 'the comfortable and tranquil days before "ladies" had been taught by strict necessity, or the desire to be of use in a changed and troubled world, that to be idle was a reproach, almost a disgrace, and that to clean windows and scrub floors was honourable occupation.'

It is worth giving some examples of MEM's fine powers of description. In many of her novels the reader can almost see, hear and smell the scenes she describes. The countryside was beautiful to MEM whatever the season. In spring 'The luxuriant growth of the green banks was spangled thickly with primrose stars; the hedges above them, only green as yet in sheltered or sunny places, were powdered white with the blackthorn bloom; all the little rivulets and ditches and brooks were full of gurgling, running water … and in the branches of the budding lilac the blackbird sang.'(*Moonlight*). Edward Barnard, fishing on the riverbank on a summer afternoon in *There Once was a Prince* saw 'A dragon-fly, magnifical in its shimmer of blue and green

180

and gold, with fairy gossamer wings,' and watched gnats 'gracefully curtseying to the light rippling of the river ... The harsh cry of the lapwing, discordant amid the music of the murmuring river, hum of insect, song of bird, startled now and again the warm air' which was 'burdened with the sweetness of lilac blossom.'

On the banks of the river at Thorpe where Dr Clough takes Nancie and Ronnie Love in his boat one summer day, there were 'meadows burnished with buttercups, powdered with daisies, where cows stood knee-deep in the enamelled grass.' At Jane's aunt's farm in *Gran'ma's Jane* '[f]locks of pigeons were cooing on the gold and green stained granary roof, high up in the elm trees the rooks were cawing; the air was rent with the blaring of a calf wanting to be fed, and the bellowing of the cow who had lost her calf; a score or so of white ducks sunning themselves in the uneven roadway, ran with wild quackings and splashed into the shallow waters of the weedy pond.'

The nurse treating old Bob in *Last Haysell* describes 'The rose of the sanfoin and the scarlet of the poppies, and the white of the bladder campion – sheets and sheets of it! Bob, no carpet woven in Eastern countries, where they make them for kings, you know, was ever half so gorgeous.' 'How the bees are all a-hum in the white clover and the air full of dancing tiny flies ... How the lime trees by the road, and the elder bushes in the hedge are a-bloom, the scent of them and the clover and the hay all mixed together.' Bob, the old countryman who has experienced this year after year, is much more interested in the mechanics of the haysell, which horses are being used and who is riding the cutting machine.

MEM could even make winter sound romantic, 'Nature, redressed and superlatively beautiful that morning, lay netted in the jewelled veil cast by the hoar frost,' and 'a frosty morning when each evergreen leaf had been frilled with a fluting of crystal ... in the still pearl-coloured air,' (*Heart Smiter*), or 'The dripping trees and hedgeways, the long grass beaten white with the rain, the swollen ditches by the roadside, the water running, dark and turbulent beneath the floating cresses.' (*Moonlight*) Less attractive is her description of winter's smell as 'the aroma loved of sportsmen of turnips rotting in the ground.' (*Fortune's Cap*)

In *Confessions of a Coward and a Coquette* the atmosphere of menace is established even before the heroine arrives at Kirk Hall by an evocative description of a night-time journey – 'each [isolated cottage] with its lighted window making the darkness darker as we passed, through a park ... between an avenue of trees half a mile long, then to jolt through a gate (I screamed then, for we caught the post in the darkness and it seemed that destruction had come at last; it seemed, too, that the deluge had come, for the low-growing branches of the two trees guarding the gate dashed in our faces and sent a shock of cold water down our backs) ...' Later the snow hides the dismally neglected garden. 'I looked upon a beautified landscape, where all squalor and untidiness and neglect were mercifully hidden, where the distinctions of rank lawn and grass-grown paths and weed-choked flower-beds were subtly disappearing, where heaps of dark decaying leaves were transformed into mounds of crystal whiteness ...' MEM is anxious to keep up the suspense and remind the reader of the ugliness that permeates Kirk Hall and that the snow can only mask.

MEM loved gardens and flowers. She has Charlotte Poole thank her predecessor at the cottage 'for the luxurious Carmine Pillar, for the chaste Thalia, for the Crimson Rambler, and the delicate sweetness of golden-hearted Euphrosyne; for Helen Keller, that rose of love's proper hue, 'celestial rosy red'; for the creamy gold of the Gloire de Dijon and the innocent pink of Clio; for the Delphiniums, their long spiky heads blue as the sky; for the Phloxes with their ruby and white beauty as yet held in store, I acknowledge my obligation to t'other woman.'

Nurse Brunton in *Patten Experiment* 'was a flower lover ... Big plants of pale and dark blue delphiniums were there, the tall flower spikes as high as the cottage door. There were yellow marigolds, cheerfully self-assertive, great bushy mallows with their myriad blooms of rose and white; round the window a monthly rose was trained; by the tiny gate was a tall sunflower or two, not yet in bloom. Sweet-scented stocks and asters, purple and white, loved of the poor, filled up the spaces left by the larger growths.' In Aunt Marion's shrubbery in *Arnold* '... here and there amid the shining aconite leaves a tall cowslip pricked up a yellow head, and high above the delicate young leafage of the nut bushes, a laburnum rang its fairy bells.'

MEM understood the power of lists to convey abundance. Mr Tilly loads his cart for market with 'Hampers of late blackcurrants, of early apples, trays of cut roses, of musks, and heliotropes, and geraniums in little pots; great pyramidal nosegays of cornflowers, of yellow lilies and red and purple stocks, decked with the green and white streamers of the Lady's-garter and backed by the long leaves of the Filii Mas.' (*Memories of Ronald Love*) To a small child, the fair in 1850s Norwich consisted of 'enchanted lanes of endless length, where on either side, in charming variety and lavish luxuriance, toys, peppermint rock, and gilded gingerbread grew. Where the confusion made by the shouting of hoarse, strange voices, the blare of the showman's whip, the beating of the big, alarming drum, rose to little brains, intoxicating them with strange, half-fearful delight.' (*Gran'ma's Jane*) Widow Eke's country shop sold 'Every conceivable article which could be wanted by the labouring class – her only customers ... Her coal store was in an outhouse; once a week the remains of a pig mingled with the drapery goods hanging from the shop ceiling; loaves of bread lay cheek-by-jowl with iron-clamped boots and shoes; kettles, boilers, and other ironmongery-ware were stowed away with rolls of bacon under the counter; outside the crowded little window, weather permitting, ready-made clothing depended from hooks.' (*Out in Life's Rain*)

With the same use of detail, MEM also gives us a very clear picture of cottage interiors. Nurse Brunton's cottage in *Patten Experiment* was a model of comfort and order, if not of refined taste. 'There were the six red-coloured, highly-varnished deal chairs standing on the border of red brick outside the square of bright-coloured carpet; there was the chest of drawers and the round centre table of the same evil-smelling material. Upon these reposed, each upon his mat, and at regular intervals from his neighbour, butter-dish, Bible, glass decanter, a gay-coloured tin which had once held biscuits, a pair of china dogs, with blue bows about their necks, and various specimens of glass ornaments which John Pedlar brings round, with cheap laces and pins and combed out orange and magenta mats, to charm the treasured savings of the year from the pockets of the labourers' wives. On the drab-coloured walls, papered, as the crinkly set of the paper showed, by the thrifty hands of Nurse Brunton herself, were hung pictures of a scriptural theme, calculated to make an artistic person extremely wicked, some mourning cards in frames of gold; a nurseryman's coloured advertising abomination ...'

By contrast, the kitchen at Honeypot Cottage was dirty and comfortless. 'The kitchen was large, with a low ceiling, heavily raftered, which with the walls had once been white. The numerous doors were ill-fitting and the place was full of draughts; through the door which opened into the garden the snow had drifted, a ridge of it lay white against the dark-coloured bricks. Such furniture as there was was mean and rickety. But the fire, confined with a few loosely-placed bricks, burnt brightly on the wide open hearth ...' The tablecloth was always dirty and askew, the table was never cleared, let alone scrubbed and Mrs Jaggerd's cooking was no better than her housekeeping. For her first meal at Honeypot Rose saw her 'stir some potatoes in the black grease in which the herrings had been cooked.' All the Shropham cottages had red brick floors. Keeping them scrubbed and red was the hallmark of the careful housewife who fought a constant battle against soot from the fire, cooking spills and muddy boots. It was a thankless struggle in which Mrs Jaggerd – and many like her – never bothered to engage.

Country entertainments feature in several of MEM's stories and no doubt she had attended many. 'Warby's Frolic' – the party given in Warby's barn to celebrate his daughter's marriage – seems a dismal affair to Rose Abra, newly arrived in Dulditch. The barn is decorated with 'branches of evergreen nailed there after some primitive scheme of decoration' and banners celebrating 'The Hapy Pare'. (Similarly mis-spelt banners celebrate Monica Dove's wedding – MEM did sometimes repeat herself). The men drink, the women watch and 'The air grew thick with the smell of boiled pudding, the odour of human beings unused to baths, of garments, which, when not on their owners' backs, supplemented the scanty clothing on the beds of rooms whose windows were never opened.' James Massey is shocked by the crudity of the performances at the concert in Hilby, set against 'an under-current of giggling, whistling, and the scraping of heavy boots on the gritty boards.' He was embarrassed for the performer of a comic song 'the burden of which was to the effect that "he couldn't keep still". By way of illustration, he jumped and floundered about the little platform in his huge patent boots, in a manner to inspire the liveliest apprehension as to its power of supporting him.'

MEM was also very good at descriptions of dress; for most of her life, clothes were an important marker of social position. Quality was all important, shabbiness less so. Over-bright colours and extremes of fashion were not genteel. So Totty, Jane's vulgar stepmother, wore a 'much-flounced dress of purple "shot" silk over a huge crinoline' and her hair was 'combed over wide pads at the side of her head; at the junction of the pads at the back was pinned a large, fancifully concocted velvet bow.' Daphne Snare's mother, Nellie Dyson, was 'apparelled in cheap garments, vulgarly fashioned to a five-years-ago mode. Her skirt, intended for walking length, trailed at the back upon the road; the sleeves of her coat, puckered at the shoulders, rose towards her ears. Her dark, much-curled hair was flattened to the forehead by a veil tied tightly over her toque, pushed backward upon the head and adorned with gold ornaments and bits of fur.' This is a woman who had once loved cheap finery but has fallen on hard times and her shoddy garments have not lasted well.

Old Mrs Drummond in *Confessions of a Coward and a Coquette* is 'tall and stooping, thin and bony, with pale, much-wrinkled face …wearing a plain dress of black, a black silk apron, jet bracelets upon her skinny wrists and a white cap with black flowers upon her head – a harassed, mournful-looking woman' – and a suitable mistress for the dreadful household over which she presides.

Arthur Gosling, the flashy London cousin who visits the Freemans in Hilby, was 'a young man, attired in dark trousers and a long, shiny, black frock-coat, whose feet were thrust into slippers of violet and gold, and whose lank hair was adorned with smoking-cap and long tassel of the same colours.' Such garments were totally out of place in a farmhouse and mark Arthur out as a flamboyant townie. Mr Gibbon, the Days' lodger, 'wore the light-coloured, large-checked suit affected at that period by young men escaping temporarily from the black-frocked livery of shop or office, his hair was brushed smoothly back and shone with brilliantine, his moustache was glossy with the same admired preparation.' He is about to propose to Deleah Day, but his dress marks him out irrevocably as a member of the prosperous working class and emphasises why she will not find him a suitable consort.

Men dressed to suit their rank and the occasion as this description of George Boult demonstrates. 'Since having been made a magistrate, it was to be observed that certain changes had taken place in the appearance and attire of the successful draper. He affected now the light-coloured tweed suit of the country gentleman, rather than the black decorous garments of trade. A deerstalker replaced the tall hat to which his head was accustomed, and he wore it, as was the fashion among the younger generation at that period, ever so little on one side. His short beard was trimmed to a point, his moustache turned upwards at the ends, on his hands were gloves of tawny-coloured leather … [he was] strangely rejuvenated and quite up-to-date.'

Pretty, silly Nancie Love, Ronnie's mother, is not a lady but she knows how to dress. For her trip to the market with her husband she dresses carefully and modestly in the hope of catching the eye of her former protector, Dr Clough. 'Full white muslin sleeves, put on beneath the wide ones of her peach-coloured dress met the neat gloves at the wrist with a little band of black velvet to emphasise the contact. In the neck of her bodice, worn low and open in the old days, white muslin was softly folded, pinned to each shoulder was a scarf of gauze of the same colour as her dress, embroidered at its fringed ends in pink roses and green leaves. The bonnet, not at all calculated to protect the pretty head from the sun, was of peach silk with an inner wreath of roses.' It is a perfect description of a fashionable summer outfit of the 1850s, suitable for a young girl going to a garden party – but not for a married mother helping her husband on his market stall. MEM's readers would have understood the meanings of dress in ways which are foreign to us in the 21st century.

But in most ways her stories are still very readable. MEM's use of language is surprisingly modern and her comments could be caustic. '[T]he loss of a wife when there is no money to pay a housekeeper is a misfortune even to the James Strakers of this world.' 'What [Mrs Pearson] looked on as her own duty was so exceedingly easy to herself that she could never understand or sympathize with the rest of mankind, who seemed generally to shirk theirs.' 'Mr Pearson ... like all idle men, never had a moment to spare.' Pollie Freeman was 'not sufficiently accustomed to tears to shed them scientifically or with decent quiet.' Everard Barrett was 'considered a handsome man by himself and his friends'; Angela Mayes' uncle 'was a man who never performed the smallest service for himself that others would undertake.' In *Mating of a Dove* the schoolmistress is always referred to as 'Article 68', the reference number by which the mistress of the Swilly Fen school was known to her superior officers and the members of the School Board; thus MEM emphasises the young woman's total lack of personality.

Mrs Petres in *When a Man Marries* 'was the especially favourite resort of the insect fraternity.' People called on the newly-married Olivia Sturt 'with the laudable intention of getting what amusement they could out of the situation.' The Curatage in *Cedar Star* 'was quite a modern house of a very ornate architecture, its chimneys and frequent gables being almost painfully picturesque, its windows showing the maximum of mullion and the minimum of glass.' 'The lady who reigned over Hazelborough, was of ancient lineage ... but she was not a very likeable or pleasant person, and her manners were the reverse of agreeable. If beauty live by kindness, it was, perhaps, owing to a deficiency of the latter quality in her bosom that comeliness was so completely absent from her face.' During the war MEM wrote sarcastically of 'ladies patriotic enough to wish to do *something* as they say, but who do not wish to leave their supremely comfortable homes.'

She could also coin apt phrases. The dragonfly in the passage quoted earlier is 'magnifical' – both magnificent and magical. Jane's father was 'he who, camel-like, drank for thirst past, present and to come.' Little Philip Margetson's face was often 'weeping-ripe' when he was teased. A barn was 'swallow-haunted', clouds were 'ragged edged', London's streets were 'cruel, crowded and callous'. Mrs Harleigh was not 'lovable-looking'; a bad-tempered old lady's expression was one of 'black frostiness,' Miss Walker in *Cedar Star* had 'gooseberry eyes and Betty had 'aggressive hair.' *Our Mary's* wrists were 'beef-red.' Charlotte Poole describes her writings as 'scribblements'. Mrs Whitley was Perdita's 'more than mother.' Lally Burne's wedding dress had a 'tinny satin train'. Satin used to be treated with oxide of tin to make it rustle like better quality silk, so the phrase perfectly encapsulates the Burnes' love of cheap showiness.

Just occasionally, MEM's language echoes a bygone age – 'a down-pin' or a 'mum-chance' was a miserable person, people were 'crowded home' (accompanied), 'told off' (told, not remonstrated with), 'as fast as you like' meant willingly, to 'span into' was to kick, 'poking' was to hide away, to 'apostrophise' was to name, to 'dish' was to destroy, a fuss was 'a piece of work' and so on. 'Gays' was the Norfolk term for coloured illustrations in a book or magazine. 'To play tame cat' was to live with someone and sponge off them. You could weep or grumble 'a good few'; 'cold shoulder' and 'cumber' could be used as verbs. She uses quite a lot of young people's slang; a girl could be a 'oner' or an 'out-and-outer', she might be 'not quite one's cut', or someone who didn't 'gee' with a particular young man. People could be 'gone' about each other, or reject a partner because they had no 'go' in them, but for the most part the meaning of such unfamiliar words and phrases is clear from the context – and there are remarkably few of them.

This means that MEM's writings are still very accessible to the 21st century reader, though they are now very much period pieces, undemanding but seldom what she would have called 'trumpery'. They remind us of a time when a girl's reputation was all-important, when the poor 'made their obediences' to 'the quality' on pain of losing their jobs, and when members of the upper classes devoted time and effort to finding out about every stranger they encountered because 'breeding' and 'connections' were considered to be of more importance than observed behaviour. MEM was personally devout but aware that her church failed in its duty towards many of its followers through arrogance, idleness and ignorance. It was a stance which shocked many of her readers, but there are still Cyprian Everys and Anna Pearsons among us, and even today her work would probably make disconcerting reading for some clergy and their congregations.

MEM tried to make her readers think and question their values, she wanted them to recognise cruelty and injustice and to try to understand those less fortunate than themselves.

But she was illogical. She longed for a golden age that, in her heart of hearts, she knew had never existed. 'Those were peaceful days of leisure,' Charlotte Poole muses in *Astray in Arcady*, 'in which the good farmer and his helpful wife made their comfortable living, and passed their days of alternate labour and ease. Then no injurious amount of game was raised to ruin crops and to make ill blood with landlord and neighbour ... For the manufacture of beer, barley was a necessity; the baker depended on English-grown wheat; the butcher on English beef and mutton. Produce was sold at a reasonable profit.' She carefully ignores the fact that the protective legislation that used to prevent foreign imports coming in to lower prices for the farmer also meant that the price of bread in a bad year could rise to a point where the labourers starved because they could not afford to buy it.

MEM even became dubious about the value of educating the children of the poor. 'What is it good for?' she has Mrs Chisholm ask. 'What is it they learn in school that stands by them and is of use to the world they live in? The village school used to cost the parish a hundred a year, and now it costs two hundred. What is the better of it? The children learn like parrots, and know no practical use to put their knowledge to.' Her conclusion – and MEM's – was that they learnt 'to hate the class above them. That is what the labouring class has learnt, so far, from our improved educational system.'

MEM also criticised the old age pension through the voice of old Joe Stark. When it was introduced in 1908, the pension was means-tested and only awarded to people who had no savings and no other income. 'Folks was allust liars, but t'rough theer a-settin' their hearts on th' five shillun a week, blowed if ain't fit to lie theirselves into hell,' Joe tells Charlotte Poole. 'This here pension is a-goin' to be the ruin o' th' banks ... Them as ha' made shift ter save 'll hide th' matter. 'Taint ter be looked for they'll hamper themselves wi' bank-books ter tell th' tale.' Over a century later, few of us have any doubts about the value of universal education, or that the welfare state should provide for the old (and to be fair to MEM, by the time she wrote *Things I Can Remember* she recognised that the old age pension was a boon to the poor) but it is interesting to see what people thought about these benefits when they were new and untested.

So politically, MEM remains an enigma. She knew better than most how difficult life was for the poor but she nonetheless

188

disapproved of them agitating for better wages. She was dubious about the state intervening to give children a basic education and to alleviate grinding poverty in old age. While she recognised that 'You may find a George Eliot amongst the farming class, a Robbie Burns in his peasant dress may sing as he follows the plough', she could not bring herself to trust labouring men, even men of ability like Joseph Arch, to make political decisions that would benefit their class. She despised the women's movement while admiring and writing about strong, capable women. 'I am perfectly certain women are capable of voting,' she told Tom in 1907, 'but I don't care tuppence whether they get the vote or not,' and she threw the petition she had been sent into the waste paper basket. In another letter she was surprised to find that one of her stories – the letter does not identify it and is undated – was taken up by a group of 'females in Norwich who have nothing better to do' as evidence of her support for 'the great work.' She affected to have no idea what they were talking about. MEM was intelligent and perceptive and com-passionate, but she was also Mrs Fairman Mann of Manor Farm, daughter of William Simon Rackham of Town Close House; there were issues she simply could not allow herself to contemplate.

MEM's attitudes may be dated, but her descriptions are today valuable in ways she could not have imagined when she wrote them. For the social historian she provides an authentic picture of rural Norfolk in the agricultural depression of the 1880s and 1890s, and a nuanced portrait of the overwhelming importance of class distinctions in the period before the Great War. In her later works she shows us a country that was changing rapidly in ways that were often un-comfortable for its older inhabitants. She captures the Norfolk dialect for a world in which regional dialects are almost extinct. And for the general reader, her books are still – as they always were – 'a good read'.

Chapter 9. Tout passe 1919-1929

MEM did not make life easy for herself. At some time in 1919 she and her daughters moved again – with all their accumulated papers, belongings and furniture – to another house in Sheringham, Greenlands, on Nelson Road perched high on the cliff top. This time they bought the house rather than renting. Rack's last war letter is dated April 19th 1919, but soon after that he left the navy and came home to live with his mother and sisters and he may well have helped them to buy it. Maybe he had insisted they find somewhere bigger so that family and friends could come to stay, but it does appear to have been an extraordinarily large, grand, uncomfortable house for four people, none of whom were young. MEM was seventy-one by this time,

Greenlands, the Manns' house in Sheringham
They lived there from 1919 to 1929

Rack forty-seven, Bertie forty-five and Margery forty-three. The views from the house must have been stunning but it was cold and draughty, quite a long walk into town and a long steady climb back. Greenlands is large and has brickwork decorated with a distinctive pattern of flints – it may have been new when they moved in. Nelson Road is full of stylish, individual houses, most dating from the early 20th century. As far as Margery was concerned there was a distinct advantage – she had a big garden and she could keep goats on the cliffs nearby.

But despite the size of the house, MEM was no longer very keen on having visitors. She was still in contact with Tom Ordish, but she had almost given up writing so he was no longer managing publication matters for her. He had retired from the Patents Office and his health was failing. In August 1923, after decades of refusing her invitations, he suggested visiting. It was obviously many years since they had seen each other. 'I am quite well,' she replied, 'but old age is rather a tragic business, even when one tries, as I do, to make the best of it … I won't plague you with a list of my disabilities. We shall have many things to talk of when I see you but you must speak very distinctly or I shall only <u>pretend</u> to hear you. About your coming, I would say with all my heart "come here" but for your comfort I believe it would be better for you to have a bedroom elsewhere and take your meals with us.' She goes on to tell him that their one spare bedroom is up three flights of stairs and draughty. This is difficult to believe; perhaps it was an excuse or perhaps only part of the house was furnished.

'Rack is still with us and has become quite a skilled landscape painter….' MEM went on. During the war Rack had bought some paints and an easel and taken up painting in an attempt to relieve the boredom of life on board. Art seems to have run in the family – MEM's brother Harry could draw and her nephew Simon was an accomplished artist. 'Bertie still does pictures for Caley's Cracker Boxes,' she continued, 'and Margery passes her time between preparing our meals and the cliff where her goats are tethered. My widowed grand-daughter is with us now.' (Mary Dorothea had married Donald Hedges in 1922.) 'She was only married for 4 months. It is so sad to see her in her widow's dress – she was such a happy, darling child…she has no money and is trying to find something to do. She is extremely beautiful and he was such a dear man…' But none of these inducements was enough; Tom's visit did not take place and he died the following year.

One of Bertie's drawings for Caley

Another letter she sent him is full of nostalgia. 'It is 10 years since we left Shropham. It will always be home to me. All of us were too old to up-root and I don't think we take kindly to an alien soil. Often I try to picture myself in the dear family rooms, sitting to tea

191

in the garden, turning in the lodge gates, driving up to the door, Taylor running to the horses..... Rack is staying with some friends in Scotland. Bertie is very busy – she has a lot of illustrating to do now besides the cracker pictures which she has done for many years. Margery is a sort of household drudge, poor thing, as we have only one servant and the house is large, but she is as willing and unselfish as ever. I am the only idle one...I have tried to get "The Fields of Dulditch" republished without success. They tell, faithfully, of a countryside absolutely altered and I had thought therefore that they should have a sort of value now. But it appears not... I hate the winter here. It is so cold...What do you do? I read a great deal...' She had almost given up writing, but that year, she told Tom, she had a story published in *Storyteller* for which she received twelve guineas.

Apart from the sorrow of Tom's death, 1924 was a good year and MEM was to have two marriages to celebrate; her younger granddaughter, Leslie, married Guy Vallance, and at the ripe old age of fifty-two Rack had finally found himself a wife. His bride was Hilda Gould, who was the daughter of a Norwich chartered accountant and had been a nurse in London. Her family had some doubts about the marriage – Rack's 'wicked uncles' were still remembered in Norwich – and Hilda had to persuade her father that her husband-to-be did not take after them in any way. We do not know how the couple met, but amongst the hundred-plus wedding presents that the *Eastern Daily Press* claimed they were given was one from Saxlingham W.I. of which Hilda had 'recently been president'. This would suggest she had lived in or near Saxlingham before her marriage – and Saxlingham is not far from Sheringham. They were married on April 10th at St Mary's Baptist Chapel in Norwich, from her parents' home in Ipswich Road, within walking distance of Town Close House where MEM had lived as a girl.

At thirty-seven Hilda was a comparatively elderly bride and her dress was suitably subdued – an outfit of grey embroidered georgette tulle trimmed with blue with which she carried a sheaf of pale pink roses. There was something of a hiccup because the best man, Captain Gibson, presumably a naval friend of Rack's, didn't turn up, but the ceremony went ahead without him. They sang *The King of Love my Shepherd is* and *O Perfect Love All Human Thoughts Transcending;* Hilda entered the church to the bridal march from *Lohengrin* and the couple left to Mendelssohn's *Wedding March*. Her going-away dress consisted of a coat-frock of navy blue repp, a matching hat, a navy blue coat trimmed with grey chenille, and sable furs. MEM must have been overjoyed and Rack had made an excellent choice. Hilda was very caring, reliable and loving, a great help to MEM in her final years and later to Margery and Bertie too. She was also quite wealthy.

Rack and Hilda moved to Tasburgh, then a small village, which lies about eight miles south of Norwich. They lived at Tasburgh House, a big, rather ugly building built in 1913 in the 'arts and crafts' style, and set in extensive grounds. They had a car and a chauffeur, and they both drove, so it was comparatively easy for them to visit MEM in Sheringham or to take her back to stay with them. Rack retired from the navy at the end of the war. He did not need to get a job and lived the life of a gentleman, devoting much of his time to painting and archaeology. In the 1930s he helped excavate the Roman fort at Caistor and then took responsibility for excavating the site of a Saxon burial ground nearby – in those days many archaeologists were enthusiastic amateurs and it was a much less scientific pursuit than it is

today. He also mended the pots he found with plaster of Paris, and stored the finds from the dig at his home until they were taken by the Castle Museum in Norwich.

Rack and his daughter, Diana, 1925

We do not know whether MEM attended Leslie's wedding in Wilsford in November – the journey to Wiltshire was not getting any easier and MEM was seventy-seven. Guy Vallance was a pilot officer in the RAF and the couple were to live at Risalpur, which is now in Pakistan, not far from Peshawar. Once out there they had a baby boy, Martin, MEM's first great-grandchild. Some of Leslie's letters survive. One thanks MEM for her Christmas presents: 'For thirty years, Gran's present has been <u>the</u> thing at Christmas' and in the same letter it becomes clear that her husband was estranged from his parents 'They don't even write to Guy at Christmas.' Later letters described how wilful little Martin was 'Thank goodness he likes wearing his topee, otherwise I don't know how we would get him to wear it' wrote Leslie, and she sent pictures of the little boy with a donkey.

Leslie Vallance with her son, Martin, MEM's great grandson

There were two more important family events in 1925. Rack and Hilda had a baby – a little girl whom they called Diana, MEM's third granddaughter. And her eldest grand-child, Mary Dorothea, the young widow, remarried. Her husband was Gerald Grantley Moore. Gerald was a divorcé so they could not be married in church and it is not clear whether Charles Hewitt even attended the wedding – he was certainly not one of the witnesses. It took place in Marylebone Registry Office and Mary gave her address as the Quebec Hotel, Bayswater Street. Gerald described himself as an 'advertising agent,' a new and slightly suspect profession. Mary was a beauty but she seems to have inherited some of her mother's instability – in any event she was not good at choosing husbands. The marriage lasted barely two years before she divorced Gerald for adultery.

For the last fifteen months of her life MEM kept a diary. It starts on February 2nd 1928 and the last entry comes a few days before her death in May 1929. The entries are very brief, but it is possible to see the pattern of her days and who her friends were at that stage in her life, and it is probable that she had spent the previous few years in much the same way. Although she was eighty that year she was obviously still very able, both mentally and physically, apart from her deafness. She was still fit enough to walk the considerable distance downhill into town, and uphill back, most days and to go along the muddy path across the fields to the church on the windswept headland most Sundays. But, wherever she went, she always had either Bertie or Margery, or someone else, to accompany her.

She had a close circle of friends and neighbours on whom she called almost every day, or who called on her – and they all lived nearby. Mrs Derry, her closest friend, lived almost next door. Janet, who also lived on Nelson Road, was Hilda's elder sister and she seems to have suffered from some form of mental illness or learning disability. For much of the time she had a nurse 'Sister Ling' who may have been a distant relation of MEM's – her grandmother was Maria Ling before she married. MEM wasn't just sitting at home doing nothing, but her horizons had narrowed.

She often included quotes in the diary – sayings that echoed her own thoughts no doubt. In fact the very first entry in the diary is 'Tout lasse, tout casse, tout passe.' (Everything passes, nothing lasts forever). But her frame of mind is most clearly shown in the quotation she wrote on the inside of the back cover: 'That sorrowful curse of the human race is the flight of time, of beauty, of faculties.'

Much of the diary is quoted here, though not every single entry, as it is the closest thing we have to her voice in her final years.

MEM's Diary 1928-9

February

6th   *Note attached to a suit in a Parisian's Tailor's window. 'Quite English. Very snob.'*

9th   *B and I called on George and the Keppels.*

13th   *Pouring rain. I shopped with Margery. Valentines from Margery and Bertie. Mrs Denny stayed to tea.*

14th   *A valentine from John Aspergh. And one from David Denny. A fine day. Town with Margery. Janet brought me flowers.*

David was Mrs Denny's schoolboy son which means Mrs Denny must have been considerably younger than MEM.

The giving of valentines and Valentine's Day presents to friends and family now strikes us as rather curious, but it is only in comparatively recent years that valentines have become the preserve of lovers. In MEM's childhood, presents were the norm. In a letter home from school in 1870 her brothers told her they had saved up to buy valentines for their parents but were worried about what they should give seven-year old Eddie. A few years later Mrs Rackham told her daughter that her friend, Mrs Clabburn, had been given a new brougham as a Valentine's Day gift.

15th   *Letters from Dolly. Wrote to her. Mussel called. Nurse Ling called to tell about Janet. Not so well.*

'Mussel' or 'Mussels' was probably a retired servant. MEM's mother had had a servant of that name when she lived in Attleborough

6th   *Called on Mrs Denny. Dr Edwards came. David ill. Called on Janet. She out.*

17th   *Janet and sister called. Mrs Denny called. Miss Calder, Miss Bateman, Miss Jackson to tea. Letter from Hilda.*

18th	*To tea with Mrs Denny. Letter from John Aspergh.*
19th	*Marg and I went to church. Janet and sister home with us. Quite a spring day*
20th	*Rack, Hilda, Diana and chauffeur to lunch and tea. Janet and Sister Ling all afternoon. Diana quite a darling. All well. R has 5 teeth out on Saturday*
22nd	*Ash Wednesday. Paid conservative 1/- Heard from Mary about Lord Victor Paget and his new post. Wrote to her and Dolly. Mrs Denny's little dog Renee died. Called to enquire about Mrs Gentry.*

Lord Victor Paget was the heir to the Marquis of Anglesey. He became something of a celebrity by marrying an American Gaiety Girl, Olive Mary Meatyard, in 1912. She subsequently divorced him, and he made a much more suitable marriage, to Bridget Colebrooke, in 1922. In 1928 he was awarded the Grand Cross of the (Royal) Victorian Order which is probably what MEM is referring to here.

23rd	*Called to see Janet.*
25th	*Mussel came. Mrs Denny came. A lovely spring day.*
26th	*B & I to church. Janet and 'sister' came.*
27th	*Began spring cleaning. Mrs Denny came.*
28th	*Heard from Mary. A quite happy letter.*

By this point Mary's second marriage had ended in divorce which must have been quite shocking for MEM. She had had to accept the fact that Hugh might divorce Nina to marry Bertie, and that Mary's second husband was a divorcé – but at a time when few couples separated and she herself did not approve of the break-up of marriages, to have three divorces come so close to her own family must have been quite upsetting.

March

1st	*'All men are alike and no man is old until he is dead.' Arnold Bennett.*
2nd	*Letter from Dolly. C.C. elections. Voted for Lady Suffield. Mrs Denny came.*

The Qualification for Women (County and Borough Councils) Act of 1907 had enabled women who were ratepayers to become County and Borough Councillors, following on from the Act of 1894 that had allowed them to serve as Rural and Urban District Councillors. The

Dowager Lady Suffield was the first woman to be elected to Norfolk County Council, in 1920. She represented Cromer. By 1928 there were three women County Councillors out of a total of fifty-five.

3rd	*Sat in garden. David came in afternoon. Mrs Denny out.*
4th	*Marg and I to church. Lovely spring day. Bertie sat all afternoon in garden to read. M & I went for a walk on the cliffs after tea.*
5th	*Getting dining room cleaned for distempering tomorrow. Janet and 'sister' brought hyacinths. They are leaving for Hindhead tomorrow.*
6th	*Heaven may lie about us in infancy – it is no reason why we should lie about it in old age.*
7th	*To town with B. After tea called on Mrs Denny & Mussels – she with alarming numbness of arm. Heard from Mrs Carling about Lord Carson.*

Edward Carson (1854-1935) was an Irish barrister, judge and Ulster Unionist politician, and was the barrister who acted for the Marquis of Queensberry when Oscar Wilde brought an ill-advised libel suit against him. His cross-examination destroyed Wilde and led to his eventual imprisonment. Carson was Solicitor General for England 1900-5 and thereafter a member of the Privy Council. He became the prime mover in Ulster's anti-Home Rule campaign and vigorously opposed the partition of Ireland. He retired in 1929. It is not clear what Mrs Carling had to say about him.

8th	*Letter from Rack. Read Life of Horace Walpole of Aymer de Valance 'who threatened with ejection from the Abbey might find a resting place at Strawberry Hill.' Apparently his monuments are in bad taste!*

Aymer de Valence, was the second Earl of Pembroke c. 1275 – 23 June 1324. Presumably he was a distant ancestor of her grandson-in-law, Leslie's husband, whose full name was Roper Guy Aymer Vallance.

11th	*B & I to church thro' snow, blizzard and gale.*
12th	*Spring cleaning my bedroom. Called on Mussels. Mrs Denny called while I was out. Wrote to Mary.*

13th	*Marg and I to Trevor's shop to see carpet for drawing room. Mrs Denny came.*
14th	*B & I to Trevor's. Bought drawing room carpet. Finished cleaning my room.*
16th	*Went to Wrightly Whights to see cinema. Letter from Mrs Louise Wright about my books. Lob asked in marriage.* [Lob was their dog!]
17th	*Arrival of Lob's fiancé. A fiasco. Alas. Wedding postponed. Sine die?*

In spite of everything she could still be witty. And it sounds as if she was still receiving the occasional fan letter, even though most of her books were out of print and she hadn't published anything new for a decade.

19th	*Anniversary of my dear father's death.*
20th	*A present of 'Fair Buttons' from my cousin Jessie.*

Norfolk 'fair buttons' are biscuits, local to Norfolk. They are made of a pastry of white flour, brown sugar, ginger, lard, baking soda and golden syrup, rolled and cut into two inch rounds

21st	*Janet and 'nurse' came home from Hindhead. Janet depressed. Walked town with B. The nurse leaves today. Salvation Army man called - 5/-*
22nd	*Retired to bed with sickness. Better at noon. Janet came. Hall cleaned – Bertie's room ditto. Letter from Hilda. Heard from Simon.*

Simon was her nephew, her brother Frank's son, and would have been forty-three. He was a clever young man and a talented artist, but he had a withered arm which meant he never fulfilled his potential. He became a bank clerk. He and Bertie were good friends and wrote to each other frequently.

24th	*Town with B. Walked home with Janet. Miss Calder in afternoon. Wrote to Frank*
25th	*Tea with Mrs Denny and David. He and I called on Janet. Jamie [could be Janie] there for 3 weeks. David came home with me.*
26th	*Fairman's birthday. Kitchen chimney swept.*

It is possibly significant that she refers earlier to her father as 'my dear father' but adds no such endearments for Fairman.

28th   Mr Fitch called. Heard from Dolly.

Dolly's husband, Charles Hewitt, had been ordained in 1900. He left Marlborough College in 1920 and became vicar of St Mary's in Wilsford, a tiny village, little more than a hamlet, about nine winding country miles south of Marlborough. For Dolly it was a disaster. While Charles was teaching at the college they had lived at Preshute, a pretty little place on the edge of town and a short walk from the centre. There she and the girls would have had a social life – many of the other masters would have had wives and families, and Marlborough was a prosperous town with well-to-do inhabitants. Wilsford is picturesque but isolated, set in the middle of a heath, and too far from town for a family without a car to visit very often. For someone suffering from depression – as Dolly obviously was – it was to be the last straw.

29th   Bertie and Marg to cinema. John Barrymore in Don Juan.

John Barrymore was a film idol of the 1920s.

30th   Marg and I to town after tea. Letter from Frank.
31st   B & I to town. Called on Mrs Denny about Derby Sweep ticket.
*   April*
3rd   Jessie sent 'rock' from Norwich Fair. Mrs Astley-Cooper came.
*   David came.*
4th   Heard from Leslie – now at Wilsford. Quite a miserable letter.
*   Heard from A P Watt*

Leslie seems to have been home from India and staying with her parents in Wilsford. She and Guy and Martin may have been home on furlough, but we know that Leslie's marriage was not happy and it sounds as if she is alone.

That MEM had heard from Watt is significant for it shows that she was still in contact with the publishing world. Founded in 1875, A.P. Watt is the longest-established literary agency in the world. 'Mr Watt' had been MEM's agent for many years. It may be that she was trying to get some of her books republished – she had earlier told Tom that she felt *Fields of Dulditch* had historical value because the world of the farm labourer had changed so dramatically in the post-war period. Or perhaps she had written something new. Either way, she was unsuccessful. A few years earlier, in 1924, Fisher Unwin had turned down a book she had sent them. 'It is possible that if you could give me one of your good strong novels, as you gave us to publish in the past, that we could have taken it up ...' he told her. The book they rejected may have been *Mattie, a Portrait.* Of MEM's unpublished works, this is the most assured and the style is the closest to that of her later work. The subject, however, would probably not have appealed to, or even been understood by a 1920s audience. The world had become much more egalitarian since MEM's solicitor brother, and her hero, Randal Saddlebow, shocked their families by marrying shop girls.

5th   *Janet brought lovely violets. Took B's scenario to be typed. Called on Janet.*

She was obviously still supporting Bertie's attempts to write.

6th   *Good Friday. Too late for church. Service 10 instead of 11. David brought me a present! Col and Mrs Coppin called. Tried to garden.*
7th   *Mary's birthday. Called on Mrs Astley-Cooper. They gave me a bag.*
8th   *Easter Sunday. Stayed to communion. Mrs Denny gave me a handkerchief sachet.*
9th   *Mrs Denny and Mrs Astley-Cooper came to tea.*
10th   *Marg and I shopping. I bought a black Jaeger coat.*
11th   *Heard from Rack and Hilda. Hilda coming Friday for the day. Janet called. Heard from Mrs Baillie Reynolds.*
12th   *Called at Natalie to see the Russell Goulds. To tea with Mrs Denny. Col. And Mrs Coppin came after   tea to see Bertie's pictures.*

Russell Gould was Hilda's younger brother and was an accountant, like his father.

13th   *Hilda and baby with Nanny and chauffer to tea. I had an upset with Janet (rather sad) in the morning.*
14th   *Heard from Simon.*
15th   *Marg and I to church. Bitterly cold. Went to see Mussels. Home to find Janet. Janet and I reconciled I hope.*
16th   *Heard from Hilda and Leslie. Town with Margery. After tea went to Astley Coopers. Mrs Denny and David there*

17th	Ticket from Simon. 343238. Simon, Marg, and Bertie a quarter between them. Mrs D paid 15/- I paid 5/-. Mrs Denny to have ticket.
18th	B and I to town. Mussels came for me to witness her signature. Bitterly cold.
19th	Wore a Primrose dress for Disraeli. [April 19th was Disraeli's birthday]

It would seem that MEM was a member, or at least a sympathiser, of the Primrose League. It was a Conservative, religious and Imperialist organisation, founded in 1883 by admirers of Benjamin Disraeli, and used his favourite flower, the primrose as its emblem. It was active until the mid 1990s. Members had to swear an oath on joining:

> 'I declare on my honour and faith that I will devote my best ability to the maintenance of religion, of the estates of the realm, and of the imperial ascendancy of the British Empire; and that, consistently with my allegiance to the sovereign of these realms, I will promote with discretion and fidelity the above objects, being those of the Primrose League.'

20th	Plus ca change, plus c'est la meme chose.
22nd	B & I to church. I called on Janet in the afternoon. She out. Called on Mrs Astley Cooper. Mrs Denny came to tea.
23rd	To town with Margie in the afternoon. Packed in the morning. Saw Janet. Very cold to me. Does not think she will have time to call to see Hilda who comes tomorrow.
24th	Hilda came to lunch. Drove me to Tasburgh in time for tea.
25th	Motored to Norwich to see about drawing room carpet etc.
26th	… Heard from Bertie and Mary.
27th	Shopped in Norwich in Woolworths. Went to Costessey to see Russell Goulds.

The Norwich branch of Woolworths had opened since they left Shropham and this may have been her first visit. F.W. Woolworth & Co. originated in Pennsylvania. The first British branch was founded by Frank Woolworth in Liverpool; he was an Anglophile who claimed to have traced his ancestry back through the Founding Fathers to a small farm in Woolley, Cambridgeshire. When he first came to England in 1890 it was to go to Stoke-on-Trent to buy china and glassware for his shops, but in his diary he also noted his love of the

201

country and his aspiration to bring the Woolworth name to England, 'I believe that a good penny and sixpence store, run by a live Yankee, would be a sensation here.' The first store opened in 1903 with fireworks, a full orchestra, circus acts and so on and sold out on the first day of trading. By 1923 there were 130 stores country-wide. Woolworths finally closed in 2009 with a loss of 27,000 jobs.

28th   *Motored to Norwich. Went to St Andrew's Hall (W.I.) and had tea with them. Perfectly lovely weather all week.*

29th   *Church at Tasburgh with Rack and Hilda. Diana <u>naughty</u> to her guests.*

30th   *Hilda drove me home.*

MEM and Diana in 1928

The Women's Institute was founded in 1915 with two clear aims, to revitalize the lives of women in rural communities and to encourage women to become more involved in food production during the war. The WIs were a boon to rural women, an opportunity to socialise and learn new skills, and for the social classes to come together. MEM could probably see how it would enhance women's lives in villages like her beloved Shropham, though she might have found it rather too democratic for her taste. Hilda had been president of her local Women's Institute (the president at that date was usually someone with some social standing in the community) before her marriage and it looks as if she was still involved with the organisation.

May

1st   *To town with Margery. Bister painted front door. Goat had three kids ... wish them born dead to save Marg the trouble. A rather miserable letter from Leslie.*

2nd   *To town with Bertie to say goodbye to Mrs Astley Cooper. Called on Mrs Denny. David howling with toothache his school begins tomorrow.*

3rd   *Called on Miss Jeffries to see her flowers. She out. Wrote to Leslie. Paid Rack's insurance £4 17s. 11d. David came.*

4th	*Heard from Dolly. A very sad letter. Wrote to her and Edith. Called on Janet. She not so well. East wind but sunshine.*
5th	*Heard from Winnie.*
6th	*Lovely day. National Anthem in church and the vicar spoke of the King in his sermon. David came in the afternoon. I went to see Janet. Mrs Denny after tea.*
7th	*Clearing drawing room. Present of apples and asparagus etc from Mrs Denny. She came after tea.*
8th	*Heard from Leslie. Not happy. Talks of going back to India in October. Janet came.*

This sounds as if Leslie had left Guy for a spell but was planning to go back to him. We know the marriage was unhappy, but the couple did not divorce until 1933, very shortly after the birth of their second child, a daughter, Gabrielle Leslie. Fortunately MEM did not live to see the divorce of a second granddaughter.

9th	*Bitterly cold. Tearing East wind.*
10th	*Mrs Gentry called for Diocesan 5/-. Janet came to say she had found a servant to replace Mildred. Bitterly cold.*
12th	*Heard the sad news of Dolly's illness.*

Dolly had overdosed on the sulphonal which she had been taking for years for her insomnia and was desperately ill.

13th	*Did not go to church. Waiting for news of Dolly.*
14th	*Heard Dolly died yesterday. May 13th. My Mother's death May 14th. Mrs Denny came.*
17th	*Poor Dolly buried today.*

The inquest into her death must have been arranged very swiftly as she was buried just three days after she died. The coroner recorded that Dolly died of 'an accidental overdose' but it seems unlikely that it was really an accident – certainly her descendants believe that it was suicide. Until 1961, committing suicide was a crime, and the Catholic church and some extreme evangelicals considered it a sin. In earlier times suicides, like criminals, were not buried in consecrated ground; even in the 1920s attitudes were ambivalent and the funerals of suicides often took place after dark. To spare the feelings of the bereaved, doctors usually therefore recorded suicides like Dolly's as 'accidental' or as taking place 'when the balance of the mind was disturbed'. However, it looks as if Dolly knew what she was doing –

she waited until everyone was out and the house was empty. Charles was at an archdiaconal visitation and he later told MEM that he would never be able to face going to such a meeting ever again. He had idolised Dolly and her death broke his heart. 'Of course, she never ought to have married me;' he wrote, 'she ought to have married someone younger and brighter and on whom life's responsibilities weighed less heavily.'

Charles buried his wife in the graveyard of his church, but MEM did not travel down for the funeral – she was an old lady and the family probably thought it would be too much for her.

It is difficult to know exactly why Dolly felt desperate enough to kill herself. The feeling of being trapped, together with a sense of worthlessness is frequently given as a reason for suicide – and Dolly must have felt trapped, or at least marooned, in Wilsford. She was, or had been, a beautiful woman who enjoyed socialising – not ideal qualities for a country vicar's wife. Charles was a serious man and probably rather dull, and there had been earlier difficulties in the relationship. In a letter to MEM he once described the 'torture' of being taken to see a Charlie Chaplin film at the cinema. He hated slapstick humour and couldn't understand why others enjoyed it – which gives an impression of a rather humourless individual. Their children had grown up, married, and left home, but Mary's second marriage had just ended in divorce and Leslie's relationship was unhappy. Dolly may have felt that she had failed both as a mother and as a wife.

Then there was the drug that she was taking, against which Rack had advised so strongly many years before. It was dangerous and cases of sulphonal poisoning were not uncommon. Its action is uncertain, often failing to produce sleep when taken at bedtime but making the patient drowsy the following day, and it was unwise to use it continuously for more than a few days at a time. Dolly had been taking it for years. It disturbs the digestion, causes giddiness and a staggering gait and may even paralyse the legs and feet – the Hewitt's maid said that the sulphonal had affected both Dolly's speech and her ability to walk, and that latterly she had 'only lived for the drug'.

After the funeral, Charles came up to Norfolk to see MEM and he spent some time in Tasburgh with Rack and Hilda.

19th   *Letters from everyone. Janet came. Rack and Charles gone to Tasburgh.*

204

20th	Ascension day. Margery to church with me. 'Never has anyone been less a priest than Jesus, never a greater enemy of Forms which stifle religion under the pretext of protecting it.' Renan

Renan's book was very controversial because he asserted that the life of Jesus should be written like the life of any historic person, and that the Bible could, and should, be subject to the same critical scrutiny as other historical documents. It enraged many Christians, but this quotation is an echo of the thoughts MEM had expressed in her story *An Open Air Service*.

23rd	Charles came for the day from Tasburgh.

The rest of the month is blank – understandably so – but it is obvious that Rack and Hilda and MEM's many friends and neighbours were rallying round and supporting her at this desperately sad time.

June

1st	Hilda, Rack and Charles came.
2nd	Hilda drove me to see Rhododendrons in flower.
3rd	Charles went to church with me. Trinity Sunday.
5th	Margery went with me to hear the RSPCA Lecture. Janet came. Very depressed.
7th	Mr and Mrs Denny came to tea.
8th	Charles left. Very sad. Hilda away yesterday and tomorrow.
9th	Simon and Mrs Hugh Bell came after supper.
10th	Hilda came to church with me. Simon came after supper. Wet, cold and windy.
12th	A plague of snails in the garden. Comme il est habite, ce petit escargot? Qui porte le maison sur son dot.
14th	Bitterly cold. Rain & wind. Hilda's birthday. Simon and Mr Bell in evening.
15th	Rack and Hilda left. Nannie and baby here until Tuesday. Mrs Denny came. Simon and Mr Bell in evening.

This is another indication that MEM and her daughters no longer felt able, or wished, to entertain visitors. Whatever the reason, when Rack and Hilda, or Diana and her nanny stayed in Sheringham they went to a hotel, and it seems that cousin Simon was also staying somewhere other than MEM's house.

16th	Simon and Mr Bell came to say goodbye. Wet all week with exception of one day.
17th	Marg to church with me. A Strange parson. I hope we never have him again. Still have fire in drawing room. Very cold.
18th	Baby's birthday. 2 years old. Came in morning for her presents. Called on Mrs Denny.
19th	Hilda came to lunch. Took baby home in afternoon.
20th	'They told me Heraclitus much worse you were dead.'

Heraclitus of Ephesus c.535 BC - 475 BC was a Greek philosopher famous for his insistence on ever-present change in the universe, as in the famous saying, 'No man ever steps in the same river twice'. This illustrates just how widely read MEM was.

24th	B to church with me. Janet came to make friends again. David came. A lovely day. Brought flowers.
25th	Miss Calder came. Tea in garden for the first time this year.
26th	Marg & I in town. Drenched to the skin in tremendous rain all day.
27th	Gale all night & today. Leslie sent photo of herself and son. Called on Miss Calder.
28th	Had tooth stopped. Marg went with me. Called to see Janet. She in bed for the day.
29th	Evelyn Moore came to tea.
30th	B & M went to see 'Dawn' at the cinema. Evelyn Moore went with them.

Dawn, made in 1928, was a silent war film directed by Herbert Wilcox and starring Sybil Thorndike, Gordon Craig and Marie Ault. Based on a play by Reginald Berkeley, it told the story of World War I martyr, Edith Cavell. Sybil Thorndike starred as Cavell, a nurse who risked her own life by rescuing British prisoners of war from the Germans. When Edith Cavell was captured and sentenced to be executed it sparked international outrage, even from neutral nations. One of the most controversial British films of the 1920s, *Dawn* was heavily censored because of its brutal depiction of warfare and its anti-German sentiments.

July1st	Margery to church with me. Mr Jackson preached. High wind.
2nd	Had another tooth stopped. Mrs Denny called – sent her strawberries in return for her roses. Wind still high.

4th	With Strawberries to Miss Calder. Margery went with me to tea to Miss Moore.
5th	Helen came for the day bringing Tony and Vivienne _unexpectedly_ V. wet and windy.

We do not know who these people were – but it does look as if unexpected visitors now made MEM uncomfortable.

7th	Took Mrs Denny peas and lettuces. A miserable letter from Mary.
8th	B to church with me.
10th	Bertie and I to see water lilies at Nirvana (the Denny's house). Heard from Rack also from Richard Pryce. £1.. 6..0 from Little Mrs Cummin.

She was still getting some royalties and it sounds as if her play was being performed again.

12th	Margery and I shopped in evening. Very hot. Mrs Denny came. Went to see Mussel.
13th	Heard from Charles and Leslie about the money to be allowed to girls. Sat on sea wall in evening. V hot.
14th	Marg and I shopped in evening. Mornings too hot. Janet came. Sat on sea wall. 80 in the shade. Drought.
15th	Too hot to go to church. Sat on sea wall in morning and evening. (in child's hand) David came morning and evening.
16th	Sudden high north wind. V cool.
17th	Wrote to Mary about money. Sent Priest 7s-6d.
18th	Too hot for town. Day show at Mrs Alderman's. B & I went. Called on Mussels. Janet called.
19th	garden perishing for want of rain.
20th	Lovely day. Went for a picnic tea with Miss Moore. She stayed to paint. Heard from Mary. Better news.
21st	Hilda sent photos of Mrs Priest's school.
22nd	Church with Marg. V hot. Ellen Terry dead yesterday.

Ellen Terry was a famous actress. She never went to school but started acting when she was just eight years old. She was born in 1848 so she was the same age as MEM. She was also an avid supporter of the suffragettes and, perhaps more significantly, of women playwrights.

It also looks as if MEM was still in touch with someone connected with Mrs Priest's school. Mrs Priest herself had died in 1881, and the school, under Miss Paraman, had moved house at least twice and by 1928 must have been under new management if it existed at all.

23rd   Shopped in evening. Sat on sea wall. Very warm. Called on Mussels.
25th   Took Bertie's pictures to Pedlars Pack. Charles sent design of window.

'Pedlar's Pack' was a gift shop.

To the beloved memory of Dorothy wife of the Revd Charles Hewitt M.A. Vicar of this Parish, who fell asleep in Jesus 15th May 1928.

Memorial window to Dolly Hewitt in Wilsford Church

'Pedlar's Pack' was a gift shop.

Poor Charles was attempting to assuage some of his grief and guilt over losing his precious 'Doll' by having a window designed in her memory to be installed in his church at Wilsford.

28th   Margery and I called on Mrs Gentry. I called on Mussels. Bought Doll's House for Diana.
29th   To church with Bertie. Wrote to Hilda and Leslie.
30th   Letter from Frank. Madge ill again.
31st   Cold and windy.

Madge was her niece, Frank's second daughter, Margaret, who was born in 1888 and became a teacher.

August
1st   Hilda came. Dog show. Pouring rain high wind. B & M took Lob to show. He disgraced the family as usual but won 2 decent prizes.
3rd   B & I to tea with Evelyn Moore. Miss Jeffries and Miss Browne who motored us home. Mrs Denny in the evening till 10.30.
4th   Hilda met me in Norwich. Went to Wansbrough Young about new will. Went to look at Mrs Priest's school – the old house. Got to Longwood in time for tea.

5th	Church closed at Tasburgh. Lovely hot day
6th	Mrs Salter and Kathleen came to see me at Tasburgh in the morning. In the afternoon went to Intwood to find the tombs of the Rackham family.
7th	Hilda brought me home in time for tea. My front tooth fell out! Heard from Mary. Better news.
8th	Wrote to John Salter about rents etc Mrs Palmer called & I paid £1..16s..0d for the garage.
9th	Leslie, baby and Nanny came.
10th	Went with Leslie and Bertie to buy hats.
	11th V. hot. B & M bathed. Leslie went with me to see Janet.
12th	Leslie to church with me.
13th	Margery went with me to dentist.

14th **80 years old today. Rack, Hilda, Diana and Nanny came to lunch. Lots of presents. Everyone very kind.**

15th	Called on Mrs Denny to thank her for her birthday gift.
16th	Marg and I to dentist. Had my tooth put in. Bertie and Leslie to Cromer to consult Jara.
18th	Leslie and nana and Sita [a dog?] to Cromer. Lovely weather.
19th	Leslie went to church with me. After church went to Keppels to see Rev George about Rackhams in Intwood church. Wrote to Charles.

MEM and Rack were becoming interested in family history. They obviously did not know a great deal about it, but in the 18th century a family of Rackhams had lived at Intwood Hall and there were many Rackham graves in the churchyard. We do not know where MEM's grandfather, Simon Rackham, came from, but there is no reason to suppose it was Intwood. Rackham is a common name in Norfolk. MEM also believed she was related to Arthur Rackham, the artist; she told Tom he was 'a connection' and wrote to him and he sent her a picture. However, if they were related it can only have been very distantly and no family link between them has been traced.

20th	Wrote to Mrs Bradbury about Rackham Pedigree. Raining nearly all day.
21st	Rain and wind. Leslie and I called on Janet.
22nd	Nana and Ena (their servant) went to Cromer for the afternoon.
23rd	B & Leslie to cinema. The Chinese Parrot.

The Chinese Parrot was a silent film, the second in the Charlie Chan series. Marion Nixon was the leading lady.

24th   *Leslie and Mrs Hill called. Leslie and B to cinema – Chang. Picnicked in Marl Pit, Pouring rain.*

A dinosaur skeleton was found there in 1858. It doesn't sound like a very good place to picnic in the pouring rain, but Bertie and Rack had both become very interested in archaeology.

25th   *Tea in garden. Rained as we began. Deluge.*
26th   *Leslie came to church with me. They all bathed or paddled in the afternoon.*
27th   *Leslie, Viki and nana went. 9.50 train in morning. Bertie took down poem with flowers in to Dolly's grave. Mrs Denny came to tell us Mr Denny had broken his leg.*
28th   *Heard from Rack. Had a cheque from A V Watt. Mrs Denny came in evening.*
31st   *Hattie and Madge came.*

Hattie was Frank's wife, MEM's sister-in-law, and Madge was his daughter.

September
1st   *Sat on sea wall with Hattie in morning – went for a walk with them in evening. Sat on the leas.*
2nd   *Hattie and Madge left after breakfast. Marg and I sat on sea wall. Church in evening.*
3rd   *Called on Mrs Denny.*
4th   *Called on Mussels and Janet. Janey a friend there.*
5th   *Heard from Madge R. She had driven to Shropham on her way home. Went with B & M to Carnival procession. Stood in Mrs Coles garden. Mrs Merriman called to take me for a motor ride. Went to Blakeney.*
6th   *Mrs Denny came after tea. David brought plums and tomatoes.*
9th   *Marg. To church with me. Rain as we came home.*
10th   *Called on Mrs Denny. Heard from Rack.*
11th   *Mrs Astley Cooper came to say goodbye. Heard from Mrs Yates and Winnie.*
12th   *Mrs Denny came. Heard from Leslie.*
13th   *Mrs Salter and Kathleen came. They brought ducks and peaches and plums and tomatoes.*

14th	*A wire from Mary to say she was coming for weekend. Another wire to put off until tomorrow.*
15th	*Mary came. Mrs Denny & her cousin Mary came.*
16th	*John Salter [see 8th August] and his wife to lunch etc. Mary to church with me in evening.*
17th	*Town with Mary in morning. Tea in garden. Lovely weather.*
18th	*Hilda, Dianne and Nannie to lunch. Went after tea. Took Bertie. All went to sands in afternoon. Janet came to tea. Mary went home.*
19th	*Margery and I alone. Went town in morning.*
20th	*Heard from Mary.*
21st	*Heard from Hilda. Had a long talk with Mrs Kepple about her Col. Unthank etc. Sent Mary her £5 for last quarter.*

She seems to have been giving Mary and Leslie a quarterly allowance.

22nd	*Hilda drove Bertie home. Left after tea. Bertie brought presents from Woolworths.*
23rd	*Bertie to church with me. Harvest Thanks giving. Called on Mrs Denny. Mr D to be brought home in ambulance tomorrow.*
24th	*Very wet and high gale. To town with Margery. Col and Mrs Coppin came to call.*
25th	*Called to enquire for Mr Denny. The Coppins came to ask us to tea tomorrow.*
26th	*Dr Roche called to tell me Janet had gone off again. I went to see her after towning [sic] with Bertie when I returned Rack and Hilda and Janet and all arrived having come over about Janet. All stayed to lunch. Bertie to tea with Coppins.*
27th	*Mrs Bridgewater came to see fossils. I called to see Janet. Sister Ling there.*

The beach at Sheringham yields corals, echinoids, brachiopods and oysters. Shark remains have been found including the odd tooth, vertebrae and also a spine, although these are not common.

28th	*Col. Coppin came to mend chair and electric bell.*
29th	*Went to see Mr Denny with his broken leg. Raining hard and cold. Mrs Denny came after tea.*
30th	*Went to see Janet after church with Margery. Preacher preached 'An innumerable number of Angels'. Evelyn Moore came after tea.*

No servants, no money, only Susannah who also came. Wrote to Charles. 1st fire.

Evelyn Moore, also mentioned on August 3rd, has not been traced nor what tragedy had befallen her.

October

1st	*To town with Margery. Col and Mrs Coppin & Mr & Mrs Dell? came to tea. Took away the stray black cat that we wanted to get rid of.*
2nd	*The Coppins came in the morning & took feather bed.*
3rd	*Mrs Stores called to thank us for our care of the stray cat. I called on Mrs Denny.*
4th	*Heard from Charles. B to lecture carrying fossils and bones.*
6th	*Simon was coming today for a week. Wired to say too ill. Heard from John Aspergh and Mary. Called on Mrs Denny. She out. Called on Mrs Gentry who witnessed new lease of Waly (Shropham tenant) B & M gone to cinema. 'Resurrection'*

Mr and Mrs Gentry also witnessed her will.
The film was directed by Cecile B. De Mille in 1927. The last sequence, the *Resurrection*, was in technicolor – the first ever example of its use.

7th	*Clocks back last night. Summer over. Bertie to church with me.*
8th	*Wire from Simon. Expected him to tea then supper. Then discovered he had wired 'tomorrow'. Went to see Mrs Denny.*
9th	*Simon came. Ill, in time for tea. Went to see Janet who declined to see me. Saw sister Ling who said Janet very queer.*
10th	*Wrote to Hilda about Janet, Simon away till teatime.*
11th	*Pouring rain. Simon home all morning. Leslie's farewell letters. Is to sail next Wednesday.*
12th	*Mrs Bridgewater sent peaches. Simon ill sat at home all day. Saw Mr Denny took him fruit, which he refused, also papers which he said he did not want. Went to see Janet who asked me to tea. She quite all right.*
13th	*Simon left. His visit spoilt by bad weather and bad health.*

Poor MEM!

14th	*To church with Margery. David came in the afternoon brought oranges and apples.*

15th	*Saw Sister Ling. Tells me Janet is to be sent away.*
17th	*To town. Bertie, Raining. A P Watt sent cheque for Noel. Called on Mussells.*

Noel was a story she had had published. It is interesting as it seems to be the only thing she had had printed in a decade. No copy seems to survive, but it does appear in the list of stories for which A.P. Watt negotiated the American rights.

18th	*Hilda came to lunch. Janet to go Northampton Asylum. Mrs Denny came in evening.*
19th	*Bertie went with others to dig fossils. Heard from Mary and from Charles about sisters sailing on 17th. Still very sad. Wrote to him. Mrs Denny sent oranges.*

It sounds as if Leslie was taking Mary back to India with her. However, by the beginning of 1929 Mary was back in England.

20th	*To town with Bertie. Came home by sea. Col Atkinson sat with me and had a long talk. Went to see Mrs Denny and after to Janet. She very quiet and sad. Heard from Simon. Read H.G Well's 'Mr Blettsworthy on Rampole Island' On the whole think it is a great book.*
21st	*Bertie to church with me. Mrs Denny brought roses.*
23rd	*Heard from Winnie. Going to have a second opinion. Hilda came over to tea and stay the night.*
24th	*Hilda left to take Janet to Northampton and returned to say Janet would not go. Mussels came.*
25th	*Gardened in the morning. Hilda came to say goodbye. Pheasants from Madge Harvey.*
26th	*Saw Sister Ling & did shopping for Janet who is in bed. 2 doctors yesterday. Wrote to Madge Harvey.*
28th	*To church with Margery. Hilda motored over & came at supper time ready to take Janet tomorrow.*
29th	*Janet gone.*
30th	*(Dolly's birthday) Hilda came. The car had broken down at midnight coming back from Northampton. In the evening sister Ling came to say goodbye. Little Jimmy came with his school report.*
31st	*To town with Bertie. Went to see Mr Denny. He gets better. Cut back fuchsias. A lovely day. Heard from poor Charles.*

November

1st	*All Saints Day. Margery went to church with me. In afternoon went with M to Natalie to see after chickens. B out to lecture at night.*
2nd	*Took all morning to clean drawing room after the worst smoking chimney we have ever had. Went shopping in afternoon.*
3rd	*Rack came to stay till Wednesday.*
4th	*Bertie to church with me. Cannon Usher? Preached a fine sermon of which I could hear every word. [She was deaf, so this was obviously worthy of recording.] Wrote to Simon.*
5th	*Rack and B walked to Manton to buy roses. Wrote to Warbrough Young about Will etc.*
6th	*'How can we tell that this world of ours is not some sort of planet from hell?' Julian Huxley.*
7th	*Heard from Mary. Hilda, Diana and nanny came. Took Rack away with them. Wrote to Frank, Warbrough Young, etc.*
8th	*V cold. Wind and rain. Soot down in drawing room, Got money from bank (House Keeping). Paid bills.*
9th	*Took my Will to be witnessed by Mr & Mrs Gentry. Heard from Rack. Bought 500? Peat £2..5s*
10th	*B and I shopping. V. cold*
11th	*Armistice day 10 years ago. Marg. with me to church. Wrote to Leslie.*
12th	*Town with Marge. After tea went to call on Mussels.*

December

12th	*Heard from Charles. The window to Dolly is in. He very unhappy. Heard from Simon. B with me to buy Christmas presents.*

Dolly's friend, Winifred Auld, went to see Charles in Wilsford the Easter after the window was installed and she wrote to tell Bertie about the visit. She thought the window very beautiful and the woman in it looked like Dolly. Charles had told Winifred that he had feared for years that Dolly would take an overdose. He was obviously still heart broken – 'He really is the most pathetic old dear,' wrote Winifred. Dolly's grave was heaped high with flowers and he kept talking about 'my poor little Doll'.

13th	*Heard from Colonel Auld about Winnie. She very ill after operation. I did not go out. Too cold. Wrote to Charles.*
14th	*Felt ill in afternoon. No tea or supper. To bed with brandy and ..?..and hot water bottle.*

15th	*Towning with Bertie. Bought Xmas presents. Heard from Rack.*
16th	*To church with Margery.*
17th	*Lovely bright day, no wind. To town with Margery. Willie Auld. Winnie better.*
19th	*Rack sent presents*
20th	*Ena gone home with mumps. So nice for Xmas! 3 weeks infection.*
21st	*Charles sent turkey. Every day worried with Xmas cards and presents*
23rd	*Could not go to church. So much to do. Rack and Hilda came for tea. Diana could not come because of mumps.*
24th	*Flowers from Mrs Self. And presents from everyone. Did not go out. Ena being ill makes for a lot of work for Margery as well.*
25th	*A very quiet Christmas – but very peaceful. Loads of presents from my dear children. Did not go out.*
26th	*Mr Denny came on his two sticks. Toothache and swelled face. Bad night.*
27th	*The Keppels called. B & M out. I with swelled face etc. Lovely weather.*
28th	*Face still swelled and uncomfortable. Mrs Denny came in at teatime. Heard from Rack and Mary and Charles.*
29th	*Bertie shopping alone. Face still swelled. A week of sitting by the fire with toothache.*
30th	*Pouring rain all day. No church.*

1929

The year started badly. At eighty, MEM was having to endure a freezing cold house and burst pipes. She then had news that her eldest granddaughter had been seriously injured.

4th	*Mrs Denny came. Miss Hanley came. Boiler went wrong. Kitchen flooded so no hot baths etc*
5th	*No fire in kitchen. V cold . Wire from Charles. Mary injured in a hunting accident. More wires. A letter. Mary in nursing home with concussion.*
6th	*Snow. No kitchen fire. Bertie ill. A wire from Charles. A dreary beginning to the New Year. May it improve!*
7th	*Letter from Rack, Leslie, Charles. No better news. Mary dangerously ill.*
8th	*A wire to say Mary out of danger.*

On New Year's Day 1929 Mary was out hunting when her horse stumbled and fell, just as they were crossing a road. Mary landed on her head, sustaining severe concussion, a gaping wound and a damaged eye. She was taken to a nursing home in Reading and her father was summoned; he wrote to MEM with the news 'There seems to be no respite from disaster for my unfortunate family ... My darling Dolly has at any rate escaped this.'

Charles sounds somewhat bewildered to have discovered that Mary, just eighteen months divorced, had a new 'partner', Captain Angus Miller, and it was Captain Miller who drove him from Wilsford to Reading to see her. For a week, Mary's life hung in the balance and Charles sent MEM regular bulletins by letter, postcard and telegram. By March, Mary was at home in Wilsford, bored and indolent. Charles writes about her as if she were a young girl rather than a woman of thirty-one, promising to 'make' her write to her grandmother. The ongoing problem was her eye. To begin with she couldn't open it and various specialists were consulted. It would take at least a year to heal, they said, and the lid would probably always droop – but Captain Miller had other ideas. After a short stay in Wilsford, Mary went back to London, stayed with him in his flat and had 'electrical treatment' on the eye which appears to have worked. Charles visited her in London and reported to MEM that Angus's flat was in the block occupied by Austen Chamberlain and there was a policeman permanently on duty at the door. Captain Miller seems to have supported Mary through her illness but the relationship came to nothing.

9th	*To town with David!!!! Charles writes confirming yesterday's better news.*
13th	*Bertie to church with me. I stayed sacrament.*
14th	*Called on Mrs Keppel. Postcard from Charles saying Mary was going on satisfactorily.*
15th	*Fire in kitchen after 10 days without.*
21st	*Heard from Leslie sending snaps of Silki. From Charles not at all good news. Mary still delirious. Mrs Denny came to tea.*
27th	*Not at all well. Giddy. Did not go to church. Walked with Marg instead.*
28th	*Heard from Rack. Went to town with Marg. Feeling better. News of Mary rather bad all last week.*
31st	*Pouring rain. Mrs Denny came. Sent book Literary Agency Cambs.*

It seems she was still writing and trying to get work published, but without success.

February

1st   *Went shopping. Pouring rain. Cold. Post card from Charles. Specialist to Mary who says he is satisfied. Heard from Frank.*

2nd   *Miss Calder ill. Went to buy her an oil stove.*

11th   *Bitterly cold. Went to town with Margery. Heard Mary better and being moved to London*

12th   *All pipes frozen. No baths. Pouring water making a river of the garden. Baker's people finally turned off the water main. No fire in kitchen.*

13th   *St Valentine's Eve.*
For old time's sake
And old love's sake
And the life that used to be!!
Snowing. All pipes frozen. Wired Hilda not to come tomorrow. Heard John Aspergh's daughter is dead.

21st   *Terrible burst in pipes in kitchen and lavatory. Everyone the same. B went last night in the dark and brought back a stove from Bakers. Mrs Denny came. Wrote to Frank.*

22nd   *Went to see Mussels. Her pipes also gone wrong. Still no fire in kitchen.*

March

19th   *My dear father died in 1881.*

21st   *Finished Spring cleaning all but the kitchen and drawing room. Ena and I put down the stair carpet. Lovely spring day*

It is interesting that Bertie and Margery are never recorded as having helped with major cleaning jobs in any way – though that does not mean that they didn't. And 'Ena and I' may well mean 'I watched Ena' – it is difficult to believe that an old lady of eighty who needed someone to accompany her wherever she went was much use at laying carpets.

23rd   *Bertie and I went to see Charlie Chaplin in The Circus. Enjoyed it very much.*

The Circus is a silent film of 1928 which was written and directed by Charlie Chaplin with Joseph Plunkett as an un-credited co-writer. The ringmaster of an impoverished circus hires Chaplin's Little Tramp as a

217

clown, but discovers that he can only be funny unintentionally, not on purpose. The production of the film was said to have been the most difficult experience in Chaplin's career. Numerous problems and delays occurred, including a studio fire, the death of Chaplin's mother, as well as Chaplin's bitter divorce from his second wife Lita Grey, and the Internal Revenue Service's claims against Chaplin's for back taxes, all of which culminated in the filming being stalled for eight months. *The Circus* was the seventh highest-grossing silent film in cinema history taking in more than $3.8 million in 1928.

25th	*Cleaned pantry. Started distempering kitchen.*
26th	*Fairman's birthday. Miss Jeffries came. Heard from Winnie. She to have an operation on her nose.*
27th	*Bertie and I bought Easter Eggs. Finished Spring Cleaning all but the drawing room. Wrote to Rack.*
29th	*Good Friday. Went to church. Could not hear a word.. Lovely day. Heard from Simon*
30th	*To tea with Mrs Denny. Took Easter offerings. Called on Mussels. Wrote Charles.*
31st	*Marg and I to 12 o'clock service. For Communion.*

Easter was difficult for Charles. Dolly had been artistic and decorating the church was 'always a labour of love with my darling and her taste was so exquisite and her industry so unflapping that it was always a picture.' Laura, his housekeeper, and Gladys Hoton from the village did their best – but it wasn't the same.

April

1st	*April Fool <u>twice</u>. Present from Mrs Denny.*
7th	*Margery's birthday.*
8th	*Mrs Denny to tea. Heard from Leslie, Hilda and Rack. He excavating at Caister.*
10th	*Wind and rain. Drawing room smoked. Miss Moore came. Heard from Mary. Says she is better but doesn't sound happy. Bitterly cold N.E wind raging. Have not been out for 2 days. Heard from Winnie. She still ill.*
	'Tis a month before the month of May
	And spring comes slowly up this way.'
	It does indeed!
15th	*Mrs Coppin came. Col C very ill. Temperature 103*
16th	*Evelyn Moore to tea. Heard from Mary. Very unhappy.*

18th	*Hilda came for me. She drove to Caister to pick up Rack on way home. Saw the amphora he had dug up. Diana, Rack and I played Ring a Ring of Roses on the lawn. Warm lovely day.*
19th	*Very warm. Played with Diana in the garden. Went to Woolworth's in the afternoon. Went to Caister in afternoon for Rack.*
20th	*Went to Norwich in morning. N.E wind v cold.*
21st	*Rack Hilda and I to church.*
22nd	*Drove to Caister. A day there. To Attleborough Hall in afternoon. Cold but sunny.*
23rd	*Hilda drove me home. Took tomato plants.*
24th	*Raining. First time for weeks. Bitterly cold. Did not go out. Mrs Coppin came. Heard from Winnie. Her operation over.*
25th	*V.Cold. Bertie to be with Miss Moore. Her house haunted. Mrs Denny came. Turned out drawing room and my room.*
26th	*Mrs Coppin came. He much better. Heard from Charles. Wrote to Frank.*
28th	*Church with Bertie. She went to Coppins.*
29th	*Cleaning drawing room. Sweep came. Heard Mary coming on Friday and heard from Leslie. Pouring rain.*
30th	*Finished spring cleaning drawing room.*
May	
1st	*Lovely day but cold. I went to see Miss Jeffries' flowers.*
2nd	*Bitterly cold east wind. Went to see Mussels. Paid Baker's bill £19..19s. Bitter weather all week.*
	'It is often more cruel to ignore than hate.'

And that is the last entry in her diary.

When MEM became ill, Hilda went over to Sheringham to help nurse her and was apparently greeted by Bertie with 'At last. No more bed pans!' It is unlikely that Margery complained but Bertie avoided unpleasant jobs whenever she possibly could.

MEM died on May 19th. Her body was taken to Shropham where she was buried in the churchyard. As in their life together, Fairman was sidelined. Whilst MEM's position is in the centre of their plot Fairman is not by her side – he is squashed into a corner. The service was taken by the Reverend Harcourt Anson – a vicar whom she had never known. Her obituary appeared in a Norfolk newspaper some ten days later.

For MEM and her daughters, life had not lived up to its promise. MEM had not had a particularly happy marriage and though she had enjoyed considerable success in her lifetime as a novelist, her fame had already started to wane before she died and she was finding it impossible to get her work published or re-published. Bertie had lost the love of her life, Hugh, and was not a famous artist – just a good enough one to earn some sort of living as an illustrator. And Margery? Well, Margery was perhaps the most content of them all as she had expected less from life and was happy with what she had. Bertie wrote a Christmas poem about her:

> *The tawdry lantern gilds the munching goats,*
> *And Marg'ry is enhaloed as she leans*
> *Feeding them their evening meal of oats.*

Fortunately, having had to bear the unbearable in Dolly's suicide, MEM did not live to see the mess both her older grand-daughters made of their lives. In 1933, six years after her divorce from Gerald Moore, and after her abortive relationship with Angus Miller had ended, Mary married again. Her third husband was Joseph Wickham, a widower who sold glue for a living and whose father was a tea planter – it is possible that she met him through Leslie and Guy's Indian connections. They moved to Colchester. However, within four years he too had left her for another woman. Heartbroken and humiliated, Mary killed herself by putting her head in a gas oven in the kitchen of a London flat. She left a pathetic suicide note: 'I cannot face life without you. I cannot live on your money when I mean nothing to you any more. I am only a burden. It is so awful to think that I failed you so badly … I would have done anything in the world to make you happy, and in doing so, made myself happy, too… The torture I have suffered since you turned so terribly against me has broken all the courage I had. I don't blame you for anything. Thank you for all the happiness you have given me.'

Leslie finally divorced Guy Vallance in 1933, and in 1938, the year after her sister's suicide, she married a teacher, Charles Alison, taking her two young children with her – by then Martin would have been eleven and Gabrielle five.

Martin joined the RAF and became a pilot like his father, but he was killed in a plane crash in Germany in 1950 when he was still in his early twenties. Charles Alison died the following year. A year later, Gabrielle, then aged nineteen, became the girlfriend of an unstable young man from Cornwall, Miles Giffard. Miles had a long history of mental health problems and, though well-educated, had never held down a job. One November day he asked his father's permission to borrow the family car to drive to London to see Gabrielle – but his father refused. Miles stayed at home getting drunk while his parents went out for the day, and when they returned he bludgeoned them both to death with a piece of lead pipe he had found in their garage and tipped their bodies over a cliff into the sea. He then took the car and drove to meet Gabrielle. The bodies were found the next day, and shortly afterwards Miles was arrested at Gabrielle's family home, 40, Tite Street, Chelsea; details of his girlfriend and her family would have been in all the papers alongside descriptions of the gruesome murders. He was found guilty and hanged in February 1953. Though she later married and had children, Gabrielle never forgot him and kept the letters he wrote to her from prison until shortly before her own death in 2008.

Overwhelmed by the horrors that had befallen her two children and the death of her husband, all within the space of a couple of years, Leslie, like her grandfather before her, became an alcoholic and (according to her grandson) embarked on another unsatisfactory relationship and made at least one unsuccessful suicide attempt. She died in 1986.

Rack died in 1944 at the age of seventy-two. Three years earlier, in June 1941, he had written proudly to Bertie that he had spent five hours one day cutting the grass (Tasburgh House had huge grounds which have now been swallowed up by a mid-20th century housing estate) and was 'not at all tired. Not bad for sixty-nine!' But in 1944 he had an operation from which he never recovered – Bertie kept his last letter alongside her mementos of Hugh. Though he was often critical of her (particularly of her figure drawing because, he said, she knew nothing about anatomy) they were very close and she missed him sadly.

MEM would have been heartbroken if she had known of the decline of her other two children. Bertie and Margery were left very badly off after their mother's death. They sold Greenlands and used the money to build themselves a small house, which they named 'Three Corners', further out of town along Nelson Road. To the horror of the new owners, a skeleton (from Rack's days as a medical student) was left behind in the Greenlands attic; Bertie collected it, sat it in a wheelbarrow and pushed it up the hill to Three Corners. The sisters made

221

sure there was no spare bedroom in their new house so that they would not have to entertain overnight guests, and each had her own domain so that they only came together at mealtimes. It sounds as if they became quite reclusive in old age and it is perhaps significant that no-one in Sheringham has any recollection of either of them. After Rack's death in 1944 Mill Farm was sold to a Miss Morfoot and Margery and Bertie each received a quarter share of the proceeds – £782 9s. 10d. each – which must have made their last years a little easier.

In 1955 Bertie was killed in a horrible accident on the Bere Regis level crossing behind their home. Like MEM, both she and Margery became very deaf in old age, and Bertie was also short-sighted. She apparently neither heard nor saw the train bearing down on her on the ungated, single track level crossing, and though she was taken from the scene alive she died soon after from multiple injuries. Her little dog was with her at the time and escaped unscathed – a sure sign, her niece Diana believed, that the death was accidental. Bertie, she felt sure, would never knowingly have risked her pet's life. Leslie was less certain and suspected suicide. It is certainly difficult to believe that Bertie would not have felt the vibration of the train on the track and smelt the smoke – but perhaps she fell and could not get out of the way in time. We have no way of knowing.

Margery was left alone, and though she and Bertie were very different they had understood each other well. Hilda and Diana visited but she found their visits stressful and was stubborn in her refusal of their help. She would never even allow them to take her out for lunch. When Diana offered to stay in Sheringham to look after her she made excuses – no-one could stay in the house, Bertie's room must be left just as it was when she died so Diana could not sleep in it. It was equally unthinkable that Diana should stay in a hotel; Margery had no need of help, she liked being alone – and so on.

The winter of 1959-60 was bitterly cold and though the neighbours helped as much as she would let them, eighty-two year old Margery was beginning to struggle. On the 20th of January, 1960, she decided she had had enough and, like her niece before her, she took her own life by putting her head in a gas oven. She had planned carefully. Her final letter to her cousin, Madge Rackham (who had invited Margery to live with her) contains detailed instructions about thanking the neighbours, cleaning the house and having her cat put to sleep. She left food to be put out for the birds and further instructions for Hilda and Diana. Meticulous and self-effacing to the last, Margery was anxious to cause as little trouble to anyone as possible – though she had reckoned without the emergency services. The police and ambulance services levied a £3 fee against her estate and Sheringham Council charged £2 for carrying out an inquest. Suicide was still a crime in 1960.

My Dear Madge,

How I hate to hurt you – you have always been so kind and sweet to me – still lately I have felt my health and strength are on the wane and I have decided that I would rather go into the unknown without a prolonged and painful illnes ...

Remember I have had quite a happy life. I have not wanted anything in my old age and I do not really think I ever felt lonely. I loved Bertie and missed her so much when she went...I do not feel I could bear to live with anyone else.

My two neighbours have been wonderful to me – please thank them one day....and see that my little black cat is put to rest as gently as possible.

How I hate making you all unhappy – but this will pass, and the brighter days lie ahead for you.

With all my love
Margery

As her mother, Mary Elizabeth Mann, had put it so succinctly at the beginning of her diary,

'Tout lasse, tout casse, tout passe.'

MEM's grave in Shropham churchyard
It has recently been renovated.

Appendix 1

MEM's novels and publication dates

Title	First published	Re-published**
The Parish of Hilby	1883 Elliot Stock	1903 Methuen
Confessions of a Coward and a Coquette	1886 Ward Downey	
Mrs Peter Howard	1886 Smith Elder	1903 Methuen
A Lost Estate	1889 R. Bentley and Co.	1904 Methuen
One Another's Burdens	1890 R. Bentley and Co.	1904 Methuen
A Winter's Tale	1891 R. Bentley and Co.	1904 Methuen
Perdita	1893 R. Bentley and Co	
In Summer Shade	1893 H. Henry and Co	1902 and 1914 John Long
Susannah	1895 H. Henry and Co	1899 Fisher Unwin
There Once was a Prince	1896 H. Henry and Co	1904 Methuen
When Arnold comes Home	1897 H. Henry and Co	1904 Methuen
The Cedar Star	1898 Hutchinson	1919 Methuen
Moonlight	1898 Fisher Unwin	1911 Hurst and Blackett
The Patten Experiment	1899 Fisher Unwin	
Out in Life's Rain	1899 Hutchinson	
Among the Syringas	1901 Fisher Unwin	
The Mating of a Dove	1901 Fisher Unwin	
The Fields of Dulditch★	1902 Digby Long	
Olivia's Summer	1902 Methuen	
Gran'ma's Jane	1903 Methuen	
Fortune's Cap	1905 Hurst and Blackett	
The Parish Nurse	1905 Collins	1905 Methuen
The Eglamore Portraits	1906 Methuen	
Rose at Honeypot	1906 Methuen	
Memories of Ronald Love	1907 Methuen	

The Sheep and the Goats	1907 Methuen	1912 Daily Mail
Heart Smiter	1908 Methuen	
A Sheaf of Corn*	1908 Methuen	
Avenging Children	1909 Methuen	
Astray in Arcady	1910 Methuen	
Bound Together*	1910 Mills and Boon	
There was a Widow	1911 Methuen	
Men and Dreams*	1912 Mills and Boon	
Mrs Day's Daughters	1913 Hodder and Stoughton	
Through the Window*	1913 Mills and Boon	
Grandpapa's Granddaughter	1915 Mills and Boon	
When a Man Marries	1916 Hodder and Stoughton	
The Victim	1917 Hodder and Stoughton	
Pedlar's Pack*	1918 Mills and Boon	

* indicates a collection of short stories

** 'Re-publication' only refers to books re-published in MEM's lifetime, not those that have recently been re-printed.

Appendix 2

Compilations of MEM's short stories

Fields of Dulditch (1902)	A Sheaf of Corn (1908)	Bound Together (1910)
Our Mary	Women o' Dulditch	Old Billy Knock
A Dulditch Angel	Clomayne's Clerk	Mittens
Ben Pitcher's Elly	In a Tea-Shop	A Dulditch Sabbath
A Dulditch Courting	A Chalk-mark on the Gate Part 1	Harriet Dixon's Afternoon Off
The Witch of Dulditch	Ditto Part II	Rattle's Wife
Donald Peck's Love Affair	"As 'twas told me"	White Chintzes
A Dulditch Rose	Freddy's Ship	Miss Alpe's Headache
Wolf Charlie	A Nerve Cure	Perhaps – ?
The Family of Woodman Harper	The Private Ward	To London Bridge
The Lost Housen	Dora o' the Ringolets	The Coming of King Ackerman
The Gal La'rences	Pink Carnations	The Eerie
Some of the Shipwrecked	A Little White Dog	A Letter Delayed
	It Answered	Home Returning
	To Bertha in Bombay	Ten Shilling's Worth
	Auntie	A Family Party
	Willy and I	The Empty Chair
	A Broken Boot	The Brown Great-coat
	When Deep Sleep Falleth	The Wedding Day
	Cares of a Curate	

Men and Dreams (1912)	Through the Window (1913)	Pedlar's Pack (1918)
A Man and a Dream	The Old Birds	A Boy and Girl Marriage
Jacko's Holiday	Mrs Carabay's Curious Dream	Penniless Percival
His First Day at the Sea	Three of the Best	My Cousin Violet's Husband
"Forty-five"	The Five Pound Note	Mrs Varley's Parrot
Back to the Land	That Man and That	Captain Drake

	Woman	
The Doubting Heart	The Beauty Specialist	Old Abel
A Country Churchyard	Blazing Away at the Birds	The Abode of Peace
"K.B."	The Letter He Kept Back	A War Marriage
A Homecoming	Letchfield	Just for Fun
Levenses	Going First Class	Bob
Ordeal by Fire	The Eleventh Hour	An Undelivered Message
The Mother	The Conservative Van	HMS Fairy
The Country Doctor	The Sunday After	An Enigma in Pink
The Red-haired Girl	The Setting Sun	Daisy's Daddy
The Four Maries	Ella's Fortune	An Amazing Offer
The Man Who Wouldn't Take "No"	A Gentleman at Large	Died of His Wounds
Rats	Blue Beads	
Easy as Kissing	The Smallholder	
Hector Alexander	Medlars	
The Last Haysell	The Girl in the Red Frock	
Queen of the Pheasants	A Golden Summer	
The Idle Peasant		

Appendix 3

Rackham family

Names in **bold** are those of people who played a significant role in MEM's life.

MEM's grandparents and parents

Simon Rackham, (c.1783-1844), cloth merchant, married **Maria Ling** (c.1799-1852) in 1815. They were MEM's **paternal grandparents**. We do not know who Simon's parents were, whether he was born in Norwich or in the county, whether he inherited his business or whether he established it. No members of the Rackham family were witnesses at his wedding which may or may not be significant. He married into a Norwich merchant family – Maria Ling was the daughter of William Ling and his wife Elizabeth, née Miller, and at the time of her father's will (1846) she had living siblings called William Samuel, Henry, Elizabeth and Charlotte who were, of course, MEM's great aunts and uncles. Simon and Maria had two sons.

(1) Henry, baptised 1816. We know nothing about him.
(2) **William Simon Rackham** (1817-81) traveller, merchant, draper, Manchester warehouseman. He was **MEM's father**
On October 16, 1845 he married
Mary Ann Elizabeth Smith (c.1827-1892). She was **MEM's mother**. Her brother James was a draper and in partnership with WSR and the Chamberlin family. Their father, John Smith ('merchant draper'), had preceded him as a partner in the firm.

Maria Rackham, née Ling, MEM's grandmother, married Robert Sheppard, Manchester warehouseman of Norwich in 1846 after the death of her first husband.

MEM and her siblings, children of William Simon and Mary Ann Elizabeth Rackham, née Smith

(1) **William Simon** (1846-1903) solicitor, m.1. 1878 Fanny Elizabeth Newman (1850-1900) daughter of Thomas Newman, a shoemaker who employed 11 people. m.2. 1901 Katherine Gardiner. No children.
(2) **MEM**. Mary Elizabeth 'Polly' (1848- May 19, 1929) novelist, m. 1871 Fairman Joseph Mann (1837-1913) farmer and they had 4 children
(3) **Henry** 'Harry' (1849-1895) worked in the family business and then for the LCC. He never married.
(4) **George** (1851- 1900) m. 1878 Edith Mary Salter (1853-?) He also worked for the family business and then became a farmer and later an innkeeper. No children.

(5) **John** (1855 - 1898) Frank's twin. Emigrated to S. Africa. He never married.

(6) **Frank** (1855-1931) John's twin. m. 1883 **Harriette Ann Warner ('Hattie')**, daughter of Fairman J. Mann's sister, Harriet. They had eight children:-

(i) **Simon** (1885-)	(v) Phyllis (1890-)
(ii) John (1886-)	(vi) Ruth (1892-)
(iii) Barbara (1887-)	(vii) Geoffrey (1897-)
(iv) Margaret (1888-)	(viii) Philip (1900-)

(7) **Edward Clement** (1863-1897). He was a constant worry to his parents and may have had learning difficulties. He emigrated to Canada. He never married.

Mary Elizabeth Rackham ('Polly') married Fairman Joseph Mann in September 1872.

They had 4 children:-
1. **Fairman Rackham Mann** (1872-1944), naval surgeon. He retired in 1919. In 1924 he married **Hilda Mary Gould** and they had one daughter, Diana.
2. **Mary Berthalina 'Bertie'** (1874-1955) artist. Unmarried.
3. **Margery Poppie** (1876-1960) nurse and poultry farmer. Unmarried.
4. **Dorothy Warner 'Dolly'** (1878-1928) m. **Rev Charles Edward Bolton Hewitt,** teacher at Marlborough College and Vicar of Wilsford from 1920. He died in 1946. They had two daughters, Mary and Leslie.

MEM's grandchildren and great-grandchildren

1. **Mary Dorothea Hewitt** (1898-1937) m.1. 1922 Alfred Donald Hedges (2nd lieut. RFA, retired) He died later in 1922. He was a member of the tobacco family, Benson & Hedges. m.2. 1925 Gerald Grantley Moore, advertising agent. They divorced in 1927. m.3. 1933 Joseph Wickham, glue salesman.
2. **Margery Leslie Hewitt 'Leslie'** (1900-1986) m. 1. 1924 Roper Guy Aymer Vallance ('Guy') Divorced 1933. m. 2. 1938 Charles W. Alison, teacher.
Leslie and Guy had two children:-
(i) Martin (c.1926-1950)
(ii) Gabrielle Leslie (1933-1986) She has living children and grandchildren
3. **Diana Mann** (1925-2011) married Ivan Hyde. No children.

Appendix 4

Mann family, Fairman's family, MEM's in-laws

Fairman's grandparents and parents

Joseph (d. *c.*1835) and Margaret Mann were Fairman's **grandparents**. Joseph took on the tenancy of Manor Farm (then called City Farm) in 1809. He built the present house there *c.*1822. They had children, including two sons.

> (1) John Mann (1785-1845) who took over the tenancy of Manor Farm from his father. He married 1. Hannah Chapman in 1807 2. A widow, Mary Bolton, in 1829. She had a son, George, from her previous marriage. This son became John Mann's heir and took the name **George Bolton Mann**. He married and had one daughter, **Edith**.
>
> (2) **Fairman Mann,** (1800-1866), **MEM's father-in-law.** He married **Berthalina, née Eagling** (1799-1874) They lived at Rockland St Andrew where he was a farmer, shop-owner and innkeeper. They had 5 children.

Fairman's siblings, children of Fairman and Berthalina Mann

(1) Sarah (1823-1874). She married Thomas Ordish, a London stationer, and moved with him to Fulham. They had 6 children, the second of whom was **Thomas Fairman Ordish 'Tom'**, MEM's great friend and supporter.

(2) John Eagling (1826-1899). He farmed the family lands in Rockland and lived at Kirk Hall. He married 1. Emma Land by whom he had 4 children. 2. Lila Lammacraft by whom he had a large family.

(3) Harriet (1827-1899). She married James Warner, a farmer at Scarning and they had 4 children, one of whom, **Harriette ('Hattie')** married MEM's brother, Frank Rackham.

(4) **Fairman Joseph (1837-1913) MEM's husband.**

(5) Eliza (1844-1929). She married her brother-in-law, William Warner, who farmed at Scarning. They had no children.